JUSTICE

THE VIRTUES: MULTIDISCIPLINARY PERSPECTIVES

Series Editor

Nancy E. Snow

Professor of Philosophy and Director of the Institute of Human Flourishing, University of Oklahoma

Published

Justice

Edited by Mark LeBar

Forthcoming

Honesty, Integrity, and Truth-Seeking

Edited by Christian Miller and Ryan West

Humility

Edited by Jennifer Cole Wright

Sustainability

Edited by Jason Kawall

JUSTICE

Edited by Mark LeBar

OXFORD
UNIVERSITY PRESS

OXFORD
UNIVERSITY PRESS

Oxford University Press is a department of the University of Oxford. It furthers the University's objective of excellence in research, scholarship, and education by publishing worldwide. Oxford is a registered trade mark of Oxford University Press in the UK and certain other countries.

Published in the United States of America by Oxford University Press
198 Madison Avenue, New York, NY 10016, United States of America.

CIP data is on file at the Library of Congress
ISBN 978–0–19–063175–8 (pbk.)
ISBN 978–0–19–063174–1 (hbk.)

CONTENTS

SERIES EDITOR'S FOREWORD

Typically, having a virtue means being disposed to having certain kinds of perceptions, thoughts, motives, emotions, and ways one is inclined to act. The end of the twentieth and the beginning of the twenty-first centuries have seen an upsurge of interest in the topic of virtue. This is true not only in philosophy but also in a variety of other disciplines, such as theology, law, economics, psychology, and anthropology, to name a few. The study of virtue within disciplines is vitally important, yet the premise of this series is that the study of virtue in general, as well as of specific virtues, can be enhanced if scholars take into account work being done in disciplines other than their own.

Cross-disciplinary work can be challenging. Scholars trained in one field with its unique vocabulary and methods do not always move seamlessly into another discipline and often feel unqualified to undertake the task of serious cross-disciplinary engagement. The upshot can be that practitioners of disciplines can become "siloed"—trapped within their own disciplines and hesitant to engage seriously with others, even on important topics of mutual interest.

This series seeks to break the silos with fifteen volumes on specific virtues or clusters of virtues. For each book, an introduction by the editor highlights the unity of writings by identifying common themes, threads, and ideas. In each volume, the editor seeks to include a chapter from a "wild card" discipline, a field one would not expect to see included in a collection of essays on a particular virtue. We do this both to highlight the diversity of fields in the study of specific virtues and to surprise and challenge readers to broaden their horizons in thinking about virtue.

The audience for this series is practitioners of different disciplines who seek to expand their thinking about virtue. Each volume contains chapters that are accessible and of interest to scholars from many disciplines. Though the volumes are not comprehensive overviews of the work on virtue that is occurring in any given field, they provide a useful introduction meant to pique the curiosity of readers and spur further engagement with other disciplines.

Nancy E. Snow,
Professor of Philosophy and Director of the Institute for the Study of Human Flourishing, University of Oklahoma

CONTRIBUTORS

Zinaida Besirevic is a Ph.D. candidate in the cognition and development program at the University of California, Berkeley, Graduate School of Education. She holds an M.A. in education from UC Berkeley, an M.A. in philosophy from San Francisco State University, and a B.A. in international relations from the University of London. Her research is in the field of moral development, with a focus on reasoning about human rights.

Sarah Brosnan is a professor of psychology, philosophy, and neuroscience at Georgia State University. She studies the evolution of decision-making behavior, using an experimental economic approach to compare responses across multiple species, primarily in human adults and children and nonhuman primates. A major focus of her work explores how individuals decide in what situations and with whom to cooperate, particularly when they receive a different outcome from a social partner.

Audun Dahl is an assistant professor of psychology at the University of California, Santa Cruz. His research investigates the development and application of basic moral concerns with human welfare from infancy to adulthood.

Matthew A. Edwards is an associate professor of law in the Zicklin School of Business at Baruch College (City University of New York). He earned a J.D. degree, magna cum laude, from New York University School of Law and a B.A. in political science, summa cum laude, from SUNY-Binghamton. His scholarship focuses largely on normative legal theory and behavioral law and economics. His work has appeared in journals such as *Administrative Law Review, Stanford Journal of Law, Business and Finance, Cornell Journal of Law and Public Policy, Berkeley Journal of Employment and Labor Law, Washington Law Review,* and *Notre Dame Journal of Law, Ethics and Public Policy.*

Jon Garthoff is an associate professor and the director of graduate studies at the University of Tennessee Department of Philosophy. He works primarily in ethical theory and political philosophy and is especially interested in how psychological capacities—including those possessed by many nonhuman animals, such as perception, consciousness, and judgment—figure in our best understanding of ethics, politics, and law.

Ryan P. Hanley holds the Mellon Distinguished Professorship in Political Science at Marquette University. A specialist in the history of moral and political philosophy in the Enlightenment period, he is the author of *Adam Smith and the Character of Virtue* (Cambridge University Press, 2009) and *Love's Enlightenment: Rethinking Charity in Modernity* (Cambridge University Press, 2017) and the editor of several volumes, including *Adam Smith: His Life, Thought, and Legacy* (Princeton University Press, 2016), the Penguin Classics edition of Adam Smith's *The Theory of Moral Sentiments* (Penguin, 2010), and, with Darrin M. McMahon, *The Enlightenment: Critical Concepts in History* (Routledge, 2010). He is also a recipient of fellowships from the Mellon Foundation, the Earhart Foundation, the National Endowment for the Humanities, and the Arête Initiative and is currently at work on a monograph on the political philosophy of Fénelon and a translation of Fénelon's political writings.

Mark LeBar is a professor of philosophy at Florida State University. He holds a Ph.D. in philosophy from the University of Arizona and works in moral, social, and political philosophy. His book *The Value of Living Well* (Oxford University Press, 2013) is a development of contemporary eudaimonist ethical theory. He coedited *Equality and Public Policy* (Cambridge University Press, 2014), and he is the editor of the journal *Social Theory and Practice.* He has published in journals including *Ethics, American Philosophical Quarterly, Philosophical Studies, Canadian Journal of Philosophy,* and *Pacific Philosophical Quarterly.*

May Sim is a professor of philosophy at the College of the Holy Cross. She is the director of the Boston Area Colloquium in Ancient Philosophy and president of the Metaphysical Society of America (2013). She is the author of *Remastering Morals with Aristotle and Confucius* (Cambridge University Press, 2007) and more than forty essays comparing Eastern and Western philosophies in the areas of metaphysics, ethics, education, the environment, human rights, and wisdom. She is the contributing editor of *The Crossroads of Norm and Nature: Essays on Aristotle's Ethics and Metaphysics* (Rowman and Littlefield, 1995) and *From Puzzles to Principles? Essays on Aristotle's Dialectic* (Lexington, 1999). Her current works include two books, one on a Confucian account of human rights and another on metaphysics and ethics, East and West.

Alan Thomas is a professor of philosophy at the University of York in the United Kingdom. Educated at Cambridge, Harvard, and Oxford, he has held visiting appointments in the United States,

Canada, and Australia. He is the author of *Value and Context: The Nature of Moral and Political Knowledge* (Oxford University Press, 2006), *Thomas Nagel* (Routledge, 2008), and *Republic of Equals: Predistribution and Property-Owning Democracy* (Oxford University Press, 2017). He has also published journal articles on moral, political, and social philosophy and on the philosophy of mind.

Elliot Turiel is the Jerome A. Hutto Professor of Education in the Graduate School of Education and an affiliated professor in the Department of Psychology at the University of California, Berkeley. He has served as associate dean and interim dean in the Graduate School of Education and has also been on the faculty at Columbia University and Harvard University. His research focuses on moral and social development, with an emphasis on distinctions between moral understandings and concepts of social conventions. He has also studied connections between culture and morality, including how people in lower positions on social hierarchies think about cultural practices of inequality. His books include *The Development of Social Knowledge: Morality and Convention* (Cambridge University Press, 1983) and *The Culture of Morality: Social Development, Context, and Conflict* (Cambridge University Press, 2002).

Thomas Widlok is professor of the anthropology of Africa at the University of Cologne in Germany. He holds an M.Sc. and a Ph.D. in social anthropology from the London School of Economics and Political Science and has previously taught at the universities of London, Heidelberg, Durham, and Zurich. His publications include work in comparative hunter-gatherer studies (Africa and Australia) and in cognitive anthropology, religion, and economics. Recent publications on virtue have appeared in *Anthropological Theory*, *HAU—The Journal of Ethnographic Theory*, and *A Companion to Moral*

Anthropology (Wiley, 2012). His latest monograph is *Anthropology and the Economy of Sharing* (Routledge, 2017).

Bart J. Wilson holds the Donald P. Kennedy Endowed Chair in Economics and Law at Chapman University's Economic Science Institute. His recent research as an experimental economist tests Adam Smith's theories of human nature as found in *The Theory of Moral Sentiments.* His research also uses laboratory experiments to explore the formation of markets and property rights systems. He has published papers in *American Economic Review, Proceedings of the National Academy of Sciences,* and *Evolution and Human Behavior.* His research has been supported with grants from the National Science Foundation, the Federal Trade Commission, and the International Foundation for Research in Experimental Economics. Before joining the faculty at Chapman, he was an associate professor of economics at George Mason University, a research scientist at the Economic Science Laboratory at the University of Arizona, and an economist at the Federal Trade Commission. He received his Ph.D. in economics from the University of Arizona.

Paul Woodruff has taught philosophy and classics at the University of Texas at Austin since 1973. His books include *Reverence: Renewing a Forgotten Virtue* (Oxford University Press, 2001, 2nd edition, 2014), *First Democracy: The Challenge of an Ancient Idea* (Oxford University Press, 2005), *The Necessity of Theater* (Oxford University Press, 2008), and *The Ajax Dilemma* (Oxford University Press, 2011), which concerns justice and disparity of rewards. He has also written plays, poetry, short fiction, and opera libretti, as well as translations from the Greek of Plato, Sophocles, Euripides, and Thucydides. He has served as chair of his department (1988–1991), director of the Plan II Honors Program (1991–2006), and inaugural dean of the School of Undergraduate Studies (2006–2012). He was educated at Princeton and Oxford. He served as a junior officer in the US Army in Vietnam from June 1969 to June 1970 and has recently published two plays that grew out of that experience, in Vietnam (1971 and 1974), *The Vietnam Plays.*

JUSTICE

Introduction

MARK LEBAR

It is hard to overstate the significance of justice in thinking about how our lives together should go. Concerns about justice of one sort or another are ever-present in the news and in our social relationships. Sometimes these are large-scale concerns (ethnic cleansing, war crimes, sexual harassment), while at other times they are small-scale (slights, broken promises, tokens of disrespect).

From long ago, we have thought of justice as something that can not only characterize (or not) our societies but can also characterize us. The first study of justice in Western history is Plato's *Republic*, and though the account of the just state he offers is interesting in its own right, his project is (officially) one of understanding what justice is in us; that is the challenge that Socrates confronts and the central concern of the work.[1] But in philosophy, over the past half-century or so, questions about our justice as individuals—justice of character, we might say—have been greatly eclipsed by questions about what makes societies just. Such questions certainly merit attention, but so do questions about our own just dispositions and actions, as do questions about the deep connections between them. And given the centrality of justice to our social lives, it is plain that these questions are not merely philosophical. They merit thought and study from a variety of perspectives.

This book is a sampling of just such a variety of thinking about justice as a trait of character. It surveys a range of questions, research methodologies, and results, from a variety of social sciences and humanities. One thing that we hope will strike the reader is the scope of inquiry it reflects. This includes disciplinary breadth, including not only philosophy and political theory but also economics, psychology, anthropology, biology, and law. Yet it also includes breadth in the range of questions. How do we become just? What do we inherit from our animal kin by way of capacities for justice? How can we think about becoming just in an unjust world filled with imperfect people? In what ways are children on the path to becoming just adults? Can law make people just? All these and more are explored in the chapters that follow.

One thing the reader may be surprised to find missing is any extended discussion of John Rawls or his important work on justice. This is because Rawls's work, influential as it is, is almost entirely concerned with the justice of institutions and societies. It is not an exaggeration to say that Rawls began a stampede that has overrun the older tradition of thinking about justice as a virtue of character. A search in the Philosopher's Index for works on justice since Rawls's magnum opus *A Theory of Justice* yields more than seventeen thousand entries; restrict it to discussion of justice as a virtue, and the yield falls by almost 95 percent. It need not denigrate the moral, philosophical, and social significance of Rawls's work and his legacy to think that there is a place for returning to ask about how we can become just as individuals or what that aspiration might mean.

This volume includes several chapters by philosophers on these topics, but it lacks what an extended philosophical exploration of justice as a virtue might perhaps be thought to consist of. What, philosophers might ask, are we even thinking of when we use the term "justice of character"? Though that is not the focus of this volume, there must be some concept common to the treatments of the various chapters, or we would risk talking past one another. What is that common core?

A careful conceptual analysis would inevitably be controversial and require a study in its own right, but we can perhaps navigate by some fixed points in the landscape. Plato begins his discussion of justice in *Republic* with examples that will echo in the chapters to follow: a just person repays his or her debts and gives to each what is his or her due.[2] Once Plato has hit on his recipe for the just psyche, he observes that it has what he takes to be the hallmarks of justice: a person so constituted would not steal or commit treachery or break faith.[3] Aristotle's thinking is more complex, but he believes the just person is not "grasping" for honors or wealth or the like.[4] In the chapters that follow, we see similar widely shared notions at work: Bart J. Wilson writes of respect for property; Thomas Widlok of distribution and sharing; Turiel, Dahl, and Besirevic of truthfulness; Sarah Brosnan of fairness. May Sim's discussion of the Confucian tradition focuses on *yi*, a matter of right treatment of others, including fair distributions and respect for the property of others and indeed a kind of respect for the self-determination of others. Those broad strokes will have to suffice for bounding our quarry; perhaps the best we can say is that justice of character will be that quality that brings about such character in its possessors. But even the more philosophical chapters here will do less by way of *identifying* what justice is than by considering how we can, or do, or may, *become* just.

We begin, appropriately enough, with some history. In chapter 1, "Growing toward Justice," philosopher Paul Woodruff takes us back to where Western thinking about justice began, with reflection on Plato's work on the subject. The enterprise of becoming just, Woodruff argues, requires contributions both from the individual aspiring to be just and from the community of which that individual is a part. Woodruff takes his inspiration from Plato in three ways. First, justice unites a community and prevents it from tearing itself apart. Second, it gives to each what is due. Third, justice in the individual and justice in the community are mutually reinforcing. But to these Platonic notions Woodruff adds a reminder: as humans, we are imperfect, and part of justice in imperfect creatures like us is recognition of that very imperfection. Our need for virtue, and for justice in particular, grows out of universal human needs that are met in a variety of ways in different cultures. Some cultures can be inimical to virtue; others provide environments in which we can practice the habits that grow nearer to virtue, without ever realizing it perfectly.

Growing just is something we are capable of, Woodruff argues, and we need to do so. For this, we need exemplars, from among those around us when we are young, communities that endorse this growth and its aim, and opportunities for leadership and the development of harmony with others. We need to be willing to broaden the community of those we interact with and cultivate the virtues besides justice as well. Failure in this enterprise is always a possibility, and Woodruff argues that understanding how it so often happens begins with self-knowledge. All of those factors necessary for growth are necessary and sometimes hard to get or maintain, but staying aware of our responses to what is broken is crucial to "weeding out the garden" supporting our growth.

Chapter 2 moves us forward several centuries. In "Rousseau, Smith, and Kant on Becoming Just," political theorist Ryan P. Hanley takes up the question of the degree to which Enlightenment thought about justice can inform our thinking about virtue of character, as opposed to its more familiar contributions to thought about the creation of a free and secure society. Hanley sees such contributions in the works of Jean-Jacques Rousseau, Adam Smith, and Immanuel Kant.

Rousseau's social contract view of political justice is familiar, but the moral psychology he sees as underlying the transition from natural beings to civil ones is complex. Rousseau clearly has in mind a process of cultivation and development as necessary for justice in the civil person, grounded in the twin impulses of self-love and pity. Surprisingly, perhaps, Hanley argues that this love is the source of the desire for justice, in being inclined to seek what is owed us.

Smith's views stand neither in square opposition to Rousseau's nor quite in parallel. Smith positions his conception of justice in contrast to the conception we might draw from Plato and Aristotle, as an all-encompassing virtue: perfection in conduct. Instead, Smith confines justice's attentions to harms and their avoidance, insisting on justice's "negative" nature as compatible with complete inaction. This constrained form of justice is foundational for social life in Smith's view. Thus, the personal virtue serves the purpose of social justice as security from injury. Smith concurs with Rousseau in the service of social justice to the protection of property but differs in seeing the personal virtue as in the main a corrective to self-love, as an identification with the perspective of the "impartial spectator" of our conduct. Smith's distinctive proposal is thus that we become just in large part by learning to see ourselves as others see us. In doing so, we harness not only sympathy—which makes the requisite perspective-taking possible—but also resentment (including sympathetic resentment of the harms done to others) and guilt as the sentimental engines of justice.

Finally, while Kant's conception of political justice may be better known, he did devote attention to the motives involved in individuals becoming just and in this reflects parallels with both Rousseau and Smith. Like them, Kant believed that a crucial function of the coercive mechanisms of the state is for security and the protection of property. Like Smith, he believed that preference for self poses the greatest threat to such security. Like Rousseau, he believed that the challenge was in obtaining security and freedom *together.* His version of the social contract, like Rousseau's, attempted to solve this problem.

The first of our contributions from social science begins in a different part of Enlightenment thought on justice: the writings of David Hume. In chapter 3, "Becoming Just by Eliminating Injustice: The Emergence of Property in Virtual Economies," economist Bart J. Wilson describes work in experimental economics that attempts to explore a kind of priority claim that Hume made regarding how we become just. Hume rejected the view that we are just in "giving others their due," because (he believed) nothing really is *due* others until we have settled on conventions of property. Thus, becoming just is a matter of developing those institutions and practices that ascribe to each of us some "due." Wilson's experiments cash out these conventions as a matter of rendering explicit rules that are tacitly at work in the interactions of individuals, to a considerable degree those suggested (once again) by Adam Smith. Wilson draws the evidence for this from a number of observations in experimental economics.

The first is a lab experiment in the production and allocation of fictitious goods. The researchers observe both the results of transactions in the game and the exchanges between participants as they attempt to arrive at norms for their interaction in a "Wild West" of goods without property rights attached.

The second is another lab experiment, modeled on Robert Ellickson's observations of norms that emerged among whalers on open seas that were resources for those taking whales. Dispositions not only to cooperate (or not) in property norms but also to punish noncooperators emerge in the lab as they did among the whalers. The sentiment of resentment (prominent in Smith's account of justice) is evident in the discussions among experiment participants and motivates the punishment norms that sustain emergent property norms. Wilson finds in this a template for one form of becoming just, which is participating in these emergent property systems.

But the insights of the Scottish Enlightenment are not the only ones relevant to thinking about how we make just people of ourselves. In chapter 4, "Learning How to Share," anthropologist Thomas Widlok asks how individuals build up "ethical skill," in particular the capacity to engage in rightful and just sharing practices. The aim of the research Widlok cites is to broaden the discussion of such practices to include non-European societies and cultures, as an antidote to reliance on samples from WEIRD (Western, Educated, Industrial, Rich, and Democratic) subjects. As it turns out, this considerably broadens the range of responses to research. Anthropological work outside WEIRD *cultures* also helps to reveal the biases built into other social scientific and philosophical examinations of people's attitudes toward requirements of justice.

This work helps to expose the nuance of cultural practice to a surprising degree. For example, even across a range of childhood ages, patterns of sharing among African children differ markedly between hunter-gatherer groups and agropastoralist groups. The developmental implications of these differences in culture manifest at quite a young age. This divide turns out to be more profound than the divide between "African" and "European" children. Children in agropastoral societies, whether African or European, are much more sensitive to meritocratic considerations than children in hunter-gatherer societies. As a result, the children of these groups regard inequalities in very different ways, and sharing practices vary widely in consequence.

Property is certainly one preoccupation of concern for justice, as it has always been. But so has a concern for truth-telling and honesty. In chapter 5, "Thought, Emotions, and Sentiments in the Development of Justice," psychologists Elliot Turiel, Audun Dahl, and Zinaida Besirevic explore the psychological evidence pertaining to people's choices to lie. Some of these choices amount to overt injustice, but others perhaps do not (for example, the choices of researchers who lie to their subjects about the research being done). Sometimes honesty is pitted against other moral values (think of the familiar example of "white lies"), and the decision-making in such situations is complex. How are such judgments made? Turiel, Dahl, and Besirevic focus on a process of coordination among differing considerations and goals and relate this sort of coordination to other research, bearing on (for example) rights.

The relevant appraisals engage deep concerns for the sanctity of life, respect for persons, and human dignity, all of which are intricately connected to justice. The connections with philosophical examination of these issues are varied, and some work in the neurology of moral judgments oversimplifies these connections. Much philosophical moral theory reflects the complexities of moral judgment in "hard cases," and Turiel, Dahl, and Besirevic believe these are also borne out in empirical research on how these judgments are made.

Observations about our neurological equipment for engaging in considerations of justice invite questions about the degree to which biology is involved in our capacities for justice. In chapter 6, "The Evolution of Justice," psychologist Sarah Brosnan traces some of the roots of the human sense of justice through their progenitors in other species, both near kin and more distantly related species. While this sense seems to be expressed in a variety of cultural forms, its expression also seems to be universal, which suggests that it has a biological basis. Thus, we may well be able to learn about ourselves by looking at other species.

An aversion to inequity seems especially tied to highly cooperative species; remarkably, this can occur both when disadvantaged through inequity and, in a more limited subset of species, when advantaged through it. Studying such an aversion in nonlinguistic species involves identifying and tracking responses to both comparative conditions. There is evidence that an aversion to inequity in various primate species actually may prompt the choice of cooperative partners in these species. The tie between aversion to inequity and cooperation is also borne out by research on other species (rats, domestic dogs, ravens, and crows).

These are the results of lab experiments, but there is also evidence from the wild, in canines as well as among primates. Only in chimpanzees, however, do we see strong evidence of advantageous inequity aversion. That suggests a shared emergence of the strong inequity aversions (both disadvantageous and advantageous) that we experience.

This work in social science arguably should inform philosophical thinking about the virtue of justice, and vice versa. In chapter 7, "The Dialectical Activity of Becoming Just," philosopher Jon Garthoff undertakes a synthesis of this sort. Garthoff explores connections between the psychological work on moral development of Lawrence Kohlberg and philosophical work on virtue acquisition, building on Talbot Brewer's notion of "dialectical activities"—activities whose nature undergoes increasing disclosure in our increasing engagement with them. Kohlberg is known for the idea of distinct stages of development and has been the target of considerable criticism (notably from Carol Gilligan). However, Garthoff believes that there is valuable work to be retained: *some* sort of developmental account of our moral capacities is obviously necessary. This is where Brewer's notion takes hold, as Brewer's model of dialectical activity seems especially well suited to the acquisition of virtue in ways congruent with Kohlberg's structure. Indeed, Brewer comes close to suggesting such a model himself in his discussion of the dialectical activity of friendship. Garthoff argues that the work in moral development can underwrite the dialectical activity of acquiring the virtue of justice.

Garthoff puts this model to work in considering how justice as a virtue, along the lines suggested by Woodruff, may be developed in morally nonideal conditions, those shaped by our acting wrongly, or being wrongly treated, or shaped by unjust social background conditions. The notion of dialectical activity in living virtuously, in just treatment of others in relationships that unfold over time with moral failure as part of them, is an attractive picture of the enterprise of becoming just.

In chapter 8, "Should Epistemic Injustices Be Redressed by the 'Corrective Virtues'?," philosopher Alan Thomas explores a different way we can be unjust in returning to considerations more central to philosophy proper. His target is the discussion of "epistemic injustice" advanced by Miranda Fricker. Fricker claims that we can be epistemically unjust to others in two ways: by failing to take their testimony seriously or by denying them the interpretative resources necessary to understand how they are being wronged. It is tempting to think that such injustice is a matter of institutional structures, but Thomas argues that the correct diagnosis is a matter of informal social norms and thus that the right corrective is virtue.

The virtue in question is one in which the just person focuses on status. Epistemic injustice occurs when I deny you epistemic credit by in some way implying that you were never in a position to receive it in the first place. This is a form of injustice, Thomas argues, and the antidote is precisely the just person's recognition of others as free and equal and as having dignity. On the other hand, this virtue can be cultivated only within a democratic ethos, which is part and parcel of liberal citizenship.

In chapter 9, "Confucian Values and Resources for Justice," philosopher May Sim pushes outside the boundaries of the Western tradition to consider how Confucian thought can contribute to thinking about justice as a virtue. Sim argues that, despite some arguments to the contrary, Confucianism has the resources to account for virtues that extend beyond the family, to equals and strangers. There is in fact a Confucian virtue of justice (*yi*). While it is true that these virtues are first cultivated in the family, their deep connection with self-determination allows for a recognizable framework of just familial, social, and political relations.

In Sim's view, the proper understanding of traditional Confucian virtues can provide the appropriate sort of ground for just relations with strangers, as well as the basis for the freedom and self-determination required for democracy. Sim argues that friendship is key. Among other reasons, it is the context for the development of the virtue of *xin* (trust or truthfulness), which Confucius ties to the very idea of personhood and the bare possibility of sociality. The notions of virtue and goodness that apply to all human beings assume a kind of equality that is not found in the hierarchical relations emphasized by critics. Sim argues that the relevant sort of equality can be found even in the hierarchical relations (e.g., ruler and ruled) that critics focus on. Justice and self-determination are to drive all actions, whether in relation to family, students and teachers, or political relations.

It is one thing to ask to what degree justice as a virtue of character can contribute to building a just society. In our concluding chapter 10, "Legislating the Personal Virtue of Justice," legal theorist Matthew A. Edwards considers the converse: to what degree the law is an appropriate tool for inculcating virtue. Virtue jurisprudence has come to occupy a significant position in normative legal theory; however, Edwards suggests that such an inculcation project would face major challenges, particularly in a liberal political culture committed to autonomy. Edwards begins by distinguishing virtue jurisprudence from other going concerns in normative legal theory—the standards by which we should judge legal rules, practices, and institutions. Relative to the more established schools, virtue jurisprudence is a newcomer; it similarly follows the interest of normative ethical theory in character, virtue, and authentic human flourishing. In its most striking (and controversial) form, it maintains that the purpose of law is to enable human beings to live lives expressing human virtue.

That aim also faces distinctive challenges. Still, Edwards argues that these challenges do not mean that there is no work for virtue jurisprudence to do. One of its effects has been to put pressure on the notions of well-being that can be taken for granted in the law; philosophical offerings of conceptions that do more to integrate the value of autonomy in a good life may go some way toward mitigating those challenges, for example. Second, the toolkit available for virtue jurisprudence includes more than just coercive criminal sanctions. If we think more comprehensively about the environment in which people can thrive and flourish, we recognize that legal institutions can play broader roles in realizing such environments.

The diverse array of questions and methods reflected in these chapters bears witness to the centrality of justice to human social relations in many guises. Insights from history, economics, psychology, anthropology, primatology, law, and philosophy (Eastern and Western) indicate the potential fruits of greater attention to the challenges in understanding what justice requires of us and how we as individual moral agents can better aspire to being just.[5]

NOTES

1. Plato, *Republic* bk. II.
2. Plato, *Republic* 331c–331e.
3. Plato, *Republic* 442e–443a.
4. Aristotle, *Nicomachean Ethics* V.2, 1130b3.
5. Thanks to Nathaniel Goldberg, Nancy Snow, an anonymous referee, and contributors to this volume for comments on this introduction.

Chapter 1

Growing toward Justice

PAUL WOODRUFF

INTRODUCTION

Justice sits awkwardly on a list of virtues. Virtues are qualities of character or soul that belong to individuals, whereas justice seems to be a quality of political systems or methods of distribution. But ancient Greeks even before Plato treated justice as a virtue of individual character or soul. Plato assumed that justice must be the same basic quality in a person's soul as it is in the character of a *polis*, a city-state. By contrast, Aristotle, the ancestor of today's virtue ethics, discusses only justice in distribution, offering no account of justice as a virtue of the individual soul. In this chapter, I propose to go back beyond Aristotle to Plato. Aside from his psychology, many of his proposals about justice hold promise. The theory I propose here grows from my lifelong study of Plato's account of justice. In these brief pages, I cannot fully expound or defend the theory. I have done more on its behalf elsewhere.[1] I will merely touch on its main points and proceed to my main task, which is to show how, on this theory, human beings can best advance in the direction of justice.

First, a word about the chapter title and why it refers to growing toward justice rather than becoming just. Becoming just is not possible for a human being on the theory I propose. Becoming just would be arriving at a state of justice after starting out from a condition without justice. But neither the starting out nor the arriving is possible for a human being.

Count out *arriving* at justice for two reasons. First, justice, like other virtues, is an ideal to which we humans can aspire and toward which we can grow.[2] And second, like health, such justice as we can achieve needs constant maintenance. If we cease to exercise after achieving physical fitness, we will soon be unfit. For Plato and his followers, virtue is like fitness. Those who think they have arrived at the goal of virtue, and so are doing nothing to stay there, are sinking away from it. Becoming *more* just—advancing in the virtue of justice—is the project of a lifetime.[3]

Count out *starting out* from a condition without justice because, as with any virtue, justice builds on itself; we become more just by practicing justice. No one could start at zero with justice. By nature, human beings apparently have some sense of justice, which we share with other species, as Sarah Brosnan points out in chapter 6 of this volume. That sense of justice is far from the full-blown virtue, but it is not zero, either. We also have by nature the capacity to develop toward the full-blown virtue in a supportive society.[4]

A small child who rankles at the injustice of favors shown to a sibling has something to start with toward justice, but this will lead nowhere without the support of a family and a community through which the child can learn to rankle at injustice shown to others.

The beginning from which we can start to grow this virtue must occur both in the individual (as a basic sense of justice) and in the community (as support for developing this sense into a virtue). Becoming more just is not a project that one person can undertake alone; it is a collaborative project in which an individual engages with a community, shares its practices, and endeavors to improve them.[5] Individuals and communities grow—or decline—in justice together. Justice cannot be a virtue of the solitary. How can we learn to share if we have no one with whom to share? We could not reasonably expect to be heroes of justice if we were alone with our commitments to this virtue. And we could not expect to form a just society if nature had not planted some justice in the souls of its members.

A THEORY OF JUSTICE IN THE COMMUNITY DERIVED FROM PLATO

Plato famously offers a single theory for justice, whether in a community or in an individual soul. I have derived a theory of justice in the community from Plato's. I do not think this theory can apply directly to individuals. Justice in an individual consists (roughly) in the combination of traits, habits, abilities, commitments, and values that support justice in the community. In the early part of this chapter, I will lay out the theory I propose for communities. I will focus on the individual later.

Justice in a community, on this theory, has at least five necessary features. I will summarize them now and expand on them later:

1. Justice binds a community together and protects it from civil war. Even a gang of thieves must have some measure of justice if it is stable and not riven with dissension.[6]
2. Justice gives to individuals and to groups what is due to them.[7]
3. Justice as a virtue of individuals is fed by, and also nourishes, justice in the community.[8]
4. Justice entails freedom; justice is not maintained by physical or psychological force but rather by the attractive power of justice itself.[9]

5. A way of justice in a community must be accepted as such by most members of that community. I call this the subjectivity condition.[10]

Growing toward justice is analogous (in some ways) to becoming a speaker of a language.[11] There is no learning a language without becoming a member of a community that speaks that language. Similarly, there is no growing toward justice outside a community. Justice, like language, will be different in different communities, but this does not entail unbridled relativism. A workable language must have certain features, though different, perhaps, for communities with different needs. The same goes for justice as a language of behavior; justice for a particular village must have features necessary to sustain that village. Justice holds a particular community together against the danger of civil war (though probably not in perfect harmony). To accomplish this, since we assume human beings have certain features in common, justice also must have corresponding features in common regardless of cultural difference. We may well debate what features of human beings are universal, and that debate has implications for justice. So we could not state a definitive list of the features that justice must have. Still, the features listed above serve as a useful sketch.

This theory of virtue is partly pragmatic in that it starts with a necessary condition (survival without civil war) that is measured by success in the practical world. Such pragmatism brings with it a weak strain of relativism. What works in one context may not work in another. All communities must cultivate courage in order to heed the many fears that protect human beings, while working through the ones that might prevent them from doing what they must in order to survive. But fisher peoples must take larger risks than farmers, so we should expect them to be less risk-averse than farmers. Similar differences have been found in justice across cultures, as Thomas

Widlok shows in this volume (chapter 4). Hunter-gatherers and agropastoralists exhibit different patterns of sharing.

Another consequence of the pragmatic element in this theory is that justice cannot be a matter of fixed principles. Because justice has to succeed in the practical world, it must be prepared to bend or change as circumstances require. Again, we have empirical evidence that people often operate in this way, as shown by Elliot Turiel, Audun Dahl, and Zinaida Besirevic in chapter 5 in this volume.

The relativism and flexibility of justice, however, are severely limited. Pragmatic constraints do not fully determine what counts as justice. To be accepted by a community as just (and therefore to meet the pragmatic constraint), a way of justice must always meet the very demanding condition of giving individuals their due. What this condition demands (as I will argue later here) is wisdom on the part of a community's leaders. Bending to circumstance is only acceptable if it is wisely done and wisely communicated. There is no justice without wisdom. This, I believe, is Plato's most important teaching about justice.

Justice, as a virtue of the individual soul, would then require the wisdom to judge what is due to the people with whom we have dealings; such wisdom would regulate our natural capacity to be angry at those who violate justice (including ourselves). We may imagine perfect justice among godlike people, but justice among human beings will have to be as imperfect as we are; at the same time it must offer just ways of handling our many imperfections. Human (as opposed to divine) justice entails the recognition of its own imperfection.[12]

On this theory, we know no sufficient condition for being just; it follows that we cannot know of ourselves or others that we or they are just—not with perfect epistemic justification.[13] Part of being humanly just is recognizing—wisely—that we can never have complete confidence in the justice of our judgments in the sphere of human activity. We can, however, often know injustice when we see it, as injustice usually involves a failure to satisfy one or another of the necessary conditions for justice. We may, in such cases, condemn injustice with a confidence that we cannot equal when proposing a remedy.

JUSTICE AND WISDOM IN COMMUNITY

Of the five conditions listed earlier, the one most important for our subject here is the third: the necessity of sharing justice between individuals and community. Justice as a virtue of individuals is fed by, and also nourishes, justice in the community. That is why individuals cannot be expected to grow in justice all on their own. They need families and larger communities that are also committed to growing toward justice.

In the *Republic,* Plato argues that the virtues of individuals and communities are related. A *polis* can be just, wise, courageous, and so on, by virtue of the like-named qualities in the citizens. Justice must be shared by all citizens in a just community.[14] If only some were just, the others would have to be held down by force. But if the community is held together by sheer force—that is, without justice—it will be inherently unstable. History shows that tyranny is an invitation for civil strife. So a community in which justice is not widely shared (in Plato's view and mine) will fail to satisfy the first necessary feature of justice.

As Plato argues, even a gang of thieves, if it stays together, is not without justice (*Republic* 352c4). The harmony that human justice produces need not be perfect; we do not all have to sing the same tune or even sing in the same key to be harmonious enough for practical purposes. It is necessary, however, that everyone (or almost everyone, at least a critical mass) remains committed to the project of living together as a community without civil war. Imperfect as we are, we all too often take actions that arouse others' sense of injustice to the point of anger. The virtue of justice (on this theory) allows people to get past anger and build communities. Procedural law expresses this virtue as shared by a community; in individuals, the virtue is evident mainly as a form of wisdom.

To see why wisdom is so important, we must look more closely at the nature of justice in the human realm. Consider the second necessary feature of justice, which I call the "dueness" condition. It's easy to see why justice requires that all individuals, and all groups, have what is due to them.[15] But it is hard to specify what is due in individual cases. It would be easier if justice and fairness were the same. They are not. Fairness can be obtained by following rules; justice cannot. I have argued elsewhere that there is no justice without compassion;[16] that is one reason justice is not fairness. Fairness is embodied in rules that are applied consistently (hence without compassion), whereas justice cannot be embodied in rules.[17] Rules of fairness are rather easy to apply because they do not bend for compassion;[18] justice is not easy to apply, because, like Aristotle's *epieikeia,* it must bend to circumstances, including those that call for compassion. If the rules do not bend to be appropriate for individual circumstances, then (we know by observation) people do not feel they are getting their due.[19] Practical human justice is, like other practical virtues, particularist.[20] Fools can be fair, but only the wise can be just. That is one reason I say that justice is a kind of human wisdom.

Another reason is that a way of justice must be recognized as just by the community if it is to fulfill its role of binding the community together—the subjectivity condition. But people do not always perceive that rule-following is just. In making decisions about my colleagues' salaries, as department chair, I discovered that I could not satisfy my colleagues by pointing to rules I had followed. Some of them insisted that their unique strengths needed to be recognized and that the rules did not fit them. Leaders who practice justice must aim at the wisdom needed to communicate the justice of their decisions. That's not easy. Harping on rules is not enough to show that individuals are getting their due.

Even if you give all members their due and go beyond simple fairness, you may still not achieve justice. We can imagine a society coming apart even when all are getting what is due to them—in the case in which they do not all *feel* that they are getting their due.[21] So we need to emphasize the subjectivity condition. Justice obtains only when people feel they are generally getting their due. Otherwise, a society could satisfy the dueness condition and still fail to meet the pragmatic goal. Not all societies that meet the subjectivity condition are just. A society that is culturally repressive may fail the dueness condition (e.g., by denying certain opportunities to women) and still meet the subjectivity condition (by making women believe that those opportunities are not their due).

That is why I added the freedom condition. A just community cannot be repressive. It is not given the appearance of harmony by physical or psychological force. Citizens get along in a just community because it is just, not because they are afraid to rock the boat or so psychologically damaged that they cannot see their way to rocking the boat (as in the case of people who are made to think they do not deserve equality). Hence, to achieve justice, we need the wisdom of honest persuasion, and we need to be able to see the difference between persuading people to accept a way of justice and manipulating them to do so. Plato's proposal in the *Republic*, involving the noble lie, seems manipulative, but keep in mind that he is committed—as he should be—to persuading the nonrational elements in the city and in the soul. We are not a perfectly rational species. But we are all capable of achieving the level of wisdom needed for getting along in a community over the long haul. How is that to be developed? And what sense does it make to speak of developing something that is natural?

DEVELOPING NATURAL VIRTUES: HABITS

Justice, at the human level, is one of the natural *human* virtues. But if it is natural, how can it be learned or acquired? To answer that, we need to understand the peculiarly human way in which our natural tools of survival—such as our virtues—are developed, rather than being innate. Virtue is as necessary to human life as are the social habits of other social species to their survival.[22] Plato's Protagoras had this basically right: without the social virtues, human beings can't form and maintain communities, and if they can't do that, they cannot survive.[23]

Virtue in general is a culture-based response to problems that are universal to the human situation. Take courage, for example. Fear is universal; any normal human can feel it. But, as pointed out earlier, a farming community might develop courage through habits of caution that would cripple a fishing village. So we do not have courage entirely by nature, the way bees have stings. By nature, we have the *need* for courage, as well as the faint beginnings of the virtue, what Confucians (using the metaphor of cultivation) would call a sprout; that is, we have some capacity that we can cultivate in order to grow toward courage.[24] But we are not born with courage entire. We must learn courage with the help of those around us. We humans need to acquire our tools of survival; bees have them by birth. We humans try to develop habits of virtue (though habits are not enough).[25] By contrast, bees cannot be habituated to sting, as the first attempt to practice the art of stinging would be fatal to the bee.

The sense of justice that we have by nature generally manifests itself as anger at perceived injustice, as we see in quite young children. Since we all have this anger by nature and since such anger can tear a community apart, we must develop ways of preventing or handling our anger that heal or at least do not destroy a community. That is where justice begins—as a cultural response to a universal human need. The community must find ways to cultivate justice in accordance with its culture in all of its individual members. To cultivate justice in individuals, a community must start by encouraging people to develop and maintain certain habits.

Habits must be maintained, or they ebb away. To make matters more difficult, a habit learned in one kind of situation may fail altogether in another. You may have been brave in war but become a coward in peace. You cannot rely on your virtue in the way you might rely on your physical strength. Muscle power rarely goes on holiday, though it weakens with age. But moral power seems to ebb and flow with the tide of situations.[26] Empirical evidence brings out our limitations; plainly, we would fall into hubris if we supposed that we could achieve perfection in any of the virtues. That is one reason I call this chapter "growing toward justice" rather than "becoming just." Human virtue is fragile, imperfect, and always dependent on maintenance by the individual and the community.

Furthermore, to develop a habit, you need practice and coaching. Practicing all by yourself gives limited benefits, even if you are practicing the cello. For the cello, you need the occasional presence of a coach who can warn you, for example, that your bow grip is deteriorating or your B-flat is sharp. For a habit such as courage, you depend more heavily on others than you do for playing cello. Suppose you are in a military unit that always runs at the smell of danger. Bad luck for you; the others will not give you the opportunity to practice courage, even if you have the good fortune to face danger with them—good fortune, because danger in good company would present you with an opportunity to practice the virtue. But danger in bad company is corrupting: you must either run away from the danger with your unit or stay in place and then either die alone or cultivate a habit of stupid rashness, which is not courage. You'll have only bad habits, whether you stay or follow your unit, and no habits at all if you are dead. Neither choice aids in the formation of good habits. More generally, even in life outside the military, acts of courage require communities that support courage. Stalinist Russia was not conducive to courage or honesty, as many reports show. Don't ask why Shostakovich and some other artists did not have the courage to resist Stalinist demands. Why should they put their lives and the lives of their loved ones in serious jeopardy for the sake of their art? If they did so, they would be following the call of their art, not of courage. Courage is not suicidal, nor does it sacrifice the lives of friends and family.

BEYOND HABITS: JUSTICE IN THE INDIVIDUAL

Justice, like any human virtue, is a lifelong project requiring a serious commitment; it is not merely a trait or a habit.[27] If you are a just person, you seek to develop justice and maintain it in yourself and others, find friends and companions who make similar commitments, and take joy in success, pain in failure. The clearest sign of justice is the pain you feel on giving way to temptations that should not have swayed you or the joy you feel on finding that you have come through a trying situation without a serious lapse in justice. The same goes for all the virtues.[28]

There is no such thing in the human sphere as a fixed trait that results in virtuous behavior in every situation (or if there is, it is extremely rare).[29] That's why self-knowledge is necessary for any virtue; we need to try to be aware of our shortcomings, ideally before they lead to bad action. A second necessity for any virtue is some level of action in accordance with that virtue, accompanied by pleasure. A third important condition is an abiding commitment to practice and cultivate the virtue. Action is not enough, however; we must also be oriented toward the value represented by the virtue. To grow toward justice, we must set a high value on justice, and we must take the ends of justice to be among our own ends.

Commitment, action, orientation, and self-knowledge are all necessary for justice at the human level. Much of this is captured in a splendid analect of Confucius: "The Master said, 'How could I dare to lay claim to either sageliness or Goodness? What can be said about me is no more than this: I work at it without growing tired and encourage others without growing weary.' "[30]

Perfect justice would call for us to know what is right in each situation. That is a tall order for a mere human being. If you had a moral compass, then you would always know what direction to go. But the moral landscape is not so simple as to allow for a reliable compass. A good compass would always point the right way. A bad compass might point steadily in a stupid direction. But we are surrounded everywhere by magnetic fields pulling our moral needles in variable directions. A true moral compass, then, will have a needle that spins around and won't settle when decisions are tough. Then you will have to decide what direction to go; if you go wrong, you will not be able to blame the compass. You will have nothing outside yourself to depend on; you will have to use your own judgment.[31] Then you will need moral wisdom, which is not at all like a compass. It is a combination of a moral sense and good judgment—the ability to decide where you should be going when the compass they gave you in Sunday school seems to point wrong or does not point at all. Your judgment then will be as good as you can manage at the time.

Justice is a virtue of leadership: just people care enough about justice that they take any opportunity to lead—or at least to speak out—when justice is at stake. An influential citizen or politician who is not just can cause justice to unravel. Consider the difference between the influence of US Presidents Abraham Lincoln and Ulysses S. Grant, who were committed to justice, and that of successors such as Rutherford B. Hayes, who were not. But you need not be famous or powerful to be a leader. As in the case of language usage, everyone sets an example for others, whether good or bad. Even small children can influence their human environment. We have no excuse for not acting as leaders when justice is at stake.

CONDITIONS FOR GROWTH

So far, I have offered only an elaborate theoretical hypothesis regarding the nature of justice, supported in part by empirical research but largely depending on its coherence as a theory. In this section, I consider its practical consequences for justice.[32] Under what conditions is justice most likely to grow in individuals and communities? What follows is speculative and calls for empirical evaluation. As a mere philosopher, I am not qualified to give the final word on this. Social science holds some promise in this area, but that is limited. Facts and values are inextricably bound together in any inquiry into how we may advance toward justice. Philosophy, empirical psychology, and anthropology must work together. *Caveat lector.*

Growing toward justice is difficult on the theory I have offered—so difficult that you cannot do it alone or in every circumstance. If you are growing toward justice, you have been lucky. Only some of the task has been under your control. If you have grown in human justice, you have had a family, teachers, and a community that are, to some extent, just. You have had opportunities to practice justice that allowed you to develop and strengthen your habits of justice. Be grateful for any growth in human virtue that you have been lucky enough to experience.

If my hypothesis about justice is right, we have evolved to have a need for justice by nature, and along with that need, we have evolved to have the capacity to develop the virtue—we have something from the beginning, call it a sprout or a capacity—that we can cultivate toward justice. This something includes the tendency to express anger—exhibited in quite small children—when we are not given our due.

Anger is to justice as fear is to courage, a universal emotion that is of great value to us but can be indulged to excess. Too much fear, or too little, can be crippling. Hence the need for a virtue that moderates and makes rational our habitual responses to danger. In a similar way, each of us needs to cultivate habits of anger that are conducive to harmony in our communities. This does not mean suppressing anger; we ought to be angry at injustice. It does, however, mean not being angry when a just system does not give us everything we want. Just as courage cultivates good habits relating to fear, justice cultivates good habits relating to anger over a lifetime.

How do you cultivate justice? As with plants, the ground must be fertile—that means you must have a capacity for personal growth. And the environment must be conducive—that is, your community must promote and reward moral health. You must also be prepared to do a bit of weeding. If you are growing, or have grown, toward justice, the following are probably true of you.

a. You have good examples of justice in your family or family-equivalent, your teachers, and the other people who show leadership around you.

Every elder teaches young people how to function in society. We are all responsible for our influence on others. This is a responsibility that most of us ignore. Your thermodynamics professor may think she is teaching you only thermodynamics, but she is also teaching you a way of dealing with people from a position of strength. She has power over you. Is she considering how her use of that power might influence you later in life, when you have power over others?

If you have the bad luck to be born into a community that is riven with unresolved disputes or in which the elders are consumed by selfish desires, then growing toward justice will be a challenge for you. Perhaps you would be able to recognize bad examples and react against them, using them as negative models. But, more likely, you will come to believe that people cannot resolve disputes or set a higher value on harmony than on self-interest. Then you will have small chance of growing toward justice.

Negative examples in literature, however, may be valuable. The oldest work in the European tradition begins with a scene of appallingly bad leadership. In order to save his army from plague, the commander Agamemnon must give up a prized trophy. This he refuses to do, until he decides to take a trophy away from the most valuable member of his team, Achilles. Then it is Achilles's turn to be angry, with a rage that almost destroys the army. Agamemnon sets a terrible example of unjust selfishness, and Achilles matches it eagerly. Hearing or reading the poetry of this scene, we can easily see how justice failed and why it failed.

b. Your community is willing to become more just, with the result that it will not block the advance of its members toward justice.

If I am right in my hypothesis that justice in individuals and justice in communities feed each other, then you will not be able to advance on a solitary path. You need companions on the journey. In an age or a society in which injustice thrives, we can have little hope of growth toward justice. Of such a time, Hesiod (*Works and Days* 192–198) wrote:

[For them "justice" will be in violence, there will be
No more respect. A bad man will harm his better
By telling a crooked tale and swearing an oath to it.

Hate-faced Envy will dog the wretched feet of every
Human being, spreading malice and rejoicing in evil.
And then, indeed, Reverence and Righteous Anger [*Nemesis*]
will hide
Their lovely faces behind white robes, leave the earth
With its wide-reaching roads to join the tribe of immortals
On Olympus, and abandon human beings.[33]

c. *You have opportunities to practice justice; for this, it is ideal for you to have opportunities for leadership from an early age.*

By "leadership," I do not mean authority. You exercise leadership whenever you take the lead in a group, even for a moment. The lowest-ranking member of a team may show leadership by setting an example or speaking up.[34] Part of leadership is keeping whatever team you are on working together in harmony. To do this, you must exercise justice to prevent disputes if possible and to resolve the ones that cannot be prevented. If you have successfully resolved a dispute, you will have kept both parties working on the team. This requires both wisdom and eloquence. Hesiod (*Theogony* 83–87), composing poetry at the dawn of European culture, wrote that judges must be inspired by the muses if they are to send away litigants at peace with each other:

Then [the Muses] pour sweet honey on his tongue, and the
words
From his mouth flow out in a soothing stream, and all
The people look to him as he works out what is right
By giving resolutions that are fair: he speaks out faultlessly
And he soon puts an end to a quarrel however large, using
his skill.[35]

d. *You are practicing to know yourself; from your self-knowledge, you are growing both the compassion that is essential to justice and the modesty that comes from knowing how easily you may judge wrongly.*

Self-knowledge is at the heart of every virtue.

e. *You are observing the human landscape and learning to appreciate the hidden merits of people around you.*

No matter how rebarbative you may find the people with whom you have dealings, if my hypothesis is correct, very few of them are incapable of justice. I have written of this elsewhere.[36] Give them a chance to side with justice.

f. *You are practicing good communication, both by listening to those around you and by speaking or writing, in order to approach the consensus that justice requires.*

Listening well is essential; without it, you will not be able to recognize problems that threaten the subjective aspect of justice. Speaking is also important, as Hesiod pointed out in the passage quoted earlier.

g. *You are trying to be independent in your judgments, willing to challenge an old consensus, and open to broadening the membership of your community.*

What is your community? We must not take a narrow view of this, or the survival of the species will be in doubt. Just people seek to resolve any conflict they can within the human community.

h. *You are equally committed to other virtues, such as wisdom, courage, reverence, and self-control.*[37]

Without wisdom, your judgment will be impaired. Without courage, you will not stand up for justice when it seems dangerous to do so, as it often does. Without self-control, you may be tempted to overstep the bounds of justice in seeking to satisfy your desires. Without reverence, you may be distracted by hubris into trusting too far in your own judgment.

WEEDING TO AVOID MORAL FAILURE

If I am right that all of us start with the sprouts of justice, then why do so many people not seem to produce a decent crop? What are the weeds that cause moral failure? What is it that takes nourishment away from justice? What overshadows it and keeps it from the sun? What garish flowers distract us from meeting the needs of justice? When we fail at a virtue, why do we fail? These are crucial questions for us to keep in mind as we observe our own behavior. Self-knowledge should help. "The Master said, 'That I fail to cultivate Virtue, that I fail to inquire more deeply into that which I have learned, that upon hearing what is right I remain unable to move myself to do it, and that I prove unable to reform when I have done something wrong—such potential failings are a source of constant worry to me.'" (Confucius Analects 7.3): Drawing on the sources we listed for justice, we can start to list sources of failure:

Unjust elders or leaders setting bad examples. In *Iliad* 1, Agamemnon sets a terrible example, putting his personal honor ahead of the army's mission. Not surprisingly, Achilles follows his example.

Anger stoked by bad losers, especially if they have influence on the public, as politicians and celebrities do.

An unjust community that is presented as the norm. If bullying or hazing is the norm in a group, then the victims in one generation will become the perpetrators in the next. If it is not the norm, then victims are likely to resolve never to make others suffer as they have done. A razor edge separates the two responses. Research on bullying may help us see how to get on the right side of this issue.

Selfishness. If you know how to be angry only at injustices to yourself, you will not grow toward justice. Part of growing up is learning to be angry at injustices done to others.

Tyranny. Tyranny undermines all the human virtues by making virtues unsafe to practice. Justice should never be made suicidal.

Temptations that strain human goodness. Great treasures sometimes lie waiting for us to take them, if only we relax justice for a moment. In Sophocles's *Philoctetes,* the wily Odysseus teaches a young recruit to lie in order to score victory over Troy. "One day of badness," he says, in effect, "and you can be rich in treasure and honor for the rest of your life—and, basking in your wealth and power, you will never have to be bad again." A sore temptation, to which the boy at least partly succumbs.

Overconfidence in your own justice or wisdom. This is the sneakiest weed of all. It can flourish unnoticed by the casual gardener. Weeding it out requires the ceaseless vigilance of a self-questioning Socrates.

WHERE TO BEGIN

I have no place to begin except from where I am. I have enough work to do figuring out where I am. I have no business telling my readers or anyone else where they are and what they should do next. That way lies hubris, and I am conscious enough of failures in my own life to know better than to tell others how to conduct theirs.

Any virtue is easily lost, and justice is no exception. A paradox we must learn to accept is that gains in virtue may entail losses. Every success, every victory, is an opportunity for overconfidence. That is why a wise mind is suspicious of victory. You may think that only a spoilsport would look behind every silver lining to catch sight of a dark cloud. But if I wish to be wise or just or reverent, I should always guard myself against the thought that one success promises another.

Most of us should begin by reminding ourselves that justice saves human lives by saving communities. Then we should attend to whatever is relevant to justice in our particular situations. Those of us who have opportunities for leadership should use them on behalf of justice, speaking up for justice, setting good examples, and not letting injustices go unnoticed.

In dealing with others who seem not disposed to justice, we should avoid giving sermons. Sermons make an audience deaf. We will do far better by asking the right question, in the manner of Socrates. Most notably in the *Gorgias,* Socrates asked questions that exposed deeply hidden commitments to justice in his three partners, all of whom initially denied such commitments, directly or indirectly. Socrates used shame to bring these out, but I do not believe that shame is essential to asking the right question. If my hypothesis about justice and the human condition is correct, then all normal humans (all those who are not psychopaths) have at least the sprout of justice—the capacity to feel angry when not given their due. On this, something can be built.

Individuals with whom you speak may have commitments that entail a commitment to justice that they have not recognized. For example, if they are committed to being leaders, then they have a commitment to justice, whether they know it or not. Many people who say they worship power at the expense of justice nevertheless aspire to leadership. Asking the right question might help them see that power without justice will not make them leaders.[38] Leadership consists of influence that does not depend on the use of force. Influence over free people depends on justice. Would-be leaders can be brought to see that a leader must have a team of *willing* followers and that no followers are willing if they feel unjustly treated by their boss. Would-be leaders should also come to see the value of justice in their communities by noting that a functional community always has some measure of justice in it.

So this is my concluding advice to those who would be just: For yourself, seek self-knowledge, make a strong commitment, try to act on it, so as to develop the habit, and make the ends of justice your personal ends. For others, set a good example, and ask the right questions.

NOTES

1. Woodruff 2011, 140–161.
2. The moral danger in supposing that virtue is achievable should be obvious: it is when one is most confident in one's virtue that one is most vulnerable to moral error.
3. I have argued that a virtue is not something we simply have, like a trait or a habit, because traits and habits can fail us. Virtue, in my view, involves a commitment to develop and maintain it, as well as a clear orientation toward the value that the virtue represents. In this, my view is similar to that of Kant, who says that rather than possessing a virtue, one is possessed by that virtue, See *The Metaphysics of Morals* 6.406/165; 6.384/148; hereafter *MM*. Citations of this work are by volume and page number in the Natorp edition/page number in the Gregor translation (Kant 1996).
4. This is an ancient idea, first articulated in the myth Plato attributes to Protagoras, in which Zeus gives justice to the human race and insists that it be given to all, unlike the gifts of technical knowledge, which go to specialists. *Protagoras* 322d. Plato draws on this in developing his theory in the *Republic*, which requires that all citizens have some share in justice (see Woodruff 2012).
5. We shall see later in this chapter that justice differs in some degree from one community to another; there is no justice you can practice, in order to become more just, that is not specific to a community.

6. Plato, *Republic* 352c. The first two features are familiar from Plato's initial account of justice in the first book of the *Republic*.
7. Much of the familiar modern work on justice addresses the question of what is due to individuals in a community. For my discussion of the difficulty of this question, see Woodruff 2011, esp. 140–161.
8. For the argument that this is Plato's view, see Woodruff 2012.
9. This is a consequence of the first feature, with the observation that repressive communities are prone to rebellion and not stable. It is a consequence of the second feature with the plausible premise that one of the things due to each person is freedom.
10. This, too, is a consequence of the first feature. The community's members cannot be drawn together by procedures or principles they do not accept as just. Rational agreement in only an original position would not be good enough to prevent civil discord. On the Platonic theory, all elements must agree, whether rational or not. This is so both in his utopian city of Kallipolis and in the soul. Otherwise, the rulers would have to use force, violating the fourth condition.
11. The language analogy is attributed by Plato to Protagoras (*Protagoras* 327e–328a). Human beings have by nature capacities both for language and for social virtues. The analogy does not hold for the origins of language and virtue. We start with the ability to sense injustice; we do not start with the ability to detect bad grammar.
12. Here I reject Plato's proposal outside the *Republic* that we become just by imitating the gods (*Theaetetus* 176b). Being perfect morally, the gods cannot know how to be just in the human sphere.
13. Plato makes this point by distinguishing a sphere in which knowledge is possible (the realm of Forms) from the sphere of human activity, in which only judgment, not knowledge, is possible. Even to the philosopher who returns to the cave, the shadows remain shadows and so not strictly knowable; the difference in the philosopher is that she knows what the shadows are shadows of.
14. See Woodruff 2012.
15. *To prosêkon hekastôi apodidonai: Republic* 1, 332c2. This needs to be understood generously, as Hamlet points out to Polonius, who proposes, in effect, to give the traveling players their due: "Use every man after his desert and who shall scape whipping? Use them after your own honor and dignity; the less they deserve the more merit is in your bounty" (*Hamlet*, act 2, scene 2, line 527).
16. Woodruff 2011, 98–109. Here I deviate from Platonic theory; Plato does not have room among his virtues for compassion.
17. See chapter 5 in this volume, which reviews empirical research supporting the thesis that norms of justice (or, indeed, more generally morality) are not simply a set of unconditional standards.

18. Under rules of fairness, I include equality, proportionate equality, and the difference principle but not what Aristotle calls *epieikeia*, usually translated as "equity" but better rendered as "fittingness." No principle captures that idea. Not surprisingly, Kant is uncomfortable with equity, "a mute divinity who cannot be heard"; in most cases, he says, judges cannot take equity into account, but he recognizes that the "strictest right can be the greatest injury" (*MM* 6.235/27).
19. Perfectly fair procedures can leave people seething with discontent, as argued in Woodruff 2011, 110–119. This is generally due to the resistance of fairness to making exceptions to rules and is often exacerbated by failures of communication.
20. Practical virtues are particularist in that they cannot be fully expressed by principles or by purely descriptive concepts such as fearlessness. Plato's Socrates shows on several occasions that certain concepts of virtue are deceptive fakes, such as fearlessness for courage. I call such concepts "doubles" of the virtues. In this view, fairness is the double of justice because it can be expressed as a set of principles and justice cannot. The doubles all look like the corresponding virtues but are tied to fixed principles and so do not suit all cases. See Woodruff 2011, 131–139.
21. It is an awkward fact of life that not everyone feels satisfied with a distribution that is objectively fair; that awkwardness lies behind what I call the Ajax dilemma (Woodruff 2011, esp. 85–87).
22. "Men are benefitted by virtues as bees are by having stings, even though the use of this valuable possession may be fatal to the individual man or bee. And the alternative is not: virtues for their own sake, or selfishness" (Geach 1977, vii, 16; see also Foot 2001). For ancient views on naturalism and virtue ethics, see Woodruff 2002.
23. "Zeus therefore, taking fear that our race would be entirely killed off, sent Hermes to bring Reverence and Justice [αἰδῶ τε καὶ δίκην] to the human race, so that Reverence and Justice would bring order to cities and be the communal bonds of friendship [δεσμοί φιλίας συναγωγοί]"; Plato, *Protagoras* 322c1–3). I believe that Plato takes from this the assumption about justice that guides the *Republic*. The universality of social virtues across cultures and even some species (though with important differences) supports the Protagorean hypothesis.
24. Aristotle, *Nicomachean Ethics*, book 2, chapter 1, 1103a24–25: "So it is neither by nature nor against nature that the virtues come to be in us, but we are born with the natural capacity to take them on, and we complete [the acquisition] through habit." See Sim, chapter 9 in this volume. Compare Mencius, on which see Ivanhoe 2000, 18.
25. Habits do not suffice because we exercise them only in familiar kinds of circumstance (see Doris 2002). And qualities that are not engrained as habit, but

are innate, may function as virtues. What other social animals have that is analogous to virtue is mostly not habitual (see note 22).

26. On the power of situations over moral traits, see Doris 2002. I know of no philosopher who contends that we can achieve perfection. But much in the language used by philosophers can seem to imply this. And some virtue ethics theories ground rightness on what the perfectly virtuous person would do. This fails for the obvious reason that virtuous human beings must be able to deal virtuously with moral errors they have made. Consciousness of imperfection is vital to the Socratic tradition in ethics. It is a crucial element in any human virtue (as basic to human wisdom) in this tradition, but it is not emphasized in neo-Aristotelian theories.
27. Traits and habits are not reliable. For the danger in relying on them, see notes 3 and 25.
28. Aristotle, *Nicomachean Ethics*, book 2, chapter 3, which opens this way: "We must treat the pleasure or pain one feels in actions as a sign of the virtues."
29. For the empirical evidence for this claim, see Doris 2002.
30. *Analects* 7.34. All quotations from Confucius are from Slingerland 2003.
31. This is essentially Kant's distinction between duties of right and duties of virtue; for the latter, the agent is the only arbiter. *MM* 6.383/148.
32. Much of the content of this section is shared with chapter 10 of Woodruff 2018. Growing toward one virtue is like growing toward another.
33. Gagarin and Woodruff 1995, 15.
34. On leadership, see Woodruff 2018.
35. Gagarin and Woodruff 1995, 19–20.
36. Woodruff 2011, 178.
37. By "self-control," I mean what Plato meant by σωφροςύνη, not ἐνκρατεία—the virtue that tempers desire without trampling it.
38. For an example of such a dialogue, see Woodruff 2014, 253–255.

WORKS CITED

Doris, John. 2002. *Lack of Character: Personality and Moral Behavior*. Cambridge: Cambridge University Press.

Foot, Philippa. 2001. *Natural Goodness*. Oxford: Oxford University Press.

Gagarin, Michael, and Paul Woodruff. 1995. *Early Greek Political Thought from Homer to the Sophists*. Indianapolis: Hackett.

Geach, Peter. 1977. *The Virtues: The Stanton Lectures 1973–4*. Cambridge: Cambridge University Press.

Ivanhoe, Philip. 2000. *Confucian Moral Self-Cultivation*, 2nd ed. Indianapolis: Hackett.

Kant, Immanuel. 1996 [1797]. *The Metaphysics of Morals.* Translated by Mary Gregor. Cambridge: Cambridge University Press.

Slingerland, Edward. 2003. *Confucius: Analects, with Selections from Traditional Commentaries.* Indianapolis: Hackett.

Woodruff, Paul. 2002. "Natural Justice." In *Presocratic Philosophy: Essays in Honor of Alexander Mourelatos,* edited by Victor Caston and Daniel W. Graham, 195–204. Aldershot: Ashgate.

Woodruff, Paul. 2011. *The Ajax Dilemma: Justice, Fairness, and Rewards.* New York: Oxford University Press.

Woodruff, Paul. 2012. "Justice As a Virtue of the Soul." In *Oxford Studies in Ancient Philosophy, Supplementary Volume: Virtue and Happiness: Essays in Honor of Julia Annas,* edited by Rachana Kamtekar, 89–101. Oxford: Oxford University Press.

Woodruff, Paul. 2014. *Reverence: Renewing a Forgotten Virtue,* 2nd ed. New York: Oxford University Press.

Woodruff, Paul. 2018. *The Garden of Leaders: A Challenge for Higher Education.*

Chapter 2

Rousseau, Smith, and Kant on Becoming Just

RYAN P. HANLEY

The contribution of the philosophers of the Enlightenment to the evolution of the concept of justice seems quite clear on its face. As many have chronicled, a chief concern of much Enlightenment moral and political thought was to define that polity capable of establishing the conditions of maximized freedom and security such that all citizens might be free to pursue their individual interests as they saw fit.[1] A state, in this view, exists to provide a legitimate and exclusive monopoly on coercive force that can be used to ensure that individuals uphold their contracts and are otherwise prevented from harming one another in the course of pursuing their interests. Justice thus conceived as nonmalfeasance was an important contribution of Enlightenment philosophy to the history of the concept of justice, as well as a sharp departure from ancient philosophical traditions that understood justice in the more capacious sense of the virtue that represented the summation or peak of upright behavior.[2]

This familiar account of the Enlightenment's conception of justice is right in crucial respects—but only half right. For while it captures an important side of the Enlightenment's contribution to the development of liberalism, it leaves unexplored another side of Enlightenment thinking about justice, namely, the ways in which Enlightenment thinkers conceived of the motives that lead us to act justly, motives that go well beyond self-interested fear of punishment. Put differently, where the familiar account helpfully captures the political concept of justice developed in the Enlightenment, it leaves unexplored the Enlightenment's insights into the moral psychology of justice and specifically its insights into the ways in which various of our natural sentiments and faculties might be cultivated and developed in ways that best enable us to become just.

The aim of this chapter is thus twofold. First, it provides an overview of the political conception of justice developed in Enlightenment philosophy. Second, it provides an introduction to Enlightenment philosophy's comparatively less well-known contributions to the moral psychology of justice.[3] This second aim requires examining both how Enlightenment philosophers understood our "natural" moral psychology and how they thought these natural sentiments and faculties might best be developed via education and experience. In order to render these two aims manageable, what follows focuses on the accounts of justice set forth by three key Enlightenment thinkers—Jean-Jacques Rousseau, Adam Smith, and Immanuel Kant—who all not only developed robust accounts of justice in both the political and psychological senses but whose accounts also exhibit significant and sometimes surprising overlaps.

ROUSSEAU

We begin with Rousseau. Rousseau clearly developed both a political and a psychological theory of justice, though it is the political theory that is better known today. This political theory begins with the notorious account in the *Discourse on Inequality* (*Second Discourse* [SD]) of man's transition from the state of nature to the civilized state. As is well known, the decisive moment in this transition was the invention of property: "the true founder of civil society" and all its "crimes, wars, murders, miseries and horrors" was famously "the first person who, having fenced off a plot of ground, took it into his head to say *this is mine*" (SD 43). Prior to this "first person," there was no need for justice. But "from property once recognized, the first rules of justice" came—rules that became necessary once "all saw themselves with some goods to lose" (SD 50). And this state in which individuals possessed property but lacked recourse to institutions that could protect their possessions was the worst condition of all:

> As the most powerful or most miserable made of their force or their needs a sort of right to the goods of others, equivalent according to them to the right of property, the destruction of equality was followed by the most frightful disorder; thus the usurpations of the rich, the brigandage of the poor, the unbridled passions of all, stifling natural pity and the as yet weak voice of justice, made man avaricious, ambitious, and evil. (SD 52)

Rousseau famously criticizes Thomas Hobbes for failing to see that our natural state was peaceful rather than warlike (e.g., SD 21). Yet Rousseau's own account of the state of mankind after the invention of property but prior to the invention of government offers as clear an image of the "war of all against all" as anything found in Hobbes.

If property is the problem that makes justice necessary, what solution does Rousseau propose? In short: government founded on contract. Yet the first efforts in this direction, he notes, were disastrous. The possessors of property, seeing how precarious their possession was, made a proposition: "Let us unite, to protect the weak from oppression, restrain the ambitious, and secure for everyone the possession of what belongs to him. Let us institute regulations of justice and peace to which all are obliged to conform, which make an exception of no one" (SD 53–54). But this, Rousseau would have us know, was merely a swindle of the have-nots by the haves, who tricked the poor into consenting to institutions aimed at perpetuating the domination of the weak by the strong. And avoiding this nightmare—namely, that "the multitude will always be sacrificed to the few, and the public interest to particular interest," such that "those specious names, justice and order, will always serve as instruments of violence and as arms of iniquity" (*Emile* [E] 236)—forms much of the impetus for Rousseau's positive political philosophy.

To this end, Rousseau argues that the first illegitimate contract needs to be replaced by a legitimate contract, one capable of achieving the end he calls the "most necessary and perhaps most difficult in the government": "rigorous integrity in providing justice for all, and especially protecting the poor against the tyranny of the rich" (*Discourse on Political Economy* [DPE] 154, 165). Rousseau's fullest answer to this question is to be found in the principles set forth in his *Social Contract* (SC). Full exploration of the mechanisms proposed in the *Social Contract* for the establishment of this legitimate order would go well beyond what space here permits.[4] For our purposes, the main point is that Rousseau claims in the *Social Contract* to lay the foundations for a state that can legitimately provide the justice that was unnecessary in the state of nature but indispensable to a civil society dedicated to protecting property rights. Yet less clear is the type of justice that Rousseau sought to guarantee through his social contract. Some have read him as arguing that justice exists by nature and needs merely to be activated by law, whereas others read him as arguing that justice exists solely by convention.[5] Evidence abounds for both readings. On the positivist side, the *Social Contract* opens by claiming that the "sacred right" of social order "does not come from nature; it is therefore based on conventions" (SC 131). So, too, it is argued in the *Discourse on Political Economy* that the general will "which is the source of the laws" is "the rule of what is just and unjust" (DPE 143) and that "it is to law alone that men owe justice and freedom" (DPE 146). Elsewhere, however, Rousseau suggests that justice is not conventional but anchored in a realm that transcends mere convention: "Whatever is good and in accordance with order is so by the nature of things, independently of human conventions. All justice comes from God; He alone is its source" (SC 152). This complex passage has crucial implications for the debates over Rousseau's relative positivism. Without aspiring to resolve these here, what is clear is that his political conception of justice turns on recognition of the need to create institutions and laws capable of guaranteeing the legitimate property rights that distinguish civil society from the state of nature.

With this in place, we can turn from this relatively familiar side of Rousseau's account of justice to its less familiar side: his conception of the relationship of moral psychology to justice and especially the types of moral development and cultivation that just individuals need. Attending to Rousseau's views on moral development is critical, as some of his most prominent formulations of our transition from natural beings into just beings seem on their face to suggest a sudden and almost magical transformation. Take, for example, his famous account in the *Social Contract*:

> This passage from the state of nature to the civil state produces a remarkable change in man, by substituting justice for instinct in his behavior and giving his actions the morality they previously lacked. Only then, when the voice of duty replaces physical impulse and right replaces appetite, does man, who until that time considered only himself, find himself forced to act upon other principles and to consult his reason before heeding his inclinations. (SC 141)

This passage clearly describes a decisive transition. But its implicit suggestion that this "remarkable change in man" was merely a passive byproduct of his "passage" from one state to another glosses over a long train of development that Rousseau took care to detail elsewhere. Take, for example, his account in *Emile* of the child's emergence into the "moral order." Here he says that "*justice* and *goodness* are not merely abstract words—pure moral beings formed by the understanding—but are true affections of soul enlightened by reason, are hence only an ordered development of our primitive affections" (E 235). He reiterates this claim later, saying of Emile that "the true principles of the just, the true models of the beautiful, all the moral relations of beings, all the ideas of order are imprinted on his understanding" and indeed imprinted there not simply by nature but "as a result of the cultivation of his inclinations" (E 253). These passages, calling explicit attention to the "cultivation" and "ordered development" of our "affections" and "inclinations," are central to Rousseau's theory of justice and reveal a side of this theory that goes well beyond the more familiar political account.

Of what, then, does this cultivation and development consist?[6] To see this, we need to refer to Rousseau's portrait of the natural man in the first part of the *Second Discourse*. Man in the state of nature, as we have already noted, was wholly ignorant of justice. This was partly the result of the conditions in which he found himself: as he "did not have the slightest notion of thine and mine," he lacked "any genuine idea of justice" (SD 38). But this also partly had to do with the conditions of his mind. Rousseau is skeptical of those philosophers who in studying natural man "make him a philosopher himself, discovering alone the most sublime truths, and making for himself, by chains of very abstract reasoning, maxims of justice" (SD 29). All of this Rousseau thinks well beyond natural man, limited as he is to what he has been given by nature. Two natural principles are especially important, Rousseau explains, namely, those "two principles anterior to reason, of which one interests us ardently in our well-being and our self-preservation, and the other inspires in us a natural repugnance to see any sensitive being perish or suffer, principally those like ourselves" (SD 14–15). Later, he will give each of these principles a name—love of self (*amour de soi*) and pity (*pitié*)—and their development, of course, drives much of Rousseau's story. Yet these two principles are of particular interest to us insofar as each plays a key role in Rousseau's account of our development as just agents.

We begin with pity, which plays a particularly prominent role in man's natural state.[7] Here, before the creation of political institutions, natural pity serves as a functional substitute for justice. As Rousseau explains, "pity is a natural feeling which, moderating in each individual the activity of love of oneself, contributes to the mutual preservation of the entire species." Thus, "instead of that sublime maxim of reasoned justice, *Do unto others as you would have them do unto you,* it inspires all men with this other maxim of natural goodness, much less perfect but perhaps more useful than the preceding one: *Do what is good for you with the least possible harm to others*" (SD 37–38). Several elements of Rousseau's claim deserve notice. First, pity is an instinct, which Rousseau goes on to call a "natural feeling" anterior to reason and which serves as a substitute for justice in beings incapable of reason. Second, the "natural goodness" that pity makes possible consists wholly in restraining pernicious behavior and doing "the least possible harm to others." In this sense, Rousseauian natural pity not only is an effective stand-in for a justice that has yet to emerge, but in limiting itself to minimization of harm, it also represents a sharp departure from earlier theories of justice that regarded justice as a far more extensive virtue.

In *Emile,* Rousseau expands this argument, introducing a new form of pity. Developed pity, in contrast to the natural pity of the *Discourse,* requires cognitive abilities not necessary for natural pity. But it also has a complicated relationship to self-love. Especially noteworthy on this front is Rousseau's account of how we feel when we witness an injustice:

> One sees some act of violence and injustice in the street or on the road. Instantly an emotion of anger and indignation is aroused in the depths of the heart, and it leads us to take up the defense of the oppressed; but a more powerful duty restrains us, and the laws take from us the right of protecting innocence. (E 287–288)

Rousseau packs a host of crucial concepts into this account of how we feel when we see the innocent suffer harm unjustly. First, he makes clear that in all cases that do not directly impinge on our self-interest, we naturally "wish for the happiness of others" (E 288). Second, when the happiness of others is unjustly infringed, our natural reaction is "an emotion of anger and indignation." This emotion needs to be subordinated, of course, to that "more powerful duty" we owe to the law. And as he explains elsewhere in a claim that is key for his theory of justice, this subordination itself requires that we transform pity: "to prevent pity from degenerating into weakness," it must be "generalized and extended to the whole of mankind," for only then "one yields to it only insofar as it accords with justice"—an argument that culminates in the insistence that "for the sake of reason, for the sake of love of ourselves, we must have pity for our species still more than for our neighbor" (E 253).

Rousseau's formulation suggests the complexity of pity's relationship to justice. Pity is indispensable for justice, but it needs development and cultivation to transform it beyond its natural form. In addition, pity is not merely an other-directed sentiment but one governed by concerns that emerge from "the love of ourselves." And this brings us back to the second of the two principles central to Rousseau's theory of human nature. Love of self, perhaps surprisingly, Rousseau in fact regards as the source of our desire for justice.

In *Emile,* he explicitly claims that "our first duties are to ourselves; our primary movements are centered on ourselves; all our natural movements relate in the first instance to our preservation and our well-being. Thus, the first sentiment of justice does not come to us from the justice we owe but from that which is owed us" (E 97). To underscore the point, he recounts two vignettes. The first is an infant's reaction to being struck by his nurse. After the blow, "the unfortunate was suffering with anger; he had lost his breath; I saw him become violet" and express "all the signs of the resentment, fury and despair of this age"—from which Rousseau concludes, "if I had doubted that the sentiment of the just and the unjust were innate in the heart of man, this example alone would have convinced me" (E 65–66). The second is a story he tells of Emile's reaction to affronts. "To meet and put up with a slap or being given the lie" is to suffer an injury, and "Emile knows the justice he owes himself in such a case"; "he owes himself justice and is the only one who can render it" (E 250n). Retaliation for harm done to our person, Rousseau thus insists, is justified on the grounds of the concern for self-preservation that is the effect of our natural self-love. On these grounds, he strikingly claims that "love of men derived from love of self is the principle of human justice" (E 235n) and that "equality of right, and the concept of justice it produces, are derived from each man's preference for himself and consequently from the nature of man" (SC 149).

SMITH

Smith was once regarded as one of Rousseau's opponents; where Rousseau excoriated commercial society, Smith, of course, championed it. But this oppositional conception has in recent years given way to a more nuanced understanding of their relationship, one that emphasizes Smith's debts to Rousseau and certain overlaps in their positions.[8] What follows extends this inquiry by examining a less studied side of this overlap, the parallels in their political and psychological theories of justice.

We begin with Smith's political concept of justice. Smith defines justice in a way that clearly signals his departure from classical conceptions. Smith, of course, knew these classical conceptions well; at the end of his *Theory of Moral Sentiments* (TMS), he calls special attention to "that complete virtue, that perfect propriety of conduct, which Plato, after some of the ancient Pythagoreans, denominated Justice" (TMS 269). In these ancient accounts, he explains, "what is called justice means the same thing with exact and perfect propriety of conduct and behavior," embracing at once what is generally associated with just behavior, and "every other virtue," including prudence, fortitude, and temperance (TMS 270). But this ancient definition is not Smith's. His is far more limited. As he explains in part 2 of the *Theory of Moral Sentiments*, justice concerns "actions of a hurtful tendency" which "are the approved objects of resentment, or excite the sympathetic resentment of the spectator" (TMS 78).[9] Further departing from the ancient conception of justice as an all-encompassing virtue, Smith goes on to suggest that "mere justice is, upon most occasions, but a negative virtue, and only hinders us from hurting our neighbor" and that "we may often fulfill all the rules of justice by sitting still and doing nothing" (TMS 82). Smith's definition of justice is far removed from Plato's and quite close to Rousseau's, insofar as each privileges nonmalfeasance; hence Smith's claim that "the end of the rules of justice be, to hinder us from hurting our neighbour" (TMS 175, 269).[10]

Smith clearly restricts the scope of justice. But we should take care not to assume that this restriction in scope amounts to a restriction in significance. On the contrary, Smith thinks prevention of injury indispensable to the existence of society. In a well-known passage, he thus compares justice to beneficence, concluding that "society may subsist, though not in the most comfortable state, without beneficence; but the prevalence of injustice must utterly destroy it," as society "cannot subsist among those who are at all times ready to hurt and injure one another" (TMS 86). Beneficence is thus only "the ornament which embellishes, not the foundation which supports the building," whereas justice is "the main pillar that upholds the whole edifice," without which "the immense fabric of human society . . . must in a moment crumble into atoms" (TMS 86).[11] And insofar as "society cannot subsist unless the laws of justice are tolerably observed" (TMS 87), Smith argues that justice is the only virtue whose "observance is not left to the freedom of our own wills" and can "be extorted by force" (TMS 79), that is, legitimately compelled by government.

This view of justice as the only virtue whose observance can be commanded forms the foundation of Smith's theory of government. Smith taught in his lectures that "the object of justice is the security from injury, and it is the foundation of civil government" (*Lectures on Jurisprudence* 398), and the specific sort of injury that most concerned him were attacks on the persons and the property of individuals. Closely following Rousseau, Smith explains that "the necessity of civil government gradually grows up with the acquisition of valuable property" (*Wealth of Nations* [WN] 710).[12] His key claim on this front is that government's origins lie precisely in the need to protect haves from have-nots; thus, in a remarkably Rousseauian line, he declares that "civil government, so far as it is instituted for the security of property, is in reality instituted for the defense of the rich against the poor, or of those who have some property against those who have none at all" (WN 715).[13] But not only is government founded on the need to protect property, but its capacity to dispense justice in a manner that preserves the stability and integrity of a civil society founded on a market economy becomes in time one of its principal tasks. "Commerce and manufactures," Smith thus explains, "can seldom flourish long in any state which does not enjoy a regular administration of justice, in which the people do not feel themselves secure in the possession of their property" (WN 910).[14] In this vein, he especially praises the British system, which provides "that equal and impartial administration of justice" that "by securing to every man the fruits of his own industry, gives the greatest and most effectual encouragement to every sort of industry" (WN 610). Smith even includes "the duty of establishing an exact administration of justice"—"the duty of protecting, as far as possible, every member of the society from the injustice or oppression of every other member of it"—as one of the three essential duties of government in the *Wealth of Nations* (WN 687; 708–709) and considered this point so fundamental that he intended to dedicate his unfinished masterwork to "an inquiry into what were the natural rules of justice independent of all positive institution" and constitute thereby the proper "foundation of the laws of all nations" (TMS 341–342).[15]

Smith's political conception of justice can be summarized thus: justice is a negative virtue that restrains us from harming others and the only virtue that can be legitimately compelled by government for the sake of maintaining order. But his theory of justice hardly ends here. Like Rousseau, Smith is keenly interested in the psychological mechanisms that promote just behavior, mechanisms that again go well beyond fear of punishment. In his *Theory of Moral Sentiments*, Smith sets out a comprehensive and subtle account of moral psychology, and several of that account's core elements are central to his conception of justice. Some of these are introduced in his account of the role of justice in restraining certain forms of self-love. In part 2 of the *Theory of Moral Sentiments*, Smith argues that the fundamental aim of "the sense of propriety and justice" is to "correct the otherwise natural inequality of our sentiments" (TMS 136). In particular, he has in mind "the natural preference which every man has for his own happiness above that of other people" (TMS 82).

Smith hardly denies that individuals are naturally self-interested; his economic theory is famously premised on this assumption. Yet he distances this legitimate self-interest from a pernicious selfishness that devalues others and their ends, a propensity, he worries, that can lead individuals to harm others in pursuing their interests. His point is that our willingness to indulge our self-preference "at the expense of other people" is "what no impartial spectator can go along with" (TMS 82). Invoking a core concept of his moral theory—the "impartial spectator" who provides an external and unbiased reference point to which agents can refer in their attempts to distinguish right from wrong—Smith explains that the injustice of "the man who injures and insults us" lies in "the unreasonable preference he gives to himself above us, and that absurd self-love, by which he seems to imagine, that other people may be sacrificed at any time, to his conveniency or his humour" (TMS 96). The impartial spectator thus sees what a man blinded by excessive self-preference cannot: the equal worth of others and indeed their equal rights to pursue their own interests unimpeded.

But this raises a question. If we are naturally predisposed to prefer ourselves to others and if justice in fact requires transcending this natural self-preference by occupying the position of an impartial spectator, on what resources can we draw in order to help us transition from naturally self-preferring agent to impartial and just judge? Herein lies one of the most interesting sides of Smith's theory of justice. For, as he makes clear, rising above our natures in this way requires that we cultivate certain dispositions that enable us to occupy this mature moral perspective founded on recognition of our equality with others:

> Though it may be true, therefore, that every individual, in his own breast, naturally prefers himself to all mankind, yet he dares not look mankind in the face, and avow that he acts according to

> this principle. He feels that in this preference they can never go along with him, and that how natural soever it may be to him, it must always appear excessive and extravagant to them. When he views himself in the light in which he is conscious that others will view him, he sees that to them he is but one of the multitude in no respect better than any other in it. (TMS 83)

Fear of punishment alone is not enough to make us just. Becoming just also requires that we develop a capacity to see ourselves as others see us. In Smith's own terms, we need to cultivate that sympathy which enables us to "enter into" the perspectives of spectators of our behavior and in turn allows us to see which of our actions and sentiments such spectators can and cannot "go along with"—hence his claim that we must "view ourselves not so much according to that light in which we may naturally appear to ourselves, as according to that in which we naturally appear to others" (TMS 83). When well done, place changing of this sort serves to teach even the most self-interested individual that others "do not enter into that self-love by which he prefers himself so much" and that they "cannot go along with the motive" that leads him to harm others, a realization that serves, Smith says, to "humble the arrogance of his self-love" (TMS 83). Becoming just thus requires not merely self-interested fear of punishment but transcending the self-preferential belief of one's superiority to others via spectatorship and sympathy, culminating in appreciation of the essential equality of others.[16]

Becoming just, on Smith's account, thus requires a capacity to enter into the perspectives of others—a capacity that sympathy makes possible. But sympathy is not the only sentiment needed for the moral development that enables us to become just. Two other sentiments are also crucial. The first is resentment, which itself has two key roles to play in this process.[17] In the first place, the resentment we feel when we are ourselves harmed leads us to defend ourselves against such harms in ways useful to our own self-interest. Insisting that "resentment seems to have been given us by nature for defense," Smith explains that resentment is "the safeguard of justice and the security of innocence" as it "prompts us to beat off the mischief which is attempted to be done to us, and to retaliate that which is already done," actions that have the salutary effect of forcing an offender "to repent of his injustice" and leading others, "through fear of the like punishment," to be "terrified from being guilty of the like offence" (TMS 79). Smith's views on this front, of course, parallel the hopes Rousseau expressed for Emile. But Smith also thinks that resentment is salutary in a second sense. For in addition to the resentment we feel when we are harmed, Smith thinks that we also feel resentment for the harms suffered by innocent others. This resentment experienced by spectators—which Smith calls "sympathetic indignation" or "sympathetic resentment"—plays a crucial social function insofar as it leads us to "sympathize with the natural resentment of the injured" (TMS 83) and approve of those institutions that punish those who injure innocent others. On these grounds, Smith argues that insofar as "the violation of justice is injury" or "real and positive hurt to some particular persons," it is "therefore, the proper object of resentment, and of punishment" (TMS 79).

Sympathy and resentment thus play prominent roles in our development of a capacity for justice. But alongside these two sentiments needs to be set a third, one less often noted: not simply the "sympathetic indignation of the spectator" but also "the sense of guilt in the agent" (TMS 84). On this front, he claims that "in order to enforce the observation of justice, therefore, Nature has implanted in the human breast that consciousness of ill-desert, those terrors of merited punishment which attend upon its violation, as the great safeguards of the association of mankind, to protect the weak, to curb the violent, and to chastise the guilty" (TMS 86). In making this claim, Smith goes well beyond ancient theorists who associated justice with righteousness, as well as modern theorists who associated justice with simple fear of punishment. His claim is rather that we are naturally endowed with a sense of merit that has profound impact on our psychological tranquility:

> The violator of the more sacred laws of justice can never reflect on the sentiments which mankind must entertain with regard to him, without feeling all the agonies of shame, and horror, and consternation. . . . The situation of the person, who suffered by his injustice, now calls upon his pity. He is grieved at the thought of it; regrets the unhappy effects of his own conduct, and feels at the same time that they have rendered him the proper object of resentment and indignation of mankind, and of what is the natural consequence of resentment, vengeance and punishment. The thought of this perpetually haunts him, and fills him with terror and amazement. (TMS 84)

Smith's claim is that our desires for psychological tranquility and for the esteem and affection of our fellow citizens conspire to provide powerful incentives to become just, incentives categorically distinct from both concern for righteousness and fear of punishment. Guilt or remorse—"of all the sentiments which can enter the human breast the most dreadful" (TMS 85)—can thus be seen as a psychological guarantee against injustice. It is a view that brings Smith close to the view that he attributes to Epicurus, who taught that we ought to abstain from harming others and invading their possessions lest we "provoke the resentment and indignation of mankind" and destroy our "security and tranquility" (TMS 297). Smith elsewhere makes this same claim in his own name, warning against corrupting "the future tranquility of our minds, either by shame from the remembrance of our own folly, or by remorse from the horror of our own injustice" (TMS 149). Hence the reward "most proper for promoting the practice of truth, justice and humanity": "it is not in being rich that truth and justice would rejoice, but in being trusted and beloved" (TMS 166–167). Here again, self-interest—but in the sense of the interest we take in earning and deserving the esteem of others as well as our own self-esteem—is a key source of our motivation to become just.

KANT

We conclude by turning briefly to Kant. Like Rousseau and Smith—and perhaps surprisingly—Kant's theory of justice has both political and psychological components. I say "surprisingly" because Kant's popular repute as a theorist of justice is almost exclusively owed to the political conception he sets forth in the first part of *Metaphysics of Morals* (MM), which seems to obviate any room for treating justice as a virtue or in the psychological manner seen in Rousseau and Smith.[18] But when we turn from Kant's practical philosophy to his anthropology, we see that far from being indifferent to this aspect of justice, Kant was in fact quite committed to identifying the motives that lead us to desire to become just and, further, that his account of these motives in several respects parallels those given by Smith and Rousseau.

Kant's political conception of justice is well known and can be very briefly summarized here. In his historical writings, Kant explained that the emergence of government followed the invention of private property; thus, as man moved from the natural to the civil state, there "had to arise also some arrangement for a civil constitution and public justice, first surely only in regard to great violent acts, the avenging of which was now left no longer to individuals, as in the savage condition, but to a lawful might that held the whole together" and protected property against invasions by others

(*Conjectural Beginning of Human History* 172). Quite simply, Kant told his students, "if one wants to have property, then one must have protection and security, and this occurs through the coercion of the authorities" (*Lectures on Anthropology* 216).

Kant thus far follows Rousseau and Smith. Further, like Smith, Kant thought that what made the state's monopoly on force necessary were certain dangers that stem from our natural predilection to self-preference. "This problem," he says, "is at the same time the most difficult and the latest to be solved by the human species": that "although, as a rational creature he wishes a law that sets limits to the freedom of all, his selfish animal inclination still leads him into excepting himself from it where he may," and thus "he needs a master, who breaks his selfish will and necessitates him to obey a universally valid will with which everyone can be free" (*Idea for a Universal History* 46). The challenge for Kant, as for Rousseau, was to define a system in which individuals were both free to follow their own wills and at the same time restrained from indulging in harmful self-preferential behaviors. This challenge animates his treatment of justice in the *Metaphysics of Morals*. Here he explains that "a rightful condition is that relation of human beings among one another that contains the conditions under which alone everyone is able to enjoy his rights, and the formal condition under which this is possible in accordance with the idea of a will giving laws for everyone is called public justice" (MM 450). Indeed, it is precisely the existence of institutions that dispense justice in defending private property that distinguishes civil society from "a condition that is not rightful, that is, in which no one is assured of what is his against violence" (MM 452) and in which "human beings, peoples and states can never be secure against violence from one another, since each has its own right to do what seems right and good to it" (MM 456). The state of nature is thus "a state devoid of justice" in which possession can only be regarded as "provisional" (MM 456). Civil society, by contrast, "can alone make any acquisition conclusive" (MM 416), and it is on these grounds that the treatment of public right in the *Metaphysics of Morals* is largely dedicated to rights of property possession and the legitimacy of punishments for the infringements of such rights.

Kant's political treatment of justice seems on its face to leave little space for treating justice as a virtue or as an element of our moral psychologies. But when we turn to his anthropological writings—and particularly if we do so with Rousseau and Smith in mind—a different side of his theory of justice emerges. An example of this comes in his discussion of sympathy. One of the most familiar claims of Kant's moral theory is that only those actions motivated by commitment to universal law have true moral worth, a claim that famously serves as the ground of his critique of moral sentimentalism.[19] The *Metaphysics of Morals* seems to reiterate this critique of sympathy (even though, as has been noted, it also introduces several important caveats regarding the value of active sympathetic identification).[20] But in Kant's anthropology, sympathy plays a very different role. Far from being inimical to moral worth, sympathy plays an indispensable role in our development as just beings—indeed, a role not unfamiliar to readers of Rousseau and Smith. Take, for example, Kant's treatment of sympathy in the *Observations* (O):

> A certain tenderheartedness that is easily led into a warm feeling of sympathy is beautiful and loveable, for it indicates a kindly participation in the fate of other people, to which principles of virtue likewise lead. But this kindly passion is nevertheless weak and is always blind. For suppose that this sentiment moves you to help someone in need with your expenditure, but you are indebted to someone else and by those means you make it impossible for yourself to fulfill the strict duty of justice; then obviously the action cannot arise from any virtuous resolution, for that could not possibly entice you into sacrificing a higher

> obligation to this blind enchantment. If, by contrast, general affection towards humankind has become your principle, to which you always subject your actions, then your love towards the one in need remains, but it is now, from a higher standpoint, placed in its proper relationship to your duty as a whole. The universal affection is a ground for participating in his ill-fortune, but at the same time it is also a ground of justice, in accordance with whose precept you must now forbear this action. (O 30)

Kant makes several important claims here that deserve comparison to the more familiar claims of his critical ethics.[21] But for our purposes, the most striking aspect of Kant's claim concerns the degree to which it parallels Rousseau's. Like Rousseau, Kant argues that sympathetic other-directed feeling, elevated and universalized to "general affection towards humankind," can itself be "a ground of justice." Kant's understanding of sympathy also parallels Smith's in certain respects. Like Smith, Kant finds our sympathy with injustices suffered by innocent others both natural and salutary. Insisting that "sympathy with the natural misfortune of others is not necessary, but sympathy with the injustice suffered by others is" (*Remarks on the Observations* [R] 66, 186), he claims that herein lies the origins of "the sense of justice through which we learn to distinguish what is permitted from what is forbidden." Far from emerging from reasoned consideration of the obligations of the moral law, this sense, we are told, "has its origin in the nature of the human mind" and specifically one's "ability to put oneself in the place of others" (R 173). In his most important formulation of this point, Kant claims:

> From the feeling of equality arises the idea of justice, both the idea of the obliged as well as the idea of the obliging. The former is the obligation of others, the latter is the felt obligation of others towards me. In order for the latter to have a standard in the

> understanding, we are able to put ourselves in the place of others in thoughts, and, in order for there to be no lack of motivations for this, we will be moved through sympathy for the misfortune and distress of others just as through our own. (R 91)

Like Smith, Kant thinks the place exchange that sympathy makes possible enables us to transcend our individual self-preference, to recognize our equality with others, and ultimately to develop the concept of justice itself.

Kant, like both Rousseau and Smith, sees a key role for the other-directed sentiments in the process of becoming just. But Rousseau and Smith, as we have seen, also saw a crucial role for the self-directed sentiments in this process, especially clear in their treatments of the sentiment of resentment or vengeance. Yet this commitment is also central to Kant's theory. Kant thinks it is natural for us to be enraged by injustices that we suffer: "never is anything more outrageous than injustice; all other ills that we endure are nothing in comparison" (R 91). And "from this there automatically develops the concept of vengeance," vengeance that he moreover thinks is justified and "permissible" to act on. So as not "to let the rights of our humanity be toyed with," Kant suggests that we "therefore possess a desire for justice, in order to demand personal satisfaction from the other for injury deliberately inflicted" (*Lectures on Ethics* [LE] 417). This is a clear case in which a "desire"—here the desire for justice—constitutes a sentiment that promotes rather than inhibits moral action. On these grounds, Kant even insists that "the desire for revenge is permitted, and a duty, insofar as it coincides with the grounds from which it arises, namely respect for the right of other people, and the duty to love justice which springs from that" (LE 417). All of this leads to the most important claim on this front: "hatred arising from an injustice we have suffered, that is, the desire for vengeance, is a passion that follows irresistibly from the nature of the human being, and, malicious as it may be, maxims of reason are nevertheless interwoven with the inclination by virtue of the permissible desire for justice, whose analogue it is" (*Anthropology* 371). Kant's treatment of the salutary effects of the "desire" for justice and "passion" as manifest in vengeance not only complicates familiar stories often told about Kant's rigorous distinction between reason and sentiment but also renders Kant a central contributor to the Enlightenment's underemphasized inquiry into the moral psychology of the just person.

CONCLUSION

The Enlightenment's contribution to the development of the idea of justice has long been appreciated. Yet this contribution has tended to be regarded as emphasizing what is sometimes called a "negative" view of justice as a principle that limits harms. As I have sought to show, this view, while central to the Enlightenment concept of justice, hardly exhausts it, as several key Enlightenment theorists of justice also sought to explain how we become just. And on this front, their inquiries focused on two particular points: first, identifying the motivational elements in our moral psychology that prompt us to desire to become just; and second, identifying the means by which we can best cultivate and encourage these motives.

Three Enlightenment theories of justice are especially insightful on these fronts and also overlap with one another. As we have seen, Rousseau teaches that justice and goodness demand to be seen as "true affections of the soul enlightened by reason, and hence only an ordered development of our primitive affections." In his view, the human being's affection of justice needs development via "cultivation of his inclinations" (E 235). Smith, for all his other differences with Rousseau, agrees. Smith famously argues for a conception of justice as a negative virtue that can be legitimately compelled by government in order to preserve conditions of security in which individual liberty can be maximized. Yet he also recognizes that this negative virtue, while necessary, is ultimately unto itself insufficient for realization of a just state in which harms are minimized; citizens of such a state also need to overcome the "natural preference" for themselves that Smith identifies as a principal source of harm (TMS 82). This is why he emphasizes the utility of the moral education of our sympathy and in particular its capacity to enable us to enter into the conditions of others and thereby "correct the otherwise natural inequality of our sentiments" (TMS 136). And this view is shared by Kant. In addition to offering what is arguably the Enlightenment's most important formulation of the political concept of justice, Kant in his anthropological writings develops a vision of the moral psychology of justice that parallels Rousseau's and Smith's—as seen specifically in his insistence that we must render our "general affection towards humankind" not merely a sentiment but a "principle" and thereby a "ground of justice" (O 30), as well as his suggestion that it is from the "feeling of equality" that "arises the idea of justice" (R 91).

Enlightenment thinking on justice thus has more to offer than has sometimes been assumed and therefore deserves study in its own right. But it also deserves our attention for two other reasons. One concerns how it relates to previous thinking about justice, while another concerns how it relates to how we understand justice today. On the former front, the Enlightenment's commitment to cultivating justice suggests that its concerns may not be quite so far removed from the ancient views with which the Enlightenment is sometimes contrasted. As Paul Woodruff reminds us in chapter 1 of this volume, ancients such as Plato were deeply committed to cultivating—or, as Woodruff has it, "growing toward"—justice. But insofar as the Enlightenment thinkers examined here all seem to share a version of this commitment, it may be that their concerns are not so distant from the ancients as is sometimes assumed. And on the latter front, the emphasis placed by the Enlightenment thinkers on the importance of encouraging individuals to become just also has important relevance today. The states in which we now live clearly owe much to the political thought of the Enlightenment; our constitutional governments, limited by the rule of law and committed to the maximization of individual freedom and security, owe much to Rousseau, Smith, and Kant, among others. At the same time, attending to the other side of Rousseau's, Smith's, and Kant's theories of justice, specifically their commitment to cultivating just individuals, suggests the possible insufficiency of a purely institutional or procedural approach to justice and that such an approach needs to be supplemented by the cultivation of citizens motivated by their own commitments to justice. The question of what sort of education can best cultivate this commitment to justice is, of course, one that every age needs to answer in its own way. Contemporary social conditions, which differ in obvious ways from the social conditions of the eighteenth century, open up opportunities and spaces for this education to emerge that could hardly have been anticipated by the Enlightenment thinkers examined here—as is shown, for example, by Bart J. Wilson in chapter 3 of this volume examining the ways in which commitments to justice can emerge in a laboratory's online chat rooms. But however far the social conditions of the Enlightenment may seem from our own, their concern to supplement their commitments to just institutions and just procedures with a commitment to the cultivation of just citizens offers a model for how we today might rethink the relationship between moral and political conceptions of justice.

NOTES

1. For a recent statement of the ideals of the Enlightenment, see S. Smith 2016, 9–11; see also Amartya Sen's account of the "transcendental institutionalism"

that he identifies as a principal element of Enlightenment thinking about justice (Sen 2009, 5–8).

2. On ancient versus modern conceptions, see especially LeBar and Slote 2002.
3. Michael Frazer offers an important recent inquiry on this front, though he focuses on certain discrete questions that are somewhat different from those on which I focus here. See Frazer 2010.
4. For a helpful recent treatment of Rousseau's understanding of and response to what he understood to be the "fundamental problem" of politics, see Cohen 2010, esp. 23–59.
5. For an overview of this debate, see the response given to various positivistic readings in Williams 2007, 93–122.
6. I aim to provide a much more comprehensive account of Rousseau's theory of the relationship of moral development to cognitive development in Hanley 2012.
7. Pity has long been a prominent focus of Rousseau scholars; helpful treatments include Boyd 2004; and Orwin 1997. I examine Rousseau's theory of pity and its relationship to love in Hanley 2017, chap. 3.
8. The most recent contributions to this extensive and growing literature include Griswold 2017 and Smith, Paganelli, and Rasmussen 2018.
9. The differences between Smith's definition and ancient definitions has long been noted; see, e.g., Vivenza 2001, 51–54.
10. For a helpful treatment of Smith's views on justice as a negative virtue, see, e.g., Kennedy 2005, 74–77.
11. Commentators have long emphasized Smith's distinction between justice and beneficence; I offer a response to this interpretation in Hanley 2017, chap. 4.
12. For helpful explications of Smith's views of this process, see Haakonssen 1981, chap. 7; and Pack and Schliesser 2006.
13. See Hont 2015, 52–53, 69–70.
14. On the centrality of property rights in Smith's political and economic theory, see, e.g., V. Smith 1998; Herzog 2013, 28–30.
15. The core claims of Smith's jurisprudence lectures are helpfully outlined in Haakonssen 2016. On Smith's failure to complete this project, see, e.g. Ross 2004.
16. Justice is hardly the only virtue that contributes to this project; I treat the role of self-command in Hanley 2016.
17. A helpful recent treatment of the central role of resentment in Smith's "moral psychology" of justice is given in Wolterstorff 2016; see also Pack and Schliesser 2006, esp. 58–63.
18. See, e.g., LeBar's representative claim that "in Kant we see the completion of the distinction between justice as a virtue and justice as a norm," the culmination of a project that "has threatened to swallow up" the project of regarding justice as a virtue. LeBar and Slote 2002, introduction and 1.2.

19. On this point, see esp. Frazer 2010, 112–138.
20. See esp. Fahmy 1009; Makkreel 2012, 111–112.
21. For helpful readings, see esp. Frazer 2010, 134–136, which notes the degree to which Kant's notion of a universalized sympathy is here given "a Rousseauist spin" (135); and Makkreel 2012, 102–103. Makkreel's comments on the utility of the "procedure of transposition" (2012, 109) and Frazer's on "perspectival exploration" (2010, 136) anticipate the claims I develop here.

WORKS CITED

Boyd, Richard. 2004. "Pity's Pathologies Portrayed: Rousseau and the Limits of Democratic Compassion." *Political Theory* 32: 519–546.

Cohen, Joshua. 2010. *Rousseau: A Free Community of Equals*. Oxford: Oxford University Press.

Fahmy, Melissa Seymour. 2009. "Active Sympathetic Participation: Reconsidering Kant's Duty of Sympathy." *Kantian Review* 14: 31–52.

Frazer, Michael. 2010. *The Enlightenment of Sympathy: Justice and the Moral Sentiments in the Eighteenth Century and Today*. New York: Oxford University Press.

Griswold, Charles. 2017. *Jean-Jacques Rousseau and Adam Smith: A Philosophical Inquiry*. London: Routledge.

Haakonssen, Knud. 1981. *The Science of a Legislator: The Natural Jurisprudence of David Hume and Adam Smith*. Cambridge: Cambridge University Press.

Haakonssen, Knud. 2016. "The *Lectures on Jurisprudence*." In *Adam Smith: His Life, Thought and Legacy*, edited by Ryan P. Hanley, 48–66. Princeton: Princeton University Press.

Hanley, Ryan P. 2012. "Rousseau's Virtue Epistemology." *Journal of the History of Philosophy* 50: 239–264.

Hanley, Ryan P. Unpublished. *Adam Smith on Self-Command: Utility, Dignity, and Sympathy* (unpublished manuscript).

Hanley, Ryan P. 2017. *Love's Enlightenment: Rethinking Charity in Modernity*. New York: Cambridge University Press.

Herzog, Lisa. 2013. *Inventing the Market: Smith, Hegel, and Political Theory*. Oxford: Oxford University Press.

Hont, Istvan. 2015. *Politics in Commercial Society*. Cambridge: Harvard University Press.

Kant, Immanuel. 1999. "Metaphysics of Morals." Translated by Mary J. Gregor. In *Practical Philosophy*, edited by Gregor. Cambridge: Cambridge University Press. [MM]

Kant, Immanuel. 2001. *Lectures on Ethics*. Translated by Peter Heath. Cambridge: Cambridge University Press. [LE]

Kant, Immanuel. 2007. "Anthropology from a Pragmatic Point of View." Translated by Robert B. Louden. In *Anthropology, History, and Education*, edited by Günter Zöller and Robert B. Louden. Cambridge: Cambridge University Press. [A]

Kant, Immanuel. 2007. "Conjectural Beginning of Human History." In *Anthropology, History, and Education*, edited by Günter Zöller and Robert B. Louden. Cambridge: Cambridge University Press. [CB]

Kant, Immanuel. 2007. "Idea for a Universal History." In *Anthropology, History, and Education*, edited by Günter Zöller and Robert B. Louden. Cambridge: Cambridge University Press.

Kant, Immanuel. 2007. "Observations on the Feeling of the Beautiful and Sublime." Translated by Paul Guyer. In *Anthropology, History, and Education*, edited by Günter Zöller and Robert B. Louden. Cambridge: Cambridge University Press. [O]

Kant, Immanuel. 2011. "Remarks in the *Observations on the Beautiful and Sublime*." Translated by Patrick Frierson and Paul Guyer. In *Observations on the Feeling of the Beautiful and Sublime and Other Writings*, edited by Frierson and Guyer. Cambridge: Cambridge University Press. [R]

Kant, Immanuel. 2012. *Lectures on Anthropology*. Edited by Allen W. Wood and Robert B. Louden. Cambridge: Cambridge University Press.

Kennedy, Gavin. 2005. *Adam Smith's Lost Legacy*. London: Palgrave Macmillan.

LeBar, Mark, and Michael Slote. 2002. "Justice As a Virtue." *Stanford Encyclopedia of Philosophy*. http://plato.stanford.edu/entries/justice-virtue; accessed August 26, 2016.

Makkreel, Rudolf. 2012. "Relating Aesthetic and Sociable Feelings to Moral and Participatory Feelings: Reassessing Kant on Sympathy and Honor." In *Kant's Observations and Remarks: A Critical Guide*, edited by Susan Meld Shell and Richard Velkley, 101–115. Cambridge: Cambridge University Press.

Orwin, Clifford. 1997. "Rousseau and the Discovery of Political Compassion." In *The Legacy of Rousseau*, edited by Nathan Tarcov and Clifford Orwin, 296–320. Chicago: University of Chicago Press.

Pack, Spencer, and Eric Schliesser. 2006. "Smith's Humean Criticism of Hume's Account of the Origin of Justice." *Journal of the History of Philosophy* 44: 47–63.

Ross, Ian. 2004. "'Great Works Upon the Anvil' in 1785: Adam Smith's Projected Corpus of Philosophy." *Adam Smith Review* 1: 40–59.

Rousseau, Jean-Jacques. 1992a. "Discourse on Political Economy." Translated by Judith R. Bush. In *Discourse on the Origins of Inequality, Polemics, and Political Economy*, edited by Roger D. Masters and Christopher Kelly. Hanover, NH: University Press of New England. [DPE]

Rousseau, Jean-Jacques. 1992b. "Second Discourse (Discourse on Inequality)." Translated by Judith R. Bush. In *Discourse on the Origins of Inequality, Polemics, and Political Economy*, edited by Roger D. Masters and Christopher Kelly. Hanover, NH: University Press of New England. [SD]

Rousseau, Jean-Jacques. 1994. "On the Social Contract." Translated by Roger D. Masters. In *Social Contract, Discourse on the Virtue Most necessary for a Hero, Political Fragments, and Geneva Manuscript*. Hanover, NH: University Press of New England. [SC]

Rousseau, Jean-Jacques. 2010. *Emile, or On Education*. Translated by Allan Bloom. New York: Basic Books. [E]

Sen, Amartya. 2009. *The Idea of Justice*. Cambridge: Harvard University Press.

Smith, Craig, Maria Paganelli, and Dennis Rasmussen, eds. 2018. *Adam Smith and Rousseau: Ethics, Politics, and* Economics. Edinburgh: Edinburgh University Press.

Smith, Steven B. 2016. *Modernity and Its Discontents*. New Haven: Yale University Press.

Smith, Vernon L. 1998. "The Two Faces of Adam Smith." *Southern Economic Journal* 65: 1–15.

Vivenza, Gloria. 2001. *Adam Smith and the Classics*. New York: Oxford University Press.

Williams, David Lay. 2007. *Rousseau's Platonic Enlightenment*. University Park: Penn State University Press.

Wolterstorff, Nicholas. 2016. "Adam Smith on Justice and Injustice." In *Adam Smith: His Life, Thought and Legacy*, edited by Ryan P. Hanley, 173–191. Princeton: Princeton University Press.

Chapter 3

Becoming Just by Eliminating Injustice

The Emergence of Property in Virtual Economies

BART J. WILSON

The end of justice is to secure from injury.

—Adam Smith

PROPERTY AND JUSTICE

David Hume criticizes the common view, then and now, that justice is the constant and perpetual will of giving everyone his due (*Iustitia est constans et perpetua voluntas ius suum cuique tribuendi*): "In this definition it is supposed, that there are such things as right and property, independent of justice, and antecedent to it; and that they would have subsisted, though men had never dreamt of practicing such a virtue."[1] Right and property, in Hume's account, do not give rise to justice. No, the process of developing the conventions of justice produces the rules of property. The rules of property are "altogether unintelligible without first understanding" the convention of justice.[2] Our own interests lead us to devise the rules of justice and injustice from existing principles or ideas, and once these rules are brought about on a firm and stable basis, we then feelingly approve or disapprove of actions that fit or don't fit with the rules specifically regarding property. If people had never dreamed of practicing justice as a virtue, the rules of property would never have existed.

In terms of the theme of this volume, the Humean interpretation of property is that we don't become just by following the rules of property. Rather, the rules of property follow from the process of us becoming just. Hume's interpretation, I claim, is consistent with a maxim by third-century Roman jurist Julius Paulus: What is right is not derived from the rule, but the rule arises from our knowledge of what is right (*Non ex regula ius sumatur, sed ex iure quod est regula fiat*).[3] Our sense of what is right consists in the capacity to follow rules, rules that we do not "know" in the sense that we can declare them all axiomatically but that we do "know" in the sense of being able to describe roughly what actions are consistent, or not, with this or that rule.[4] If this is not self-evident, try listing all the rules of polite conversation. Have you included what "Do not bore" or "Do not dominate" or "Be responsive" means? These may not even be first on a list of general rules of conversation, and yet when we are challenged with someone who imperviously breaks one out of the uncountable number of rules, we can call forth ex tempore the specific rule relevant for this encounter. We have a kind of a background sense, which, although quite unarticulable, allows us to formulate in the foreground a reason for why this person has attenuated the genial atmosphere.[5]

The first implication of not being able to explicitly know or specifically state the rules that govern how we act is that only *in their totality* does a whole system of rules, the practice or custom, form the sense of how to conduct ourselves rightly.[6] To embed our understanding of property in practices is to consider it as implicit in our rule-guided actions. In short, our actions are governed by abstract rules, not concrete algorithms.

The second implication is that the rules that govern our actions also govern our perceptions of actions,[7] and it is rule-guided perception that poses the fundamental problem for the emergence of property as a moral custom. While different individuals will recognize a specific set of circumstances as one of the same kind involving property, we are unable to present the precise stimulus condition that will replicably produce the same perception in different people and hence the same action in different people. Rule-guided perceptions carry the understanding in patterns of appropriate action, which conform to a sense of what is right for this circumstance. But while agents can perceive when they or others have or have not done what is right, that others share that perception is not a given. The perception of an action as one of a kind that fits a pattern of what is right depends critically on the agency being shared.

Actions constituted as a custom are shared among those who practice the custom because the common perception of the action has integrated the individual agents into a shared regularized whole, a "we."[8] Shared perceptions serve as the foundation for actions within a custom, actions that are what M. M. Bakhtin calls dialogic,[9] in continual active dialogue and multilaterally extending to and from an agent. A rule doesn't apply itself. It must be followed in real time, under ever-fluxional circumstances, and against the unarticulated background of the entire custom. The interpretation of what a rule means is done on the fly and in dialogic concert with those around the agent. The custom is what keeps the rule *active,* and the application of the rule reaffirms the custom. But *the current application of the rule also modifies the custom, for the custom now also applies to all of the novel nuances in the background.*

From everyday human intercourse, we have expectations regarding the regularity of one another's conduct. When does a rule arise? When one needs to be formulated. When does a rule need to be formulated? When someone does something contrary to what is right. An act of injustice, an *iniuria,* is an act that injures another. Such an act challenges the existing order of actions. It interrupts the regularity of everyone's conduct. Rules of property arise as remonstrance to injuries, hurts, and losses willfully inflicted on others. Returning to the example of conversation, the rule "Do not bore" is called to the foreground when we are confronted with a veritable bore in the room, and what it means to bore us to tears (say, with the semantics of Latin phrases) relies on all the unarticulable rules of polite conversation.

Hume may not have needed any further empirical validation for his theory on the origin of justice and property, but some of us need the challenge of designing experiments and observing their results to develop our thinking. As an experimental economist, I build virtual economies to see how theory and philosophy work in practice when real people are recruited to a laboratory and paid real cash to make decisions they see to be in their own interest. So when my colleagues and I became interested in how property works, we created virtual worlds in which property was not exogenously enforced to observe whether and how rules of property emerge.

Despite coming from a world with property securely enforced, our participants do not initially adhere to Hume's first fundamental law of nature. In each and every session, possession is initially anything and everything but stable. In other words, our participants are not just from the get-go. They must become just if they are to escape poverty, and they become just by eliminating the injustices of harming one another. As part of the process of becoming just, rules of property emerge "to cut off all occasions of discord and contention."[10] In this chapter, I explicate this Humean process by drawing on the spontaneous conversations of participants reported in four different economics experiments: Kimbrough, Smith, and Wilson (2010); Kimbrough (2011); Wilson et al. (2012); and Jaworski and Wilson (2013).

PLATFORM 1: THE HOMESTEAD

Kimbrough, Smith, and Wilson (2010) is the first experiment to explore how property emerges as a convention in the laboratory. Figure 3.1 displays a screenshot of the experiment. Every session consists of eight participants, each of whom controls the production of two types of fictitious goods, red and blue. In figure 3.1, person 2 controls the production displayed in the rectangle numbered 2 (and in green only on person 2's screen), which is called a field. All participants are informed in the instructions, deliberately in the passive voice, that

> When the clock expires [at the end of the period], you earn cash based upon the number of red and blue items that have been

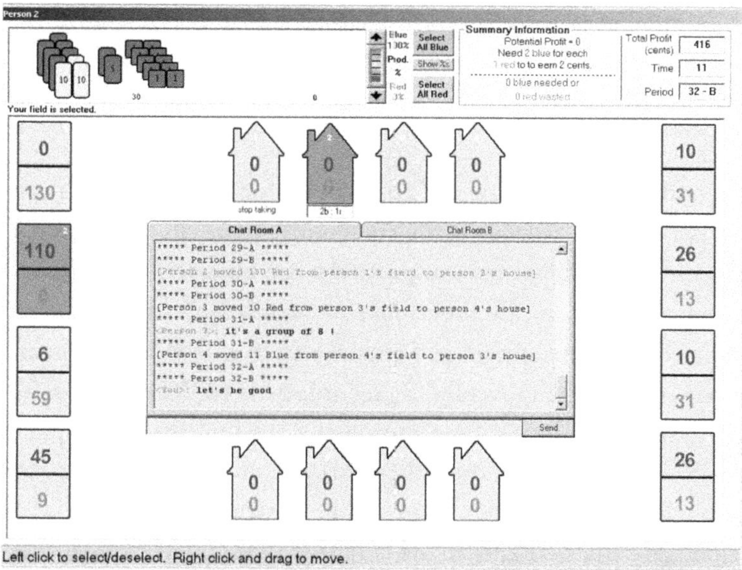

Figure 3.1. Screenshot of the homestead platform.

> moved to your house. To select items to be moved, *left* click on an item or click on the red or blue buttons at the top of the screen. The yellow highlighted items can be moved by dragging with the *right* mouse button.

Person 2's house is in green (on person 2's screen). What the participants are not told is that they can move items to other people's houses and fields and that they can move items from other people's houses and fields. The participants must discover that such movements of items are possible.

The participants are also not informed, but can discover, that odd-numbered persons (even-numbered persons) are capable of increasing returns for producing red (blue):

> For the first 10 seconds of each period, you will produce items in your green field. Using the scroll bar in the upper middle portion of your screen, you can change the proportion of each second allocated to producing red and blue. Each person's production is displayed on their field.

An odd (even) can earn 30 (26) cents in isolation, but with specialization and exchange at the competitive price, an odd-even pair can earn 90 and 80 cents, respectively. Anytime an item is moved to another person, the movement is recorded in a chat room in the middle of the screen, and anytime an item is moved from another person, the movement is recorded in red. Key for this discussion is that at any time during the session, the participants are free to chat with the other participants in one of the two publicly accessible chat rooms. The instructions for the chat room give the participants wide latitude within an explicit constraint of civility:

> Everyone in this experiment can send text messages. Everyone can read all posted messages. In the center of the screen, you can type a message in the line in either of two chat rooms and click on the Send button.
>
> Under your house you can also post a one-line message that will be visible at all times to the other players.
>
> You are free to discuss all aspects of the experiment, with the following exceptions: you may not reveal your name, discuss side payments [outside of the laboratory], make threats, or engage in inappropriate language (including such shorthand as "WTF"). If you do, you will be excused and you will forfeit your earnings.

Unlike the well-circumscribed action spaces in traditional economics experiments, this one is as wide open as the Wild West. Participants interact in real time from the moment the experiment begins until it concludes 67 minutes later. The software imposes no order of moves, except that red and blue are produced during the first 10 seconds of a period and that consumption occurs at the moment the period concludes 90 seconds later. In Kimbrough, Smith, and Wilson (2010) and Jaworski and Wilson (2013), the participants start in pairs, and without hint or notice, two pairs appear as one group of four on the screen, and finally, the two groups of four become one group of eight, but in Kimbrough (2011), all eight people are together for the entire session (which actually makes things more unsettling). The participants inhabit a hurly-burly, uncertain world. The experience is fast-paced, you might even say suspenseful, to such an extent that after a pilot session, we made every seventh period a day of rest in which nothing is produced but during which the participants can still converse with one another.

At this point, the naysayer interjects to make the original observation that the participants live in a physical world with secure property and that we gave the participants their own house and field in the virtual world. So what can this experiment help us understand about the emergence of property as a moral convention? My response is that obviously my coauthors and I are not claiming to have recreated the Big Bang of property. That would be cool but a little dangerous. Instead, we are observing how real people making decisions of salient monetary consequence interface with one another on a frontier with no externally enforced custom of property. Some groups will succeed and prosper, and some will fail and do so spectacularly. The question is, can we identify why we observe one outcome or the other from a complete historical record of what happened, including heat-of-the-moment conversations?

PLATFORM 2: THE OPEN SEA

The second platform is inspired by Ellickson (1989), who studied how North Atlantic whalers in the eighteenth and nineteenth centuries solved the problem of property for things that lie free for any taker. Wilson et al. (2012) test Ellickson's admittedly ex post explanation with an ex ante experimental design. Figure 3.2 displays the software interface for the experiment.

Each participant, first in pairs and then later without notice as a sextet, controls a stick figure that can move around the white open area in the middle of the screen. The range of vision for a stick figure is limited to the gray area displayed in figure 3.2 for Orange. White circles move randomly around the wide Sargasso Sea until a stick figure right clicks on one within its range. Five seconds later, the computer determines according to an unannounced

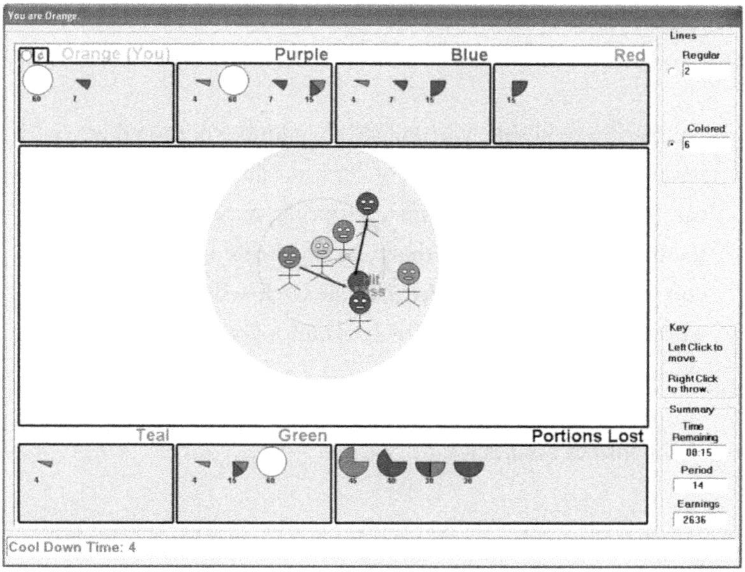

Figure 3.2. Screenshot of the open sea platform.

probability whether the stick figure is successful in hauling in the circle. Within that five seconds, however, any other stick figure within range or capable of reaching the circle can also "throw a line" and attach itself to the circle. Each whole circle is redeemable for $v = 60$ or 100 cents, depending on treatment. However, if multiple people are probabilistically successful, each successful participant only receives a $1/n^2$ portion of the whole circle. Thus, $(1-1/n)v$ of value is wasted if multiple people lay claim to the same circle that lies free for any taker.[11] After 90 seconds for "gathering"/"catching" circles, the stick figures figuratively return to port for 60 or 90 seconds, depending on treatment, and are free to discuss anything in the experiment within the same guidelines stated above.

To test Ellickson's proposition that different circumstantial conditions lead to different rules of capture, the stick figures could use two different lines to gather circles, or, as is explained in the instructions:

> On the top right side, you will see the number of lines that you have left. There are two types of lines, *regular* and *colored,* which can be selected by using the appropriate radio button next to them. Both lines work in the same way, with one exception. If you hit a circle with a *colored* line, the circle will turn your color whether or not the computer determines you are successful in catching it.

Later, the instructions state:

> You may also purchase additional lines by clicking on the Buy button next to the type of line you would like to purchase. The cost of the lines is taken out of your earnings. You will be given an initial allotment of lines. After that you will be able to purchase *colored* lines for 12¢ [or 20¢, depending on treatment] and *regular* lines for 6¢ [or 10¢].

With regular lines, the participants can implement the whaling rule which was called *fast fish, loose fish.* If a ship's harpoon was in the whale and held fast to the boat, no one else would attempt to catch that whale. However, if the harpoon was not attached to the boat, that is, if the fish was loose, then the whale was fair game for any other ship to harpoon. Ellickson noted that whalers in the North Atlantic used this rule for preying on right whales, slow-moving baleen whales that don't dive when harpooned and aren't particularly feisty.

When whaling moved off the coast of the United States, American whalers preyed on sperm whales, which have teeth, will use them on a boat, and will dive, pulling the boat down with them. With this change in conditions, Ellickson reported that American whalers switched from a *fast fish, loose fish* rule to what was called *iron holds the whale.* If a ship's harpoon was attached to a whale and identifiably so, then no other ship would attempt to catch the whale. The colored lines in the experiment allow the participants to identify the first striker. The reason the colored lines are more expensive is so that the participants can reveal their preference for a colored line to a regular line. (The participants will only choose to use the more expensive colored line if there is a valuable reason to do so. Otherwise, the cheaper regular line will do just fine.) Participants are randomly assigned to one of two treatments. In the first, the circles move slowly and are easy to catch on the first strike ($p = 0.75$). In the second, the whales move 50 percent faster and are three times more difficult to catch on the first strike ($q = 0.25$). In a subsequent third treatment, the participants first experience right-like whales for the first two-thirds of the session and then, unannounced, the same-looking circle begins behaving like a sperm whale.

WHAT IS "WHAT IS RIGHT"?

Despite the functional differences between the platforms, common themes run through the discussions of both types of experiments, and the emergence of justice follows the same process in both platforms. The students, all undergraduates, participate in only one session within a platform, and only a small number of the 480 participants would have been recruited to participate in both platforms. As the excerpts of the instructions above hint, the instructions are deliberately sparse. We beam the strangers onto an unfamiliar virtual world and ask them to make sense of one another in whatever comes next. The question is whether and how they make it work.

Not surprisingly, at the beginning of the session or when additional stick figures or houses and fields suddenly appear around them, the participants use the chat room to get their bearings. The screen is a picture in the foreground, but what is the sense that lies in the background? What subsidiary perception fits the application of the representation in focus? The chat transcripts provide a glimpse into the sense they are attempting to make.[12] Here are three examples of the first steps in that process:

D: should we be trying to help each other?
D: or is selfishness the way to go?
H: that's a super good plan . . .
H: if everyone just agrees to not steal other peoples then we will get more
A: that is very true
D: I think so too
G: true
D: I'm down
H: so just do that
. . .
G: so r we working together or against each other
H: i think we are supposed to work together
G: ok sounds fine
. . .
B: its a way to collaborate and help each other or steal from each other

Notice first that while the instructions on actions are amoral, and in the first platform are presented in the passive voice, the participants readily imbue the observed actions with morality, calling certain movements of pixelated chits and certain clicks on a circle "stealing." This isn't a rare occurrence. According to the 450-million-word Corpus of Contemporary American English (COCA), the frequency of the word *steal* is 20,296 (number 1,798 on the list and right below *politician*).[13] The four experiments discussed in this chapter include a total of 480 participants in sixty sessions who typed 175,143 words (space delimited units of text). The words *steal, stealing, steals, stole,* and *stolen* appear correctly spelled 397 times. That is 50.3 times the frequency in the COCA. A critic might say, "But of course they call this stealing. They come from a physical universe with formally and informally enforced property." The question to ask is: Why is it that the perceptions of these participants lead them to apply that word with its full moral force to these particular circumstances?

Note also how *B, D,* and *G* perceptionally parse the context into one of two big bins. Either we help each other, work together, and collaborate, *or* we selfishly work against each other and steal from each another. *D* and *G* are in part seeking clarification on what is right in this virtual world, but why pose the question? They are recognizing the background and have a subsidiary interest in the first perceptual bin, which is the first alternative in each of the three cases. Not once do I recall the question in the transcripts being posed in the form of "Should we be trying to be selfish, or is helping each other the way to go?" *D* and *G* are also raising the question as the foundation for seeking agreement on the former of the two possible answers. The problem then becomes one of integration into a "we":

E: do you want to do this the right way?
F: wht is the right way
E: the right way is I produce red you make blue then we split it nobody gets 100 percent profit but we both win
F: tht wat i been doing then u started stealing
F: [*E*] do u wanna start talkin about maximizing our production or keep fighting over it?

Integrating into a regularized whole involves changing the moral view of those who do not perceptually share the same background of what is right. Observed contradictions are one hurdle. *F* claims that *E*'s harmonizing plan is inconsistent with his or her prior actions. Another hurdle is virtual vertigo. The declaration of "im confused" is not uncommon in this type of experiment following digitization into the e-world. In platform 1, the transition is achieved by clarifying, as *E* does, how to specialize and trade. But there is also moral confusion:

D: So it would benefit us all if no one was a thief. [A]!
A: the point . . . is to make a big profit?
D: yes but to make a long term profit teamwork helps a lot

Participants volunteer for these experiments to earn cold, hard cash. Profit is the common goal. To achieve that goal as an integrated group, *D* reasons with *A* by liberating from moral disregard a principle that *A* cannot contest. Once teamwork is perceptually shared, the transition to a whole can follow quickly:

F: lets agree to not hit once someone is on it alot of money is lost
D: hahah
A: true
F: my partner and i did and it worked well
E: yup
F: agreed??
A: agreed
F: [D]??
F: [C]??
A: lol
E: haha
A: guess not
C: yea that sounds like a plan

However, with the intransigent, integration is not inevitable:

D: look, if we all stop stealing, we can all help each other maximize

...

A: yea [B] push it

D: but ... we can help you

B: no

D: what do you need?

D: how many blue for red?

D: we can give you what you need, without you hurting us

C: [B] everyone else hit it were trying to help each other

A: no one can get screwed if we don't steal

C: you aren't making ANY money now

...

D: and we have all been helping each other the whole time

B: Chill out... it is just a game

...

D: so we are reputalbe

C: uh

C: for MONEYYYYYYYYYYYYYYYYYYYY

C: real money

C: why are you even here

D: we can help you earn more

C: [B] is BALLIN

D: if you let us

D: and then, you would stop hurting us

...

C: we are working together

C: but [B] doesnt want to help

...

C: [B] why would you steal my red fopr someone else[14]
B: just because
...
B: Stop whining
D: gaah! when will it end!
C: your taking MY MONEY
C: real money

This is one of the rare cases of an obdurate "baller" chatting with or, better, antagonizing everyone else. Individuals who have not attuned themselves to the group are generally quiet to the point of ignoring pleas to engage in conversation. (They also tend to avert their eyes when they are privately paid their earnings at the conclusion of the session.) *A*, *C*, and *D* have integrated into a regularized "we" who are "working together" and "helping each other" (these are common phrases across sessions), but *B* clearly has not. *B* is interrupting the dialogue of *A*, *C*, and *D* and challenging the integration of the "we," which the "we" remonstrate as "hurting us."

Until this point, I have described the situation somewhat disinterestedly as one of disagreement in the perceptions of what is right, out of which a rule of property arises. Can either *B*'s propensity to act in a certain manner or the "we's" disposition not to act manifest itself in a custom? The reflexive answer is, well, no, both are not possible if the telos of a rule is to regularize activity and create an order,[15] as the participants are well aware:

G: teamwork evryone wins
H: right right right
...

G: in this exp. the access to other peoples stuff really just causes problems

...

H: lets make some money

G: muah ha ha ha. order fights chaos i love it!!!!

E: hahahaha

G: no taking. ask and you shall receive

...

G: the only chaos is if the other half doesn't play nicely

E: seriously people your going to mess it up for everyone because this will turn into everyone messing each others up

E: and no one winning

But why this will mess it up for everyone is a good question and relevant to answering the bigger question of how do moral sentiments undergird the rule of property that emerges.

HARM, RESENTMENT, AND PROPERTY

Consider baller *B* and the "we" of *A, C,* and *D*. The "we" perceive certain clicks of *B*'s mouse as stealing that screws them over and hurts them. If they leave the experimental session with zero earnings, they still receive $7 for showing up on time, which is more than they walked into the laboratory with. So what makes *B*'s clicks hurtful to the "we"? *A, C,* and *D* perceive themselves to be falling from a superior to an inferior position. The superior position is that there is only person who controls how much red and blue are produced in one specific field. For each person, there is also only one house that will convert red and blue items at the end of the period into cash earnings, provided that items have been moved to it. The inferior position obviously is no red and blue items in either a field or a house following *B*'s clicks and hence no cash earnings. Adam Smith summarizes the situation when placed in the context of this session:

> To disturb [the "we's"] happiness merely because it stands in the way of [*B*'s] own, to take from [*A*, *C*, and *D*] what is of real use to [*A*, *C*, and *D*] merely because it may be equal or of more use to [*B*], or to indulge, in this manner, at the expence of other people, the natural preference which every man has for his own happiness above that of other people, is what no impartial spectator can go along with. . . .
>
> Though it may be true, therefore, that every individual, in his own breast, naturally prefers himself to all mankind, yet he dares not look mankind in the face, and avow that he acts according to this principle, and that how natural soever it may be to him, it must always appear excessive and extravagant to them. . . .
>
> [*B*] is to them, in every respect, as good as [*A*, *C*, and *D*]: they do not enter into that self-love by which [*B*] prefers himself so much to [the "we"], and cannot go along with the motive from which he hurt[s] [*A*, *C*, and *D*].[16]

Part of the background of what is right, as Smith details, is that "there can be no proper motive for hurting our neighbour."[17] *B*'s clicking on the red and blue items in the fields and houses not under his control is an act contrary to what is generally right (*ius*), an *iniuria*, not just in the secondary sense of harm in the modern use of the word *injury* but also in the primary moral sense of an act contrary to what is right. With the hope of bringing him into the group, the "we" are showing up *B* in the dialogue as being callous and morally perverse so that a rule of property may emerge. In platform 1 (the homestead), the form of the rule seems rather straightforward. In one lone case, someone spells it out precisely as a rule:

E: but let's start with the rule of: don't take stuff from other people's houses or fields

While this rule may appear obvious, it is not the only possible rule of property for platform 1. When followed in real time and under fluctuating circumstances, a different rule may arise out of a minor change in the background. Recall that the design in Kimbrough (2011) differs slightly from the others in that all eight participants are together from the beginning of the session. Because the harmony of possession is more difficult to achieve from the outset in octets than in duets, every single one of Kimbrough's sessions discusses a different rule never proposed elsewhere in platform 1:

E: the fields are fairgame, lets decide on that from now on, nobody takes ANYTHING from a house, if you have stuff to share you can put it in your field

The same process is at work in platform 2. When a stick figure is the first to click on a freely roaming white circle, the first striker suffers harm (probabilistically) when anyone else subsequently clicks on the same circle. As "things," these pixels on a computer screen are within the virtual grasp of the whalers and homesteaders before a baller, *B*, snatches them away. This perception of harm is the common thread across these two different platforms and explains why clicking on an already attached circle is considered to be stealing just as much as moving red and blue items out of a creator-endowed field or house. In both platforms, the different participants perceive the actions of the baller *B* types as one of the same bad kind. Just as the "we" resent *B*, so do integrated groups of stick figures in platform 2 also resent the *iniuria* of double-clicking on circles, which can prompt them to retaliate:

B: [D] you took mine! haha

F: what ever happen to our deal??

D: hhahah im the best

D: im the master

C: i know right

A: [D] u suck

D: i learned the best from [C]

F: ok everybody only steal from [D]

C: LOL

A: k

B: haha

D: hahah hey no fair

E: deal

F: deal

C: deal

E: haha

F: blue??

F: dude come on

A: sorry

E: hahahaha

F: or dudet u in??

F: steal from [D] no one else

F: ??

A: i will

E: me 2

F: sweet

Regardless of the form of the rule that arises out of the background to fit the local circumstances, there is a compelling emotion, which Smith astutely identifies, that buttresses the sentiments regarding a rule of property as moral: "Resentment seems to have been given us by nature for defence, and for defence only.... It prompts us to beat off mischief which is attempted to be done to us, and to retaliate that which is already done."[18] In a two-page-long footnote, Smith anticipates and refutes a reluctance to accept resentment as part of a sense of moral demerit:

> Resentment is commonly regarded as so odious a passion, that they will be apt to think it is impossible that so laudable a principle, as the sense of the ill desert of vice, should in any respect be founded upon it. They will be more willing, perhaps, to admit that our sense of the merit of good actions is founded upon a sympathy with the gratitude of the persons who receive the benefit of them; because gratitude . . . is regarded as an amiable principle, which can take nothing from the worth of whatever is founded upon it. Gratitude and resentment, however, are in every respect, it is evident, counterparts to one another; and if our sense of merit arises from a sympathy with the one, our sense of demerit can scarce miss to proceed from a fellow-feeling with the other.[19]

Within the integrated community, everyone empathizes with everyone else in resenting the harm inflicted by people like *D*, the self-proclaimed master. This empathy is a necessary component for supporting a rule of property, and what makes this empathy palpable is that the individuals have harmonized into a "we." Resentment is the sentiment, the predisposition, that makes the rule of property a moral goal. The rule of property is moral, not merely because the community is in fact committed to the rule but because *the community feels compelled through (morally justified) resentment to commit to the rule*. When *E* says that "seriously people your going to mess it up for everyone because this will turn into everyone messing each others up," *E* is concerned that the commitment to the rule might erode. That it often doesn't in the presence of the obdurate is a testament to the work that morality does.[20] Resentment of harm, the mutual empathy of desiring to avoid harm, and the compelling moral commitment to a rule to avoid harm are what give meaning to property as a practice.

Because we resent the harm when things are ripped from our hands, when we are not masters of what we have, we seek to become masters of what we possess through a rule of property. Mutual empathy toward harm converts islands of individuals who *have* into individual members of a "we" who *possess*. Once we have a rule, the moral commitment to the rule sustains the rule as part of the manifest practice or tradition of property.

PROPERTY EMERGES WITH THE ELIMINATION OF INJUSTICE

As Samuel Pufendorf observed in his discussion of natural law and property, humankind is capable of "kindness by the furtherance of mutual good," but humans are also "often malicious, insolent, and easily provoked, and as powerful in effecting mischief, as [they are] ready in designing it."[21] It's not hard to find evidence to confirm the latter through comments in these experiments:

- you're all a bunch of crooks
- o! damn the heathen
- we[']re turning into vultures
- It's a madhouse! A madhouse!
- this is madness
- I'm gonna have nightmares about this tonight
- This is like lord of the flies, they leave us to fend for ourselves, lol

Every virtual economy opens with vicious chaos, and roughly only one out of every six groups ever overcomes the havoc by the time the experiment ends. Those few who do first appeal to one another's own interests and their repeated experiences with the mutual harm of war. Once the injustice of real and positive hurt becomes common to everyone, that is, once the practice of justice becomes a common virtue, they then establish regular and orderly conduct by instituting specific rules for the stability of possession. These experiments demonstrate that property is not independent of or antecedent to justice, nor is property the cause of wars and quarrels in the world. Rather, it is by becoming just through the elimination of injustice that we institute rules of property.

NOTES

Portions of this chapter appeared in Wilson (2015) and are used here with the permission of Springer (License Number: 3705431178047). I wish to thank Jeffrey Kirchner for expertly constructing these virtual worlds and this volume's editor, Mark LeBar, for comments that have substantially improved the chapter.

1. Hume 1740, 338.
2. Hume 1740, 315.
3. Quoted and translated in Hayek 1973, 72, 162.
4. Hayek 1963.
5. See Wittgenstein 1953, 422: "there is a picture in the foreground, but the sense lies far in the background; that is, the application of the picture is not easy to survey."
6. Hayek 1952.
7. Hayek 1963.
8. For more on justice as a community virtue, see Woodruff, chapter 1 in this volume.
9. Bakhtin 1983.
10. Hume 1740, 322.
11. For example, if two people are successful, each receives a quarter of the whale, and half of the value is wasted.

12. Because the participants are identified as person *i* in the first platform and by a color name in the second, to standardize the presentation of the conversations, I will use letters to denote the different participants within a session. Sometimes the context will incidentally reveal which platform the session comes from, and other times it will not. The latter case is intentional. Each panel is from a distinct session. Several but not all of the conversations are presented in the original papers, which also include many more details on the context of the specific session.
13. http://www.wordfrequency.info.
14. Moving the items to an unsuspecting location is a commonly employed strategy when possession is particularly unstable.
15. The Latin word *regula* is the common root for both *rule* and *regular*.
16. Smith 1759, 82–83.
17. Smith 1759, 82. Notice also that part of what is right is that every person in every respect is as good as another in this experiment. The closer we look, the more rules we see come out of the background to support the ones we are focally attending to.
18. Smith 1759, 79. See Hanley (chapter 2 in this volume) for more on Smith's theory of justice, including the role of resentment in it.
19. Smith 1759, 76. Samuel Johnson's dictionary (http://johnsonsdictionaryonline.com) from 1755 defines *sympathy* as fellow feeling, mutual sensibility, and the quality of being affected by the affection of another. Our word *empathy*, which wasn't available to Smith, fits better than *sympathy* for the modern reader not familiar with eighteenth-century diction.
20. *F*'s plan to "steal" only from the master of mischief *D* and no one else actually worked. Why? Because all of the others morally resented *D* and held to their moral convictions to punish him and not "steal."
21. Pufendorf 1672, 136.

WORKS CITED

Bakhtin, M. M. 1983. *The Dialogic Imagination: Four Essays*. Austin, TX: University of Texas Press.

Ellickson, Robert C. 1989. "A Hypothesis of Wealth-Maximizing Norms: Evidence from the Whaling Industry." *Journal of Law, Economics and Organization* 5: 83–97.

Hayek, F. A. 1952. *The Sensory Order: An Inquiry into the Foundations of Theoretical Psychology*. Chicago: University of Chicago Press.

Hayek, F. A. 1963. "Rules, Perception and Intelligibility." *Proceedings of the British Academy* 48: 321–344.

Hayek, F. A. 1973. *Law, Legislation, and Liberty, Vol. 1: Rules and Order*. Chicago: University of Chicago Press.

Hume, David. 1740 [2000]. *A Treatise of Human Nature*. Edited by D. Norton and M. Norton. New York: Oxford University Press.

Jaworski, Taylor, and Bart J. Wilson. 2013. "Go West Young Man: Self-Selection and Endogenous Property Rights." *Southern Economic Journal* 79: 886–904.

Kimbrough, Erik O. 2011. "Learning to Respect Property by Refashioning Theft into Trade." *Experimental Economics* 14, no. 1: 84–109.

Kimbrough, Erik O., Vernon L. Smith, and Bart J. Wilson. 2010. "Exchange, Theft, and the Social Formation of Property." *Journal of Economic Behavior and Organization* 74: 206–229.

Pufendorf, Samuel. 1672 [2005]. *Of the Law of Nature and Nations: Eight Books*. Clark: Lawbook Exchange.

Smith, Adam. 1759 [1982]. *The Theory of Moral Sentiments*. Indianapolis: Liberty Fund.

Wilson, Bart J. 2015. "Further towards a Theory of the Emergence of Property." *Public Choice* 163, no. 1: 201–222.

Wilson, Bart J., Taylor Jaworski, Karl Schurter, and Andrew Smyth. 2012. "The Ecological and Civil Mainsprings of Property: An Experimental Economic History of Whalers' Rules of Capture." *Journal of Law, Economics and Organization* 28, no. 4: 617–656.

Wittgenstein, L. 1953. *Philosophical Investigations*. Translated by G. E. M. Anscombe. Malden: Blackwell.

Chapter 4

Learning How to Share

THOMAS WIDLOK

INTRODUCTION

The anthropology of morality has recently received a major boost and renewed interest, as expressed in a number of substantial publications.[1] The themes covered in this research include topics such as values, moral sentiments, virtue, piety, care, charity, humanitarianism, violence, and punishment, and it has numerous overlaps with the key concepts that are also subject to research in other disciplines. However, there have been two ways in which the anthropological perspective has both critiqued and complemented the work in neighboring disciplines such as psychology, philosophy, economics, sociology, and so forth. One is primarily a methodological issue of broadening the sample, and the second is a broader attempt to decenter Western academic discourse on morality also in terms of its theoretical foundations. I briefly summarize these two issues before presenting some of the substantive results of anthropological research which give a sense of what we know empirically about the social and cultural conditions that enable people to build up what can be called a skill for fostering just relations. The empirical domain under consideration will be that of sharing transactions across diverse cultural settings.

The first relevant issue concerns the empirical scope of the studies that have focused on justice and other issues of morality. One of the particular benefits of anthropological work has always been that it looked at outlying cases of non-European societies and cultures and more specifically at cases of societies in which ethical knowledge had not been formalized into a codified system maintained and interpreted by a class of specialists. However, a few years ago, Henrich, Heine, and Norenzayan (2010) pointed out that the true outliers, and truly "weird" (sub-)cultures in many respects were those that had been consulted by the great majority of all works to that point; the sample of most disciplines was almost exclusively limited to the Western, educated, industrial, rich and democratic subjects (the WEIRD people), often Euro-American college students, who are in many ways the weirdest people when considering the whole spectrum of human societies and cultures. Not only psychological and economic experiments but also philosophical or sociological theories usually relied on the "common sense" of professors and students working in Western-type academic institutions. Even when experiments were not limited to students and when introspection was not limited to professors, the invocation of "the man in the street" or "the man on the Clapham omnibus" carried not only a male bias but also many other cultural biases that had for a long time remained unnoticed. The new generation of anthropologically inspired researchers, by contrast, set out to deprovincialize research from its Euro-American biases, and the results were in many ways questioning previous results. Not only did non-WEIRD people provide other responses in economic and psychological experiments, but often they were also covering the larger part of the spectrum, while WEIRD people, typically psychology undergraduates and philosophy professors, were the true outliers in the sample. Basic cognitive phenomena such as the Müller-Lyer illusion that were considered to be human universals turned out to be restricted to people living in a "carpentered" environment, that is, those who were accustomed to looking at the world in terms of ninety-degree angles, flat surfaces, and straight lines.[2] Among the experiments that scrutinized a host of other domains were also those regarding distributive justice, above all the ultimatum games and prisoner's dilemmas, experiments that have been carried out by the thousands in a host of different versions and specifications.[3] Again, the major insight was that responses were much more varied than what was initially found (and imagined) to be the case. With regard to (re)distributive justice, the expectations of self-interested individuals who would only cooperate when this produced an immediate benefit to them was less frequently encountered than anticipated.[4] Moreover, there seemed to be much greater diversity in the sample and along a number of different variables, so that there was no simple "the West" versus "the rest" opposition to be found in the results. Since this was unsettling news for many neighboring disciplines, many psychologists and economists have since taken to the streets, not just of Clapham but also of Mumbai, Nairobi, Lagos, and their rural hinterlands in order to see how subjects from these places respond to the plethora of experimental tasks that had been developed in the past.

The second point of anthropological concern with regard to decentering Eurocentric research, on which I focus in this chapter, has a more fundamental theoretical edge to it. It seems that broadening the sample for experimental research or for hypothetical scenarios is not good enough to meet the challenge of countering Eurocentric biases. As I have pointed out elsewhere, it is not sufficient to include subjects who live outside Europe and North America, who carry an "exotic" passport, or who are ethnically different.[5] For instance, people who belong to the Sudanese Nuer, a celebrated ethnographic case study, now live in large numbers in the *Western* diaspora, and some are highly *educated,* work in *industry,* have become relatively *rich,* and seek to build up a *democratic* system. In many ways, therefore, some Nuer have joined the ranks of the WEIRD people as spelled out above, so that ethnic identity or place of origin is no longer a good proxy for broadening the sample. Moreover, and more critical, there is internal cultural diversity among many groups, and there is a diversity of strategies that make up individual repertoires that are not easily captured in experimental settings. This has also become clear with regard to the so-called trust games. The size of the stakes used, for instance, seems to matter much more than previously thought.[6] If some non-Europeans appeared to be even less cooperative than the average WEIRD person, it may have to do with the fact that the money stakes played a different role in their lives or that they lived in extreme poverty in which keeping assets like the stakes in experimental games provided one of the very few opportunities to secure an individual income. In other words, people react differently to the stimulus depending on what proportion it constitutes of the monetary means they typically have available. Similarly, time depth was found to make subjects activate different strategies from their cultural repertoires, since one-off encounters were treated differently from those exchanges that were recurrent or had some other relevant time depth to them.[7] As I show below, people critically rely on clues from everyday life when they solve problems of justice or other ethical concerns. It is these clues that are systematically excluded from the design of experiments for reasons of control and comparability. The biggest exclusion in this respect is the tendency to turn ethical matters into *filosofie a solo,* that is, into an individual decision-making situation.[8]

The critique toward investigating ideas of justice and other fundamental anthropological concepts on the basis of decisions made by individuals in isolation concerns not only experimental approaches but more generally the use of "case material" in philosophical treatises.[9] Case studies in philosophy (and to some extent also in sociology and other disciplines) are usually illustrative and fictive. They are cited (or constructed) to illustrate a point and to highlight the typical features of a particular theoretical statement. This is very different from the genuine anthropological take on events[10] and situations.[11] Events in anthropological accounts are often not typical at all but are often marginal or conflictual, because that makes them particularly "diagnostic," since it shows how these events have the potential to generate either new solutions or solutions to what otherwise remain purposefully ambivalent and undecided strategies. Situations in anthropological accounts are investigated in terms of recurrent patterns, as distinct events are understood as instances of "a situation." At the same time, a situational analysis underlines the importance of particulars that emerge in the course of events (see also Woodruff, chapter 1 in this volume). Ethnographic case studies therefore serve not only to broaden the basis of the sample but more fundamentally also to reframe the problem of ethical skill. How people deal in particular situations is more than a practical "realization" of preconceived moral ideas. The particulars of a situation are not an afterthought to a moral core somewhere outside that practice, either in external material conditions (Marxism and Darwinian evolutionism), in the ideologies of the cultural codex (idealism), or in the internal deep structures of mental processes (cognitivism). Rather, habitual practice itself is seen as the core that enables people to become just. As Hanley (chapter 2 in this volume) has shown, the major Enlightenment thinkers were considering "being just" in a duality of external coercion, typically through social institutions and contracts, and of internal motivations, typically seen as hardwired in human nature or cognition. The recent anthropologically inspired research points at the domain of habits and gradually built-up skills that is situated between the received duality of changing social institutions and unchanging human psychology. As I illustrate in this chapter, the social practices of sharing and of redistributive justice are not "contractual" in the sense of externally and formally defined institutions of "the society" but are intimately connected to individual lifeways and bodies that are implicated in processes of habitualization. They are, at the same time, also not limited to the "mental" or "motivational" inner life, because they are created and maintained through repeated interaction and they generate and enable justice across particular situations rather than from some universal core located elsewhere. I first summarize some of the evidence from cross-cultural experimental data before looking at ethnographic evidence collected in egalitarian societies in which sharing is particularly pronounced. This evidence leads me to some reflections about the link between skill and personhood in the process of habitualization.

HOW DO CHILDREN BECOME JUST?

One of the anthropological complaints against developmental psychology is that, ironically, we get only a very limited sense of the actual processual dynamic underlying a "development." With regard to practices of sharing, for instance, developmental psychologists have established in their research with children that culture entrenches ideas and practices of what is considered "just" much earlier in life than previously thought. Even children as young as four years of age differ considerably across cultural samples. However, exactly how they manage to build up this cultural competence, or what I will call skill, is much less clear. The overall picture that emerges from experimental approaches remains disturbingly static. I take a recent Ph.D. project on the topic as an example, because the author, Marie Schäfer, conducted field research in my field site in Namibia and because it is one of the more perceptive and sophisticated attempts to capture culture differences. In her first comparative study of sharing behavior, Schäfer included children of five African groups.[12] She conducted a series of experimental tasks with the general pattern of two children each receiving a "treasure" (provided as a stimulus by the experimenter), and she observed the different ways in which the children dealt with uneven treasures, whether and how they sought to establish a just and fair (re)distribution. In the second study, the children received their treasures not simply as a "find" but after some effort on their part. In a variant of this study, the children were "angling" for the treasures but with (manipulated) magnetic angling gear that allowed the researcher to determine how many treasures each child managed to receive, despite their individual efforts but without them noticing.[13]

Some of the results of the first study are summarized in figure 4.1. The twelve treasures (sweets in one variant and nonfood items in another) were divided in such a way that one child would initially receive eleven treasures while the other would receive

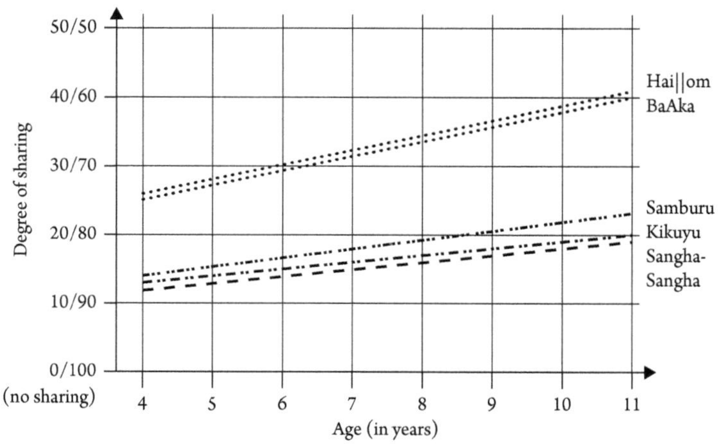

Figure 4.1. A summary of comparative experiments on sharing behavior among children ages four to eleven from two African forager and three African agropastoralist groups. (Adapted from Schäfer 2014 and redrawn by M. Feinen.)

only one. Then the children were left to their own devices to deal with this inequality. In sum, the results show that the "rich" children of two groups of subjects tended toward giving their peers as many as five of their treasures so that each of them ended up with about the same number on average, namely, six. The children in three other groups gave much less (one or two items). In all cases, sharing increased with age (ages ranged from four to eleven), so that one could say that children were learning with increasing age how to share or how to share more and in a more equitable manner. However, across all ages, the significant difference persisted between the two "fair-sharing" groups and those who shared unevenly. The difference correlates with the fact that those who shared fairly were members of two groups of hunter-gatherers (the Aka of the central African forest and the Hai//om of the southern African savannah). The other three groups (Samburu, Kikuyu, and Sangha-Sangha) were agropastoralist Bantu-speaking groups with a very different way of life, less egalitarian, and more competitive. The results do not come as a surprise to anthropologists who work with these groups, because the hunter-gatherers are known for their strong sharing ethic, whereas the other groups are known to be much more hierarchical in social organization and have an economic system that requires accumulation and strong notions of exclusive ownership.[14] In other words, it is not that the children were "cultivated" in some of the groups and remained "natural" in some of the others but rather that the directions in which they were culturally trained in their respective groups were different. Since the differences were perceivable at a fairly early age, it is also clear that we are not dealing only with formal instruction and education but rather with ways of picking up prereflectively what is considered just and fair or simply the right way of doing things habitually in the everyday settings to which children are exposed from the beginning of their life in the group.

Schäfer's second study shows that the dividing line is not between "African" and "European" but between people with a hunter-gatherer background and those with a farming background. The latter, together with the European children included in this study, tolerated unequal distribution when it was based on merit (on the work effort of children successfully angling for treasures). In other words, children from societies with a farming background (both European and African) endorsed inequality of outcome. The European children made their sharing dependent on whether the other person had actively worked for gaining a share ("angling" in the experiments), while among the hunter-gatherers, such a distinction was irrelevant for the sharing afterward. In abstract terms, meritocratic considerations that are taken for granted by many Europeans were dismissed or undermined among the hunter-gatherers. In questioning parents after the experiment, Schäfer found that European and African accumulators with a cultural background in farming explicitly justified that children would be allowed to keep what they had gained, in particular if they "worked" for it, and indeed should be encouraged to do so. She also got the impression that the children of African farmers were used to parents and other authorities distributing shares rather than they themselves negotiating them. These parents exhibited the same puzzlement that equal shares have provoked more generally among the agropastoralists who have come to dominate the world probably ever since the Neolithic revolution (see the reactions to the Parable of the Vineyard Workers in Matthew 20:16 for a well-known example). Note that it is not simply a matter of one type of society favoring equality while the other favors inequality. Rather, it is a matter of two very different ways of tolerating inequality. The agropastoralists are tolerant with regard to inequalities of outcomes, and the adults explicitly praise and support behavior that leads to unequal outcomes. Hunter-gatherers, by contrast, are tolerant with regard to unequal work efforts or unequal contributions made when allocating shares.

The experimental results match the wider ethnographic record, which suggests that hunter-gatherers much more readily accept that outcomes are enabled or disabled by more than what each individual contributes and that therefore there are grounds for individual complaints and demands.[15] Prototypically, this is the case for hunting when luck or the animal itself and not just the hunter determines whether the hunt is successful. Moreover, hunter-gatherers accept not only that uneven opportunities occur but at the same time that this unevenness requires human action in terms of sharing and redistribution to ensure a more equitable outcome that provides everyone with more or less the same share. To phrase it differently, it is not as if one society is being in favor of fairness and the other against it but rather that there are two different standards of what constitutes fairness, one based on meritocratic principles and one based on pragmatic principles of dealing with an everyday life that continually creates inequalities.

The question that we are left with is how do people in these diverse cultures create conditions for their members to become (and remain) just and fair in their respective ways? Unfortunately, the experimental setup treats the subjects very much as isolated individuals. Children are divided into age groups, but the children's learning curve is based not on any interaction or any biographical development but on the data points of the sample, which effectively isolates individuals and individual responses in order to accumulate the data points into an aggregated sequence. This common technique of natural-science-based psychology has been criticized by Ingold (2007) and others as following the "sigma principle." Summing up outcomes makes it impossible to trace any particular living individual with his or her learning environment, because it creates, instead, a "fractal" average subject with a constructed (or imagined) "development" that is several steps removed from the way learning is experienced by the individual person in his or her particular social relationships in real life.

In the following sections, I summarize the anthropological work on sharing that employs ethnographic methods in an attempt to restore the processual character of this social dynamics which is lost in the experiential situation in order to explain the emergence and maintenance of moral skills.

CONDITIONS THAT ENABLE SHARING

A large part of the anthropological literature on sharing is based on an evolutionary approach that tries to elicit what makes sharing so widespread among humans in comparison with all other living beings. Even among so-called social animals such as termites and bats or among mammals such as lions and various primates, sharing is very restricted compared with what we find among humans.[16] There are behaviors such as co-feeding, brooding, or "tolerated taking" that can be seen as forms of proto-sharing, but they are negligible when compared with the high incidence and degree of sharing among humans. They are negligible in two ways. First, human sharing can be widespread, well beyond close relatives or dependents such as mother-child or husband-wife dyads. Ethnographers have recorded sharing among hunter-gatherers in all parts of the world, where close kinship is no delimiting factor but where sharing is expanded to include nonrelatives and basically anyone who happens to be around at the site.[17] Second, human sharing is not an exceptional mode of transfer, but in foraging groups, it can account for the larger part of people's diet. Ache foragers of South America have been reported to receive up to 80 percent of their food through sharing.[18] In modern industrial society, too, the larger part of the population receives its livelihood not through selling labor but as dependents of various kinds, relying on state welfare, family, pension funds, and other transfers.[19]

Correspondingly, a number of social, political, and economic functions have been identified that can explain the high incidence of sharing among human beings. The most widely discussed are the risk-reduction function and the leveling function of sharing. Sharing can work as "social storage" and buffer the risks of failing resources, and it can equalize differences of wealth as a consequence, for instance, of the unequal distribution of hunting luck or hunting prowess, for that matter. More specifically, the discussion has centered around the theoretical ideas of "reciprocal altruism," "kin-based nepotism," "tolerated scrounging," and "costly signalling."[20] Note, however, that while these functions may explain why there is more sharing among humans than among other living beings, including closely related primates, they cannot ultimately explain why there is more sharing, say, among the Aka than among the Samburu or less sharing among shareholders in a corporation than among university students in a hostel.[21] What determines the width, depth, and modality of sharing once sharing as a practice has been "invented," as it were, and once it has been added to the human repertoire?

As a first step toward answering this question, we need to conceptualize sharing as a complex practice rather than as a simple behavior. The very basic dividing of, say, the carcass of a hunted animal can be said to be a part of sharing as a practice, but it does not adequately describe all there is to it. After all, cutting up and dividing the meat can be part of very different practices, ranging from commercial selling of meat at the butcher to the distribution of meat by a household head, or by a patriarchal leader or any other central authority, and further to reciprocal gift exchange and to sharing in the narrow sense. It is in this last sense of sharing as a technical term, defined as a practice that "enables others to access what is valued"[22] with a polythetic list of characteristics that distinguish it from reciprocal gift giving or selling.[23] The characteristics that I highlight in the remainder of this chapter are those conditions that help to cultivate sharing, namely,

(1) demanding (rather than offering), including the need to respond to demands, (2) the presence of the person demanding rather than his or her abstract membership in a group, and (3) the acceptance of one-way transfers. By looking at these three characteristics, I try to answer how a cultural orientation and disposition toward sharing and enabling others to access valued goods is created and fostered.

AGREEABLE DEMANDS INSTEAD OF PRINCIPAL COMMANDS

Among the somewhat counterintuitive but robust results of ethnographic work on sharing is that it occurs without a marked ideology of generosity or altruism. It is not, in the first instance, generous offerings (self-imposed or imposed by authorities) that prepare the ground for sharing to occur, but demands and prompts. In fact, in societies with a high incidence of sharing, there is often a reluctance to give without being prompted to do so, and there are frequent attempts to avoid sharing pressure by hiding things, attempting to ignore demands, or consuming out of sight. Giving too quickly and giving too much are often explicitly evaluated negatively. But so are demands that are out of proportion. There are negative evaluations of demands but not qua being a demand, since it is the inappropriateness and disproportion of a demand that are bemoaned. Peterson (2013) and Macdonald (2000), who worked among Australian Aboriginal groups, report how people complain about fellow group members "humbugging," that is, making out-of-proportion demands on their peers, and they criticize outsiders (including visiting anthropologists) for giving in too readily to demands, while they readily accept that all people try to evade some of the sharing pressure that is on them.[24] Pryor and Graburn (1980), who worked with Arctic foragers, established that the explicit discourse about sharing and generosity could not be seen as causing sharing behavior but was rather another factor to be included in the complex sharing practice. In their Inuit case study, those who were said to give frequently turned out to do so much less than the others. Pryor and Graburn propose that in systems in which transfers are said to even out fairly, there may in fact and in practice be less reciprocal equilibrium than in systems in which there is a constant suspicion of inequality and where therefore more attention is being given to keeping an exact record accounting for what is given and what is being received in return. Among the Hai//om San of Namibia, where I carried out most of my field research,[25] people find it strange and even objectionable to see how individuals from neighboring farming groups alternate between exhibiting unselfishness (for instance, against the old and frail) on the one hand but also at the same time exhibiting self-interestedness (against peers) on the other hand. Both seem to them disproportionate and in a sense unjust. Hai//om consider giving objects or services to people who have not asked for them to be interfering with personal autonomy, and they object against this as a possible attempt to make others indebted and dependent. Consequently, many of their acts of sharing are diffused by allowing others to take (instead of handing things over) and in particular by relying on intermediaries, usually children who carry things over to the neighbors. The fact that children frequently take on the role of intermediaries and delivery boys or girls gives us a first clue to why the Hai//om children responded in the way Schäfer found in her experiments. We are dealing with a group in which even small children tend to share fairly and evenly with their peers but in which there is very little emphasis on "free gifts" and indeed a suspicion against such behavior. Here the ethics of sharing seems to rely on something else than an ideology of generosity, as we find it in some religious or secular systems of morality that propagate almsgiving as a sacrifice in the interest of either a reward after death or for future generations. The puzzle is resolved if we consider sharing as a practical (ethical) skill of demanding and of responding to demands. We may consider this learning how to respond appropriately across situations as an empirical case illustrating what Woodruff (chapter 1 in this volume) has described in more abstract terms as "growing toward justice." Woodruff has also pointed out that this growth is particularist in nature, informed by a range of reasons for decisions that may vary from case to case, without denying that there are universals involved in the human condition. Having looked at some of the experimental data on how children acquire the skill of sharing and at some of the social patterns that emerge from the ethnography, the next section here takes a more analytic approach. I look at culture specificity and universality with regard to the importance of personal presence in the process of enskillment and growth.

PRESENCE IN ETHICAL ENSKILLMENT

There is very little or no formal instruction in hunter-gatherer groups that cultivates extensive sharing. In other words, there is not a sophistication in explicating ethical values in commandments and duties toward children (and adults). Instead, there is a realization that the skill of judging when a demand is appropriate and when it should be followed has to be learned in practice. Acquiring this skill of sharing requires social presence in at least two ways. First, children and adults learn by witnessing situations of successful and unsuccessful demands and by participating in successful and unsuccessful attempts to accumulate and to withdraw from sharing. Second, presence itself is one of the main factors for making successful demands. How social persons present themselves and their demands is not just an afterthought of accepted lawlike principles, but it is decisive for what happens in these situations. There is a considerable body of anthropological literature now criticizing the Western conception that locates culture primarily in the realm of ideas, plans, blueprints, and evaluation while everyday practice is reduced to implementation or "technical" realization.[26] The critique is raised against the conceptual dualism that separates cultural and creative ideas from passive bodies and materials but also against the assumption that plans and blueprints are prior and more fundamental than the practices they describe. Here habit or habitual practice takes center stage, replacing the determinism of material conditions or the idealism of cultural plans. Ingold (2000) has elaborated on this with regard to domains such as architecture and landscaping but also to crafts and music. Gell (1998) has put forward a similar argument with regard to art, and it is also echoed by what Lave has pointed out for learning and education.[27] They all point out that Western observers are too quick to attribute knowledge and culture to templates and blueprints that they find either in codices and ideologies or in individual mindsets or in "culture" in the abstract. Instead, they argue, the cultural achievements are actually contained as skill in the repeated practice itself. As I have pointed out elsewhere, we can put forward a similar argument for the domain of ethics.[28] One of the key points in the anthropology of skill is that practice is no longer reduced to technical execution and no longer categorically separates design from construction. In parallel, I have suggested that ethical practice is no longer reducible to rule-abiding moral behavior.[29] No investigation of good things can limit itself to collecting explicit statements, omitting the habitualization of practice across situations. A parallel example is Ingold's remark about good artifacts: they are not a matter of good design but rather what he calls "the pattern of regular movement," such as when weaving a basket.[30] In our context, the good "ethical artifact" would be described in terms of repeated virtuous acts across particular situations and not in cultural reflections about what should be done in principle. It follows that in both domains, handcrafts and ethics, the importance of formal instruction has been overemphasized. The same, I argue, holds for practical ethical skills such as sharing. Just as the knowledge of how to do things (technically) is typically not handed over as a program or a set of rules independent and in advance of practice, so is the knowledge of how to do things in an ethical way, which, like sharing, is a matter of responding to everyday sharing demands in changing social constellations. Practitioners become skillful not through their privileged access to a cultural code but simply by training and perfecting their own movements as they go along. This not only reverses the established evaluation of practitioners as inferior followers of those who formulate moral codes or technical plans and designs, but it also suggests a more diffuse or distributed notion of what constitutes a fair and rightful share and how we get to recognize what is fair and just. The emphasis has shifted from the cognitive or theoretical learning of moral values to the practical acquisition of what ought to be done as one encounters ethical problems, for instance, in situations of (re)distribution and when facing demands.

Learning to share therefore happens in the action of being confronted with relevant situations (see also Woodruff in chapter 1 of this volume). Moreover, in the process, sharing also requires bodily presence. While it can do without formal contracts and indeed without contractual thinking, physical presence is the prototypical means for prompting sharing. Explicit demands may underline the presence of a needy person, thereby eliciting a share, but frequently it is the "silent demand" of approaching someone who is able to share with the goal to make that person recognize the presence of those in need of a share.[31] The fact that presence (and the recognition of presence) is often silent is relevant insofar as this prediscursiveness also helps to explain why children learn these strategies so early in life. It also explains why sharing is typically considered a strong moral obligation even if there is no set of codified rules that would need to go along with it. The body of rules, we could say, is constituted by the embodied presence of people who share a situation. The presence-sharing nexus is continually trained when approaching people or when being approached by them. Being present is read as a silent moral demand. By contrast, turning away from people, splitting up, separating oneself, and avoiding co-presence are read as a negative response to these moral demands. In other words, the ethical enskillment includes not only the positive skill of knowing how to act morally but also the negative skill of being able to fend off demands by others that are out of proportion. What emerges from the ethnography is that ethics as a skill is not tied to realizing golden rules or other principles. Rather, it is tied to choices made in changing contexts in which the position of those who are acting and the position of those they are responding to are constantly changing. It is part of the skill to keep up with these changes. Those toward whom demands can be legitimately posed can lose whatever they possess. Conversely, those who were have-nots a moment ago may find themselves in a position in which they receive something and are immediately subject to the legitimate demand of others who have less or who are also in need. In the final part of this chapter, I explore briefly the implications of these observations with regard to the notions of personhood involved.

ACCEPTING ONE-WAY TRANSFERS

In the previous section, I took a lead from anthropological theory on art, music, and handcrafts considered as skill, and I have extended it also to cover the domain of morality and justice. The general argument is that understanding how people arrive at just behavior needs to involve looking at practice over time instead of limiting ourselves to codes and blueprints. My own view is that this is also a good starting point for resolving normative problems, but in any case, it can help us to understand why people come to accept and initiate one-way transfers that are not reciprocal and not immediately beneficial to themselves, without the need to make far-reaching assumptions about altruistic sentiments and similar dispositions. In the remainder of this chapter, I highlight two (complementary) ideas concerning personhood that are relevant in this context, since they concern notions of personhood implicit in practice rather than in elaborate ideologies or ethical codes. The first notion of personhood is that of extended self (as recently explicated by Russell Belk), and the second is the notion of finite self, as I have recently labeled it.[32]

In Belk's view, the key to sharing is that those who are close to us are treated as "part of our extended self," so that "sharing with them is like sharing with self."[33] This is why sharing takes place, above all, within the immediate family circle in highly commercialized contemporary societies. When children take food that their parents have bought and placed in the fridge, when they use the facilities of their family home, and so on, it would be wrong to consider this as following an abstract rule of reciprocity or as a two-way transfer (possibly an indirect one), because there is no movement between two units. We are also not dealing with the execution of a law of kin-based altruism, because the people who share their home and their resources in this way need not be genetically related. Rather, Belk argues, this is a single (family) unit feeding itself, an "aggregate extended self" that has been constituted through numerous everyday activities that maintain it.[34] In other words, the "ethical training" that leads people to develop sharing as a skill is based on the many everyday activities in which people extend their selves. What works most readily in many immediate families can also work more or less effectively among peers in an age set, such as the student hostels or flat shares already mentioned.[35] These everyday acts of bonding and extending the self are regularly trained in small bands of foragers but can also be anchored in commercial settings, for instance, in the practices of co-consumers sharing a brand of clothes[36] or those sharing files on the internet.[37] Extending the self in this way is by no means "natural," since there are also many activities that work against such an extension, typically when people engage in direct competition with one another or when exercising exclusivist practices such as consumption as distinction.[38] Similarly, insisting on drawing the boundaries of the ethnic or other "we" group ever more narrowly in face-to-face interaction "un-trains" widespread sharing.[39] Correspondingly, the extension of aggregate selves is found to vary across (sub)cultures and, more generally, over time and across situations.

The model of extended self can help to explain why sharing as a one-way transfer is so widespread and broad among humans and why it is so culturally diverse. Establishing personhood is not to be confused with recognizing individual selves. It requires considerable imagination and complex processes of consciousness to recognize a person, since that person need not be congruent with an individual body. As humans, we are used to the fact that one and the same individual may act as different persons in different contexts and moreover that there are "legal" persons that are either not tied to a human body (e.g., modern corporations) or go beyond individuals (e.g., clans). We have also become accustomed to objects that can come to stand for particular persons (in religious shrines or in bureaucratic or digital forms of identification). Recognizing personhood in oneself and in others is either absent or very limited among animals and therefore can explain the relative absence of sharing among nonhumans. Moreover, given that personhood is subject to cultural imagination, it is also not surprising that there is considerable diversity in the ways in which people recognize personhood and determine what it is. Again, the diversity of personhood concepts can therefore help to explain that sharing varies so widely in its intensity and breadth among human groups.

A second, complementary idea that can help us to understand the cultural variability of sharing is the model of presence and of the finite self that builds on the notion of ethical skill, as sketched here earlier. If ethical skill is "moral practice," in that it only emerges in social practice itself, as I have suggested,[40] then practical presence is the major ingredient that allows sharing to occur. One of the key features of human (co-)presence is that it is limited by the finite lives that we live. It is limited first in the sense that my presence is limited by the presence of others and by their recognition of my presence. It is also finite in the sense that every human self is tied to an aging and mortal human body, which restricts the individual self. Hence, complementary to the cultural imagination of how personhood can be extended (as described by Belk), there is the experiential realization that this extension is limited and finite. Being a finite self among other finite selves underlines that there are bound to be one-way transfers, in particular at the beginning of one's life and toward the end. Again, this finiteness is prediscursively experienced from an early age and throughout one's life. As humans grow, they acquire and give up positions, be it their status as a dependent child, as a youngster, or as a responsible adult, and they finally give up their human life among their fellow humans altogether. Learning to let go of things and to let go of a particular status vis-à-vis others is therefore an everyday experience but one that is culturally entrenched in very different ways in different cultural contexts.

CONCLUSION

This chapter began with the growing realization that much of what we know about humans, including their sense of (re-)distributive judgment, is based on a rather small sample of WEIRD people. A number of disciplines are now striving to expand the spectrum of people and cultural traditions included in comparative work. I have argued that this expansion of the spectrum has to proceed along two lines, namely, not only including "other" people but also including the fact that decision and judgments depend on clues about the "others" who are implicated in questions of judgment, for instance, when allocating and evaluating shares. I have highlighted three conditions that need to be included: (1) granting demand practices the prominent position they hold in naturally occurring social life, (2) allowing embodied presence rather than abstract principles to play the critical role they do in practice, and (3) incorporating notions of extended and finite personhood that allow people to tolerate one-way transfers. By incorporating these three conditions in our research, we can trace the process of becoming just, of building up embodied ethical skills and the capacity to evaluate the skills in others. I have focused on the sharing practices that establish inclusive social relations and in themselves involve a whole repertoire of communicative means. Making demands that are considered and recognized to be rightful while restraining those demands that are considered to be disproportionate or otherwise inadequate is an ethical skill that is largely prediscursively acquired. As a complex social institution, sharing is enabled by a host of social settings, including a high degree of spatial permeability in settlements, prevalent language pragmatics, modes of classificatory kinship reckoning, and similar modes of social relatedness.[41] By giving more attention to the details of these social settings, we are in a better position to explain not only sharing but also instances in which sharing breaks down (or has a low intensity or breadth). Part of the future research agenda will be the investigation of how much of observed injustice is due to a gradual and possibly unintentional disbanding or weakening of some of the features that this chapter has outlined as the enabling framework for sharing.

NOTES

1. See Fassin 2012; Heintz 2009; Zigon 2008.
2. Henrich, Heine, and Norenzayan 2010, 65; see also Widlok 2014, 2.
3. Andersen et al. 2011, 3427.
4. Henrich et al. 2005.
5. Widlok 2014.
6. Andersen et al. 2011.
7. Gintis and van Schaik 2013, 26.
8. Marten 1993, 14.
9. See Ingold 2015, 131–132.
10. Kapferer 2015.
11. Zigon 2015.
12. Schäfer 2014; see also Schäfer, Haun, and Tomasello 2015a.
13. Schäfer 2014; see also Schäfer, Haun, and Tomasello 2015b.
14. See Woodburn 1998.
15. See Widlok 2017 for an overview.
16. Widlok 2017.
17. See Widlok 2017.
18. Kaplan and Hill 1985.
19. Ferguson 2015.
20. Widlok 2017, 43.
21. See Widlok 2017.
22. Widlok 2017, 1.
23. Belk 2010; see also Widlok 2017.
24. Myers 1988.
25. See Widlok 1999.
26. See Ingold 2000; Gell 1998.
27. Lave and Wenger 1991.
28. Widlok 2004; Widlok 2010.
29. Widlok 2004, 59.
30. Ingold 2000, 291.
31. Løgstrup 1997.
32. Belk 2007; Belk 2010; Widlok 2017.
33. Belk 2010, 724.
34. Belk 2010, 725.
35. Widlok 2017, 104–105.
36. Belk 2010, 726.
37. Widlok 2017, 142.
38. Bourdieu 1979.
39. Widlok 2015.
40. Widlok 2017.
41. See Widlok 2010.

WORKS CITED

Andersen, Steffen, Seda Ertaç, Uri Genîzî, Moshe Hoffman, and John A. List. 2011. "Stakes Matter in Ultimatum Games." *American Economic Review* 101, no. 7: 3427–3439.

Belk, Russell. 2007. "Why Not Share Rather than Own?" *Annals of the American Academy of Political and Social Science* 611, no. 1: 126–140.

Belk, Russell. 2010. "Sharing." *Journal of Consumer Research* 36, no. 5: 715–734.

Bourdieu, Pierre. 1979. *La distinction: Critique sociale du jugement*. Paris: Les Éd. de Minuit.

Fassin, Didier. 2012. *A Companion to Moral Anthropology*. Malden: Wiley-Blackwell.

Ferguson, James. 2015. *Give a Man a Fish: Reflections on the New Politics of Distribution*. Durham and London: Duke University Press.

Gell, Alfred. 1998. *Art and Agency: An Anthropological Theory*. Oxford: Clarendon Press.

Gintis, Herbert, and Carel van Schaik. 2013. "*Zoon Politicon*: The Evolutionary Roots of Human Sociopolitical Systems." In *Cultural Evolution: Society, Technology, Language, and Religion*, edited by Peter James Richerson and Morten H. Christiansen, 25–44. Cambridge: MIT Press.

Heintz, Monica. 2009. *The Anthropology of Moralities*. New York: Berghahn.

Henrich, Joseph, et al. 2005. "Economic Man" in Cross-Cultural Perspective: Behavioral Experiments in 15 Small-Scale Societies." *Behavioral and Brain Sciences* 28: 795–855.

Henrich, Joseph, Steven Heine, and Ara Norenzayan. 2010. "The Weirdest People in the World?" *Behavioral and Brain Sciences* 33, 61–135.

Ingold, Tim. 2000. *The Perception of the Environment: Essays on Livelihood, Dwelling, and Skill*. New York: Routledge.

Ingold, Tim. 2007. *Lines: A Brief History*. London: Routledge.

Kaplan, Hillard, and Kim Hill. 1985. "Food Sharing among Ache Foragers: Tests of Explanatory Hypotheses." *Current Anthropology* 26: 223–246.

Lave, Jean, and Etienne Wenger. 1991. *Situated Learning: Legitimate Peripheral Participation*. Cambridge: Cambridge University Press.

Løgstrup, K. E. 1997. *The Ethical Demand*. Notre Dame: University of Notre Dame Press.

Macdonald, Gaynor. 2000. "Economies and Personhood: Demand Sharing among the Wiradjuri of New South Wales." In *The Social Economy of Sharing: Resource Allocation and Modern Hunter-Gatherers*, edited by George W. Wenzel, Grete Hovelsrud-Broda, and Nobuhiro Kishigami, 87–111. Osaka: National Museum of Ethnology (Senri Ethnological Studies 53).

Marten, Rainer. 1993. *Lebenskunst*. München: Fink.

Myers, Fred R. 1988. "Burning the Truck and Holding the Country: Property, Time, and the Negotiation Identity among Pintupi Aborigines." In *Hunters and*

Gatherers, Vol. 2: Property, Power, and Ideology, edited by David Riches, James Woodburn, and Tim Ingold, 52–94. Oxford: Berg.

Peterson, Nicolas. 2013. "On the Persistence of Sharing: Personhood, Asymmetrical Reciprocity, and Demand Sharing in the Indigenous Australian Domestic Moral Economy." *Australian Journal of Anthropology* 24, no. 2: 166–176.

Pryor, Frederic, and Nelson Graburn. 1980. "The Myth of Reciprocity." In *Social Exchange: Advances in Theory and Research*, edited by Kenneth J. Gergen, Martin S. Greenberg, and Richard Hartley Willis, 215–237. New York: Plenum.

Schäfer, Marie. 2014. "Cultural Variation in Children's Development of Resource Sharing and Fairness." Unpublished Ph.D. thesis, Leipzig University.

Schäfer, Marie, Daniel Haun, and Michael Tomasello. 2015a. "Cultural Differences in Children's Sharing among Peers in Five African Societies." Poster presented at the biennial meeting of the Society for Research in Child Development, Philadelphia.

Schäfer, Marie, Daniel Haun, and Michael Tomasello. 2015b. "Fair Is Not Fair Everywhere." *Psychological Science* 26: 1252–1260.

Widlok, Thomas. 2004. "Sharing by Default? Outline of an Anthropology of Virtue." *Anthropological Theory* 4, no. 1: 53–70.

Widlok, Thomas. 2015. "Ethnicity As Social Deixis." In *Ethnicity as a Political Resource: Conceptualizations across Disciplines, Regions, and Periods*, 85–96. Bielefeld: Transcript Verlag.

Widlok, Thomas. 2017. *Anthropology and the Economy of Sharing*. London: Routledge.

Woodburn, James. 1998. "'Sharing Is Not a Form of Exchange': An Analysis of Property-Sharing in Immediate-Return Hunter-Gatherer Societies." In *Property Relations: Renewing the Anthropological Tradition*, edited by Chris Hann, 48–63. Cambridge: Cambridge University Press.

Zigon, Jarrett. 2008. *Morality: An Anthropological Perspective*. Oxford: Berg.

Zigon, Jarrett. 2015. "What Is a Situation? An Assemblic Ethnography of the Drug War." *Cultural Anthropology* 30, no. 3: 501–524.

Chapter 5

Thought, Emotions, and Sentiments in the Development of Justice

ELLIOT TURIEL, AUDUN DAHL,
AND ZINAIDA BESIREVIC

In this chapter, we approach the topic of justice and of morality more generally from a psychological perspective. As developmental psychologists, we have analyzed how children, adolescents, and adults reason about moral issues, including considerations of justice, welfare, and rights. Whereas our research includes judgments regarding justice, it has regarded justice along with judgments about welfare and rights. We propose that reasoning is central to morality but not to the exclusion of emotions. Our view is in contrast with several other psychological approaches proposing that the development of morality involves the acquisition of externally established (by parents, the group, culture, society) fixed norms adhered to if established with sufficient strength. Various terms are used for that which is acquired, such as *rules, values, standards, virtues,* and *traits of character*. Typically, there is overlap in the features placed on lists of moral characteristics. Even broad concepts such as justice and fairness are listed as fixed entities that make up the morality of individuals. We propose that morality is not adequately characterized as being due to the acquisition of an unconditional, fixed set of traits or socially defined standards.

While this volume is centered on justice, we believe that it is essential to view the development of orientations toward justice in the context of moral development more broadly. Based on long-standing research on children's and adults' moral orientations, we propose that individuals reason about right and wrong in social relationships, societal arrangements, and cultural practices. Consequently, individuals do not simply adhere to rules, values, or traits and apply moral judgments in flexible ways to social situations. Instead, people approach social situations by accounting for possible varying features, and they weigh and balance different considerations and goals in coming to decisions. Therefore, decisions can involve processes of coordination.

To illustrate the flexibility of moral and social reasoning, we begin by discussing coordination in reasoning about honesty and trust, which often have direct implications for fairness and justice. We then turn to a discussion of how individuals develop their reasoning, coordination, and evaluations of moral and social issues based on social experiences from an early age. We propose that these developments involve active construction based on direct experiences with and signals from others. Individuals do not automatically accept the values or rules of their community but scrutinize and sometimes reject the messages they receive from authority figures and others. Construction, scrutiny, and rejection in moral development are evidenced by research on resistance to perceived injustices, for instance, in patriarchal societies.

Alongside processes of reasoning, emotions are central to the moral orientations of children and adults. Contrary to some current views, we propose that emotions and reasoning about moral issues are closely intertwined. In the last part of the chapter, we conceptualize the intertwining of reasoning and emotions in terms of moral "sentiments," a set of broad concerns that are central and binding for most people and are viewed as obligatory. These sentiments form the basis for both reasoning and emotional reactions. We propose three moral sentiments—the value of life, respect for persons, and human dignity—and discuss research findings bearing on these sentiments.

We believe that explanations of the development of morality based on sentiments, as well as processes of construction and reasoning, are informative for psychological and philosophical approaches to justice.

FLEXIBILITY AND COORDINATION IN MORALITY: THE CASE OF HONESTY

Honesty is often listed in the psychological literature among the values, standards, or traits of character constituting acquired morality. However, there is ample evidence that people lie and that they may even lie fairly regularly in some contexts. We can ask, therefore, when someone lies, is that person acting in an unjust way toward others? To answer this question, it is necessary to consider examples of acts that involve intentionally deceiving others. One type is when a person lies for personal gain at the expense of another. That act is usually considered dishonest and might be seen as violating societal standards or as unjust insofar as it is aimed at, for example, gains for oneself at the expense of others. A fair amount of research has been designed to study these types of cheating in children, going back to the work of Hartshorne and May (1928–1930). They and others (Grinder 1964; Lee 2013) used a variety of tasks to ascertain if children would lie or cheat in academic tests, athletic contests, and games. Studies of lying have also been conducted at later times.

The typical paradigm is that children are deceived by giving the impression that they would not be caught cheating when in fact their behaviors were actually detected. The findings are that most children cheat some of the time but few cheat most of the time or cheat rarely. As another example, surveys of high school students yielded the finding that majorities admit to cheating on exams and lying to parents and teachers.[1]

Much of the research is based on the assumption that honesty should be maintained. In that context, at various times, commentators have claimed that there is a moral failure reflected in widespread acts of dishonesty among young people. However, honesty and dishonesty are not straightforward regarding justice. An ironic example to that effect is that many researchers who studied cheating on the part of children lied to the children in order to measure children's lying. Is lying on the part of the researchers an instance of morally wrong behavior? Most likely, the researchers would say that their acts are not morally wrong and that they are justified to achieve worthy goals of scientific knowledge and understandings about children. That is, they would give priority to scientific goals over honesty.

Whatever our assessment of the actions of the researchers, this example illustrates that honesty and deception are more complex than is often presumed. Philosophical discourse was prompted to engage this complexity in reaction to a reading of Immanuel Kant's view that lying is categorically wrong. In challenging this position inspired by Kant, philosophers have rejected his conclusions regarding the case of a bystander who is asked by a murderer where his intended victim has gone.[2] Many maintain that in such a situation, the moral prescription to save a life with dishonesty takes precedence over honesty. The example is meant to show that morality, as adherence to an unconditional rule, is problematic to an understanding of moral decisions. We note that it is not only hypothetical situations created by scholars that might require morally necessary acts of dishonesty, as illustrated by deception on the part of many people in response to the plight of Jews and others during the Holocaust perpetrated by the Nazis during World War II.

It appears, then, that lying or deception cannot solely be regarded as morally wrong when matters of welfare or justice are implicated. A familiar form of lying often treated as acceptable is termed "white lies," aimed at sparing the feelings of others. Studies show that children and adults evaluate lying to spare the feelings of another more positively than self-serving lies.[3] However, thinking about honesty and deception goes deeper than white lies, as evidenced by studies that delved into how people think about honesty in various contexts. Rather than measuring whether individuals lie, the research examined how they think about honesty and the ways they draw priorities between honesty and other moral and nonmoral social goals.

One study revealed patterns of thinking about varying situational contexts and was conducted with adolescents (from twelve to sixteen years old).[4] In that study, adolescents made judgments about deception regarding what we refer to as moral, personal, and prudential activities. They were presented with hypothetical situations in which parents or peers insist on their objections to an adolescent's choice of an activity and the adolescent continues engaging in the activity but lies about it. In one set of situations, the adolescent is directed, in contrast with his or her choice, to engage in acts considered to involve injustice (racial discrimination) and harm (fighting). In other situations, the adolescent is directed to engage in acts perceived to involve personal prerogatives (whom to date, what club to join) or involving prudential or safety considerations (doing homework, riding a motorcycle).

It was found that virtually all the adolescents judged deception to be acceptable when parents directed an adolescent to engage in the acts considered unjust or harmful and that most judged it acceptable to engage in deception when parents directed activities considered to be part of personal jurisdiction. The adolescents did not accept the legitimacy of parental authority regarding the acts in the moral and personal domains. It is not the case, however, that adolescents simply do not value honesty and trust. They accepted the legitimacy of parental authority over the prudential acts and judged it wrong to deceive parents in those contexts. Moreover, it was found that most judged deception as wrong in situations involving straightforward self-interest and avoidance of sanctions. The adolescents participating in this study also distinguished between deception of parents and peers. They judged it less acceptable to deceive peers than to deceive parents regarding the moral and personal acts, because relationships with peers were seen to be based on equality and mutuality while relationships with parents are based on the power of parental authority and associated inequalities.

These patterns of findings reflect the way moral judgments include the application of different considerations in coming to decisions in situations that include varying features. The findings, which indicate that in some situations honesty is given less priority than other moral considerations such as preventing harm or injustice, are not restricted to adolescence. Adults, too, draw such distinctions and sometimes give priority to some moral goals over honesty. In one study, adults made similar judgments about deception in marital relationships involving power differences and inequalities between spouses.[5] A different study showed that physicians judge it acceptable to deceive insurance companies when that is the only way to provide adequate medical treatment to patients with life-threatening conditions.[6]

Our intention is to emphasize two general propositions about children's morality stemming from the research (and philosophical considerations) just considered. One is, as noted above, that morality is not adequately characterized as the acquisition of an unconditional, fixed set of traits or socially defined standards. Whereas honesty and concerns with trust are often high on some psychologists' lists of proposed rules or traits of character said to encompass morality, the research shows that people's application of concerns with honesty and trust involves mental activity reflected in the weighing and balancing of different moral and social considerations in coming to decisions in multifaceted social situations. We refer to this process as coordination of different considerations and goals that includes the application of moral understandings in situational contexts. Processes of coordination are by no means restricted to decisions bearing on honesty. For example, research on the application of rights, as well as equality in situations of social inclusion and exclusion, has yielded similar findings. Whereas rights (such as to freedom of speech or religion) and equality are understood and endorsed in some contexts, they are subordinated in other contexts with competing moral and social considerations.[7]

The second general proposition stemming from the research on honesty, rights, and inclusion is that processes of coordination reflect flexibility of thought in coming to moral decisions. Underlying this proposition is the idea that morality involves thought but in conjunction with emotions (which we discuss later in this chapter). The research on honesty demonstrated that in many instances, individuals judge dishonesty as wrong yet judge deception as acceptable when it is in conflict with the prevention of harm or the promotion of fairness and welfare. That research documents that individuals have commitments to welfare, fairness or justice, and rights.

Having provided evidence that reasoning, flexibility, and coordination are key features of the moral orientations of children and adults, we now turn to a discussion of how these moral orientations develop from an early age.

THE DEVELOPMENT OF MORALITY: CONSTRUCTION, COORDINATION, AND MULTIFACETED SITUATIONS

The commitments to welfare, justice, and rights are based on moral judgments that begin to be formed in early childhood, as evidenced by a large body of research that has examined moral judgments and the social experiences that contribute to their development. By at least four to six years of age, children form judgments about harm and in more rudimentary ways about justice.[8] The research was based on a perspective—philosophical and psychological—of morality as a domain that is not defined by existing social arrangements or cultural practices or by standards agreed upon in a community.[9] Judgments in the moral domain constitute a complex configuration of thought, as revealed by research that presented children with actions entailing physical harm (e.g., hitting others, pushing them down), psychological harm (e.g., teasing, hurting feelings), and fairness or justice (e.g., failing to share, stealing, destroying others' property). These acts were presented to participants in the research as intentional and as resulting in negative consequences to others. It has been consistently found that children and adolescents judge that concerns with moral issues are obligatory, not contingent on authority dictates, rules, or consensus (e.g., that the acts would be wrong even if no rule or law exists about it) or on accepted practices within a group (e.g., the act is wrong even if it were acceptable practice in another culture). Judgments about moral issues, based on these criteria, are connected with reasons or justifications concerning the prevention of harm, promotion of welfare, fairness, and rights.[10]

By early childhood, moral judgments are distinct from judgments about sanctions, prudence, the power of persons in positions of authority (e.g., parents, teachers), and the domain of social conventions and personal jurisdiction. For instance, judgments about social conventions are linked to existing social arrangements and contingent on rules, persons in authority, and existing social or cultural practices. Justifications for judgments about conventional issues are based on understandings of social organization, including the role of those in authority, rules, and customs. The domains of thinking are reflected in judgments about actual events experienced by children, as well as in interviews about hypothetical situations.[11]

In the context of the definition of morality as *not* based on existing societal standards or cultural practices, as well as the fact that children do not judge moral issues by existing rules, authority dictates, or accepted practices, it is necessary to ask how, then, children's moral judgments are derived. Along with others, we propose that children construct moral and other social concepts through their interactions with the world.[12] In this perspective, development is neither genetically nor environmentally determined but involves constructions in efforts to make sense of experiences, social rules, roles of authorities, social institutions, and cultural practices.

In this view, a major source of the development of morality is children's everyday experiences with others involving harm, fairness, equality, and adjudication of disagreements and conflicts. These types of experiences include, as some examples, children hurting one another (physically and emotionally), helping and failing to help, sharing and failing to share, including and excluding others, cooperating and failing to cooperate, and treating people equally and unequally. Moreover, children are not solely recipients of "moral" messages from adults. They interact with adults over many of the same issues and observe adults interacting with one another harmoniously and with conflicts—and sometimes around matters of harm, helping, sharing, cooperating, and equality (for a discussion of sharing activities, see chapter 4 by Widlok in this volume).

These types of experiences, social interactions, and observations are part of the development of moral judgments, as evidenced by a number of observational studies with infants, toddlers, and preschoolers[13] and older children.[14] It has been found that children's social interactions around moral events typically do not involve commands or communications about rules and the expectations of adults. Communications around moral transgressions are about the effects of actions on people, the perspectives of others, the need to avoid harm, and the pain experienced, as well as about welfare and fairness. By contrast, interactions around conventional events revolve around adherence to rules, commands from those in authority, and an emphasis on social order.

Another source of concepts of justice and their application in social situations is experiences of injustices, especially institutionalized forms of injustice and inequalities. By institutionalized injustices, we mean forms of injustice and inequalities embedded in systems of social organization and cultural practices. Most societies are organized hierarchically, with some in positions of greater power and privilege and others in positions of lesser power. In many situations, however, hierarchies with inequalities are accepted by most and are not regarded as involving injustices. An obvious example would be the makeup of an orchestra with different roles and responsibilities. Other contexts in which there is acceptance of inequalities exist in several sectors, such as in workplace or educational settings. However, other forms of hierarchy and inequalities divided along lines of race, ethnicity, social class, and gender have historically evoked concerns with justice and rights.[15] Experiences around those types of injustices are sources of the formation and application of understandings of justice—but perhaps not until adolescence and adulthood. Such understandings in later years, however, build on moral judgments formed earlier in life, moral judgments that enable a recognition of when injustices are embedded in systems of social organization and cultural practices.

We are therefore proposing that individuals do not simply accept social conditions or cultural practices as they exist but, instead, scrutinize social relationships through a moral lens. That is, people do not uncritically accept cultural practices promoting inequalities and unfair treatment, even though the practices are part of tradition and supported by those in positions of power and authority. This proposition is supported by psychological and anthropological research in patriarchal societies that maintain power differences and associated inequalities between males and females. Typically, in patriarchal societies, males are accorded positions of power over females, and restrictions are placed on many activities of females that do not apply to males.[16] A series of studies have been conducted in patriarchal cultures in the Middle East, India, and Benin designed to ascertain how females think about the power differences and inequalities in institutionalized cultural practices.[17] These included inequalities regarding educational and work opportunities, recreational activities, and decision-making in families.

Without going into the details of the research methods or findings,[18] we can summarize the thrust of the research findings. First, adolescent and adult females recognize that the social system accords power and control to males over females, that privileges and many areas of independence are given to males that are not in the purview of females, and that males have many more freedoms than females. Second, females desire freedoms for themselves and, most important, judge the inequalities based on gender to be unfair.

These judgments about inequalities in patriarchal frameworks make for conflicts in the societies and efforts on the part of females to circumvent inequalities in their daily lives, as demonstrated by ethnographic studies conducted by anthropologists in poor neighborhoods in Cairo and in Bedouin villages in northwest Egypt.[19] Both studies found conflicts in interactions between males and females and that women struggled for equality by arguing their cases and by sometimes acting covertly with deception to combat restrictions placed on their lives (including to avoid established practices such as arranged marriages and polygamy). As stated by Wikan, who conducted extensive research with people living in conditions of poverty in Cairo, "these lives I depict can be read as exercises in resistance against the state, against family, against neighbors and society."[20] The conflict and resistance on the part of females are often directed at the injustices of the inequalities they face.

It was also found in the studies in the rural Bedouin village that women were often critical of the restrictions placed on them in their daily lives. Moreover, they sought ways to avoid the control that men exerted on them, using several means, sometimes involving deception, to evade restrictions placed on their personal choices, education, and work opportunities. They also used deceptive means to avoid general cultural practices such as arranged marriages and polygamy, which they believed were unfair.

EMOTIONS IN THE DEVELOPMENT OF MORAL ORIENTATIONS

The development of orientations toward justice and other moral issues involves not just thoughts but also emotional reactions. Whereas our discussion so far has focused on children's and adults' judgments about moral and other social events, everyday moral encounters are replete with affect. Opposing existing social conditions, resisting injustices in overt or covert ways, and engaging in conflicts and social struggles involve emotions. Emotions are associated with thinking about injustices and inequalities and more generally with moral judgments. The question, then, is not *whether* emotions are involved but *how*.

A position that has taken hold in recent years in some quarters in psychology is that emotions are primary in determining many or most moral evaluations and actions and that in such situations, reasoning has little role.[21] In these perspectives, it is maintained that moral evaluations are most often based on emotional reactions, which lead to so-called intuitive judgments about the situation. Reasoning is relegated to efforts at rationalizing the judgment after it has been reached. Nonrational and unconscious processes, it is claimed, lead people to form similarly nonrational moral judgments that are more or less impenetrable to thought processes and that are influenced by extrinsic features such as the disgusting smell of the room in which they are making the judgments or good smells signifying cleanliness.[22]

In our view, the emotivist-intuitionist positions are based on the misconceptions of drawing a false dichotomy between emotional and reasoning processes and in conflating minor effects of incidental situation features with the roles of emotions. It is not surprising that incidental factors, such as primed thoughts or moods, can have a limited influence on judgments. It would be quite another matter if such incidental factors could by themselves lead to the view that it is wrong, for example, to save a drowning child. As it turns out, studies that purport to demonstrate the dominance of "emotion" over "reason" have mainly manipulated incidental affective features (e.g., made participants disgusted) and demonstrated small effects on people's judgments.[23] In short, there is no indication that the manipulation of something like disgust by itself could lead someone to think it wrong to save a drowning child.[24]

We define emotions as involving appraisals that events are relevant to one's concerns and behavioral, physiological, and motivational reactions to these appraisals.[25] Appraisals are the person's evaluations of encounters with the environment with respect to his or her concerns.[26] In this perspective, people have emotional reactions when events are interpreted (appraised) to impact the fate of their concerns (i.e. things that are important to them).

Concerns—like those embedded in moral judgments—are central to the elicitation of emotions, but they are not themselves emotions. For example, most people are concerned that people not hit each other: They maintain that it is generally wrong to hit others and accordingly prefer to avoid harm, other things being equal. Still, they do not have a continuous emotional reaction to hitting. Emotional reactions occur when events are appraised as being relevant to those judgments and their accompanying concerns. It is upon seeing one person hitting another that people may be morally outraged (insofar as they judge this particular act of hitting as wrong). Emotions follow from the constellation of events, appraisals, and concerns, including the concerns that form part of moral judgments. In this view, any type of emotion could involve moral concerns, not just "moral emotions" such as guilt or shame. Guilt or shame can be experienced in reaction to nonmoral issues as well as moral ones. As an example, one can feel guilty about violating a diet or failing to study for an exam. In our view, guilt in its moral sense would be better reframed as involving reflections on social relationships.[27] Similarly, anger sometimes may be about moral issues, such as perceived injustice, and other times may be about nonmoral issues, such as a malfunctioning computer.

We are proposing that emotions operate in concert with moral thought, not in competition with it.[28] It is because people care about moral issues that they can have emotional reactions upon judging particular actions as morally right or wrong. Therefore, emotions are not detached from judgments but instead depend on them. Emotions involving evaluative appraisals are guided by ways of judging social relationships and reflect people's aims, purposes, and goals in life.[29]

Emotions are also relevant to morality in that they contribute to the development of moral judgments through the emotions children experience and observe in others. Although there have been longstanding efforts to identify negative emotions as the bases of morality (e.g., guilt in psychoanalytic theories, anxiety in behaviorist theories, and disgust in some contemporary formulations), the primary emotions associated with morality appear to be positive ones such as affection, sympathy, and empathy.[30] In addition, emotions associated with moral judgments can be differentiated from those associated with other types of social judgments. Research addressing such differentiations has demonstrated that children attribute positive emotions to actors, recipients, and observers in connection with positive actions such as helping and sharing.[31] By contrast, the emotions attributed to transgressors of conventions are neutral or feelings of sadness. With respect to moral transgressions, children attribute hurt feelings to recipients of the acts (such as inflicting physical or emotional harm) and mixed positive and negative emotions to instigators of the acts.

Emotional experiences of various kinds contribute to the formation of moral judgments and understandings of self, other people, and events. That children attend to interactions and exchanges among people, the feelings evoked, and the effects of acts on self and others is documented in studies that examined children's reflections about events involving harm that they had experienced as either perpetrators or victims.[32]

In short, the development of orientations toward justice and other moral issues involves thoughts and emotions operating in concert. While it is analytically useful to distinguish between thoughts and emotions, this distinction should not lead us to view emotions as ontologically separated from thoughts. In response to perceived injustices, emotional outrage and compassion with victims are contingent upon—and intertwined with—judgments about what constitutes fair and unfair treatment of others.

SENTIMENTS AS A BASIS FOR THOUGHTS AND EMOTIONS ABOUT MORAL ISSUES

The joining of cognitive and affective processes in morality is particularly evident in what we will provisionally term *sentiments*.[33] By sentiments, we mean a set of broad concerns that are central and binding for most people and viewed as obligatory for everyone. The sentiments are the sanctity of life, respect for persons, and human dignity. We propose that each of these is intricately connected to moral orientations to justice, as well as welfare and rights.

The notion of sentiments captures how people are committed to protecting some concerns, react strongly if others violate them, and do not think anyone has the right to opt out of caring about them. In this sense, sentiments differ not only from other human concerns but also from general judgments or principles. Although people deem it permissible to violate the general prohibition against harming others in certain contexts (e.g., in self-defense), they do not thereby abandon the sentiment of respect for persons. Their continued commitment to the respect for persons is evidenced, for instance, by the conflicts experienced even when doing what they think is right.[34] In turn, dignity is a central concept in human rights approaches and therefore a core value of concern within systems of justice.

THE VALUE OF LIFE

The types of sentiments generally held regarding the sanctity or sacredness of life have been addressed in detail from a philosophical perspective by Dworkin (1993). He proposed that the intrinsic value of life includes the strong emotional-conceptual sense of the sacredness or inviolability of life. He maintained that people everywhere are concerned, in one way or another, with preserving lives, act to save lives when they can, make strong judgments about the loss of life, and experience intense emotions such as grief at the loss of a loved one. Although the dynamics of the issue of life are complicated because people do take lives in war and for reasons of self-defense and it is one of the condoned ways, through capital punishment, of responding to murder, Dworkin argued that it is "a fundamental idea that almost all share in some form: that the individual human life is sacred."[35] Although for some there may be religious underpinnings to the sense of the sacredness of life, it is also a secular view (in the form that life is inviolable).

Dworkin revolved much of his position on the sacredness of life around debates about abortion and euthanasia. However, his purpose in elaborating the nature of those debates, even in the context of differences about their permissibility, was to demonstrate the force of the sacredness and inviolability of life. It becomes clear that most people hold to the sanctity and inviolability of life when we consider their common positions on the taking of life immediately after birth (or late in pregnancy). Few find it acceptable to take an infant's life after birth with regard to any of the reasons or justifications (or any others) evident in the controversies over abortion.[36] Research into moral judgments needs to better account for people's sense that lives have intrinsic value and for how the sentiment develops.[37] This should be viewed as a general sentiment, because people feel very strongly about maintaining their own lives, the lives of close others (family, friends, etc.), and, in a general way, human life (including those they do not know).

There is some research that in an indirect way assessed people's orientations to the value of life and provided evidence that the value of life is a factor in decisions about fairness. Drawing on long-standing philosophical discussions regarding so-called trolley-car situations, psychologists have assessed how people make judgments about sacrificing a life to save a greater number of lives.[38] As is well known, the trolley-car situations typically include two main versions. In one, a runaway trolley car will strike and kill five workers unless a bystander throws a switch that will divert the trolley and thereby kill one person instead of five. In a second version, the bystander can push a large man standing on a footbridge onto the tracks, killing that person and saving the five. In the psychological research, individuals in an fMRI machine are asked to judge whether it is permissible to throw the switch or push the man as a means of diverting the trolley car.[39]

These studies have found that a majority of participants judge it acceptable to throw the switch and unacceptable to push the man. On the assumption that the two versions pose the same utilitarian calculation of five lives versus one, those results have been interpreted to demonstrate inconsistencies in judgments and that many moral judgments (e.g., the judgment that it is wrong to push another person) are not rational and are based on emotions. This interpretation is supposedly buttressed by findings that the judgments about pushing are associated with greater activity in different regions of the brain associated with emotional processes.

By exclusively focusing on utilitarianism as the morally relevant feature and only assessing evaluations without considering the reasons and sentiments people might bring to bear on these situations, the researchers missed an opportunity to delve into how people think about the value of life and other moral considerations in relation to judgments about fair decisions. In fact, the original purposes of the philosophical analyses of the trolley-car situations were to use them to consider the different types of moral principles that could be brought to bear in such situations. One element of the trolley-car situations that is salient but ignored in the psychological analyses is that they pose a particular type of conflict, one in which the value of life is in conflict with itself in that the taking of life serves to save life. To put it in slightly different terms, the trolley-car situations require that a strongly held value be violated in order to preserve that very value.[40]

This type of conflict is in accord with what has been referred to as "hard cases." For example, Walzer regards the question of torture in some situations as a hard case: "One of my examples was the 'ticking bomb' case, where a captured terrorist knows, but refuses to reveal, the location of a bomb that is timed to go off soon in a school building."[41] Walzer regards this as a hard case requiring exceptions to the application of rules, because it involves violating a moral goal in order to promote a moral goal. Similarly, Williams (1973) presents several hypothetical examples of situations that do not have easy utilitarian solutions because of the conflicts involved. A relevant one pertaining to the value of life with features similar to the trolley-car situations concerns a man who is confronted with the decision of whether to shoot to death one person in order to save the lives of nineteen people. What should the man do? The connection to the trolley-car situations is obvious. Solely by utilitarian calculations, it is best to sacrifice one life to save many more.

The main reason Williams constructed these types of situations, as well as the reason others had for constructing the trolley-car situations,[42] was to illuminate that from a moral perspective, the utilitarian calculation is not the only one. As Williams stated regarding the utilitarian answer, "even one who came to think that perhaps that was the answer, might well wonder whether it was obviously the answer."[43] What other answers could there be? The other answers or moral considerations to take into account include responsibility for one's actions, concerns with one's integrity, and the psychological effects on the actor. These considerations were also applied in philosophical discourse to different decisions regarding the two versions of trolley-car situations.[44]

Research that included additional variations of the trolley-car situations as well as assessment of the reasons behind people's decisions—including decisions about the switch and footbridge situations—has shown that sentiments about the value of life loom large and make for conflicts about the appropriate courses of action.[45] Indeed, the conflicts have to do with how to balance considerations about saving lives, the noninstrumental right to life involved with those who would be sacrificed, the actors' responsibilities for their actions, and contractual obligations involved in these decisions. Emotions are involved in such decisions but in concert with reasoning about just solutions in the situations so that the differences between them become salient.

RESPECT FOR PERSONS

The sentiment about the value of life may well be connected to the second general sentiment of respect for persons, which was analyzed by Piaget (1932) in his research on the development of moral judgments. For Piaget, respect for persons in relationships of mutuality and reciprocity is essential for moral concepts of equality and justice. In Piaget's formulations, however, it is mutual respect, not respect of one person for another in a superior position of authority or accomplishments, that is central in concerns with justice and fairness in serving the needs of persons and adjudicating competing interests. Piaget regarded mutual respect as a sentiment that does not develop until late childhood or adolescence, in conjunction with what he termed autonomous morality, which develops after an earlier heteronomous morality involving unilateral respect for authority, seen to define morality with fixed, unalterable rules.

The research discussed earlier here on the ways young children distinguish morality from social conventions (including authority dictates and rules) is in contradiction with Piaget's formulation of development. Piaget proposed that development proceeds from a heteronomy by which moral judgments are seen as adherence to fixed rules and unilateral respect for authority to an autonomy by which understandings of welfare and justice are distinguished from judgments about authority and rules.[46] The research has shown that morality constitutes its own domain, with a developmental pathway separate from that of the domain pertaining to conventional systems. In that context, we would expect respect in early childhood to take forms different from unilateral respect. It is well documented that young children judge as wrong acts that involve inflicting harm. Such concerns with avoiding harm might well be precursors to what we would consider respect for persons in the sense of mutuality and reciprocity. Concerns with avoiding harm may also be precursors to further development of sentiments regarding the value of life.

DIGNITY

The third sentiment, dignity, has also not been subject to much empirical study but is an issue prominent in discussions of central moral principles, especially human rights. It is prominent in Article 1 of the Universal Declaration of Human Rights, with the statement that "All human beings are born free and equal in dignity and rights." The idea of dignity is often brought to bear in discussions of women's roles in societies, the permissibility of torture, incarceration, and genocide. Moreover, in discussing the Holocaust shortly after the end of World War II, Victor Frankl seemed to draw connections among life, respect, and dignity:

> [In] a world which no longer recognized the value of human life and human dignity, which had robbed man of his will and had

> made him an object to be exterminated . . . the personal ego finally suffered a loss of values. If the man in the concentration camp did not struggle against this in the last effort to save his self-respect, he lost the feeling of being an individual, a being with a mind, with inner freedom and personal value.[47]

As with the value of life and respect for persons in the reciprocal sense, human dignity is thought to be a fundamental attribute of all persons. It is viewed as inherent to being human and therefore a basis for the universal application of justice and rights. It is true that all these notions can be framed in instrumental terms, in that some lives may be devalued for one reason or another, some persons may be deemed as less worthy or even unworthy of respect, and some may be seen as lacking dignity. However, as sentiments that are centrally linked to morality, the terms are not meant to be comparative but are seen as what ought to be accorded to all people. Nussbaum (2000; 2006) provides a detailed analysis of dignity as inherent to human existence, connecting the notion of features of human functioning that must necessarily be accorded across cultures. Nussbaum provides a working list of capabilities intended to represent human functioning that "can be endorsed for political purposes, as the moral basis of central constitutional guarantees."[48] Therefore, the capabilities describe human functions that social and political systems ought to provide as the conditions for individuals to choose to live flourishing lives. This is not the place to consider the substance of the capabilities proposed by Nussbaum. The purpose of mentioning them is to point to an effort to specify features of human functioning that are ends in themselves and are connected to the idea of human dignity. As Nussbaum stated: "The core idea is that of the human being as a dignified free being who shapes his or her own life in cooperation and reciprocity with others, rather than being shaped or pushed around by the world in the name of a 'flock' or 'herd' animal. . . . For we see a human being as having worth as an end."[49]

Therefore, when it comes to morality, the sentiments of human dignity, sanctity of life, and respect for persons can be seen as fundamental aspects of judgments. We also view these sentiments as requiring a good deal of empirical study regarding if and how individuals maintain them. We have undertaken research on the topic that is still under way.[50] The research revolves around presentation of several situations depicting potential violations of rights and diminution of dignity, as well as direct questions about the meaning of dignity. The situations described the following cultural or societal practices constituting violations of several articles of the Universal Declaration of Human Rights: class-based discrimination, torture of political prisoners or suspected terrorists, women's independent movement and dress code, and the status and poverty of minority groups in various countries. These situations were designed to implicate violations of rights and associated dignity. Indeed, many participants perceived these features and referred to emotions and sentiments (including respect). Although analyses of the results are still ongoing, it seems clear that most adolescents and adults judge these violations as wrong, that national laws should not allow violations of human rights, and that disadvantaged groups should have societal protections. Most participants also expressed an awareness of human dignity, and in response to questions about the meaning and violations of human rights, some referred to dignity.

For example, one adult female, when asked if she knew what human rights were, stated: "The right of people to have freedom, dignity, and to live comfortably without the fear of danger." She followed up in response to a question about what human dignity is and whether human dignity should be respected by everyone: "What I was saying before, the ability to feel like you are in control of your person and you are respected and valued," as well as that "we are all equal; I don't think anyone should get to take away anyone else's dignity."

Similar views were provided by adult and adolescent males with regard to the meaning of human dignity. The adult:

> I think what it means to me is just, like, you shouldn't be dehumanized, or stripped of, like, you know, your humanity or just being a . . . person or being thought of less than fully human under any circumstances.

The adolescent:

> Human dignity is, it's like what makes you human, it's your feelings or personality, basically anything that defines a human or makes you human. Dignity in my definition is like a self standard, it's individuality, so the individuality is what makes you you and makes you stop from doing something you don't want to do or that you think is wrong.

In keeping with these meanings, most participants asserted that all groups in a society should have equal rights, that everyone's dignity should be respected. Many also recognized that violations of human rights are moral rather than legal transgressions, in part because they involve violations of human dignity, stating that (restoring justice) treating people equally, requires recognizing everyone's dignity.

CONCLUSION

To understand how children become concerned with justice and other aspects of morality—that is, how morality develops in individuals—and how people make decisions with moral implications, it is necessary to consider multiple features. One is how moral judgments develop. A great deal of evidence shows that moral judgments, which begin to be formed at early ages, entail concerns with welfare, justice, and rights. The evidence also indicates that it is children's direct, everyday social interactions with others, rather than instruction from adults, that make for universal experiences contributing to moral development.

However, morality does not stand apart from everything else social to be applied in pure form. Morality is not characterized by ingrained habits or learned rules or fixed traits of character to be manifested as long as they are of sufficient strength to override self-interest or social approval. To understand how morality contributes to decisions, it must be viewed as a process of thinking that, in the complexity of social relationships, entails weighing and balancing it with other social and personal dimensions. Compounding the complexity is the fact that morality can be in conflict with itself, even with regard to a specific moral goal. As discussed here, conflicts can exist regarding the value of life when a situation poses the possibility of saving lives by sacrificing lives.

More generally, a moral goal, such as promoting trust, can be in conflict with goals of promoting people's welfare. A dramatic example is when many decided to engage in deception in order to save lives during the Holocaust in World War II. Of a less dramatic nature are situations in which physicians judge deception (e.g., of an insurance company) acceptable in order to fulfill their professional obligations to promote the health and welfare of their patients. It is important to stress that those who accept the necessity of dishonesty under some circumstances are not "dishonest" people lacking in morality. As reasoning beings, they can scrutinize the features of social situations and draw priorities among moral goals, including ones involving rights, fairness, equality, or social inclusion. Similarly, individuals scrutinize cultural practices of inequality and sometimes engage in social opposition and moral resistance.

A main point of this chapter is that moral judgments about justice, welfare, and rights are closely associated with sentiments of the sanctity of life, respect for persons, and human dignity. When actions violate moral sentiments—for instance, when one person acts unjustly toward another person—individuals can have strong emotional reactions alongside judgments and reasoning about the action. We believe that those taking psychological and philosophical approaches to justice will benefit from considering the multifaceted nature of the moral orientations of children and adults, which include flexible reasoning, judgments, sentiments, and emotional reactions regarding distinct and sometimes conflicting moral considerations.

NOTES

1. Josephson Institute of Ethics, press release, www.josephsoninstitute.org, October 16, 2000.
2. See Bok 1999.
3. See, e.g., Bussey 1999.
4. Perkins and Turiel 2007.
5. Turiel, Perkins, and Mensing 2009.
6. Freeman et al. 1999.
7. For discussion of processes of coordination, including how they apply to the well-known studies of adherence to authority by Milgram 1974, see Turiel 2008b; Turiel 2015.
8. For reviews, see Smetana 2006; Turiel 1983; Turiel 2002; Turiel 2015.
9. See, e.g., Dworkin 1993; Kohlberg 1971; Nussbaum 2000; Piaget 1932; Rawls 1971; Sen 2009.
10. See Turiel 1983; Turiel 2002.
11. Turiel 2008a.
12. Kohlberg 1971; Piaget 1932; Turiel 2002.
13. Dahl 2015; Dahl 2016; Hay 2006; Nucci and Turiel 1978.
14. Nucci and Nucci 1982; Turiel 2008a.
15. Vlastos 1962.
16. Abu-Lughod 1993; Nussbaum 2000; Turiel 2002; Wikan 1996.
17. Wainryb and Turiel 1994; Neff 2001; Conry-Murray 2009.
18. See Turiel 2015 for such details.
19. Wikan 1996; Abu-Lughod 1993.
20. Wikan 1996, 6–7.

21. See, e.g., Greene et al. 2001; Haidt 2001; Schnall et al. 2008.
22. Liljenquist, Zhong, and Galinsky 2010; Schnall et al. 2008.
23. Pizarro, Inbar, and Helion 2011.
24. For critiques of the emotivist-intuitionist view of moral functioning, see Turiel 2010; Turiel and Dahl forthcoming.
25. Lazarus 1991; Nussbaum 2001.
26. Lazarus 1991.
27. Turiel and Gingo 2017.
28. Nussbaum 2001; Turiel and Dahl forthcoming. For a discussion of other perspectives on the intertwining of thought and emotion in morality, see chapter 2 by Hanley in this volume.
29. For an informative analysis of evaluative appraisals, see the discussion of grief in Nussbaum 2001.
30. Hoffman 2000; Piaget 1932.
31. Arsenio and Fliess 1996.
32. Wainryb, Brehl, and Matwin 2005; Wainryb and Recchia 2012.
33. Turiel and Killen 2010.
34. Dahl et al. forthcoming.
35. Dworkin 1993, 13.
36. Turiel, Hildebrandt, and Wainryb 1991.
37. Turiel and Killen 2010.
38. Edmonds 2013; Foot 1967.
39. Greene et al. 2001.
40. Turiel 2010.
41. Walzer 2007, 302.
42. See, e.g., Foot 1967.
43. Williams 1973, 125.
44. Edmonds 2013; Foot 1967; Sunstein 2014; Thomson 1976.
45. Dahl et al. forthcoming.
46. A corresponding developmental sequence was proposed by Kohlberg 1971.
47. Frankl 1946, 78–79.
48. Nussbaum 2000, 74.
49. Nussbaum 2000, 72, 73.
50. Besirevic and Turiel forthcoming.

WORKS CITED

Abu-Lughod, L. 1993. *Writing Women's Worlds: Bedouin Stories*. Berkeley: University of California Press.

Arsenio, W., and K. Fleiss. 1996. "Typical and Behaviourally Disruptive Children's Understanding of the Emotional Consequences of Socio-Moral Events." *British Journal of Developmental Psychology* 14: 173–186.

Besirevic, Z., and E. Turiel. Forthcoming. "Judgments about Human Rights and Human Dignity."

Bok, S. 1979 [1999]. *Lying: Moral Choice in Public and Private Life.* New York: Vintage.

Bussey, K. 1999. "Children's Categorization and Evaluation of Different Types of Lies and Truths." *Child Development* 70, 1338–1347.

Conry-Murray, C. 2009. "Adolescent and Adult Reasoning about Gender Roles and Fairness in Benin, West Africa." *Cognitive Development* 24: 207–219.

Dahl, A. 2015. "The Developing Social Context of Infant Helping in Two U.S. Samples." *Child Development* 86: 1080–1093.

Dahl, A. 2016. "Infants' Unprovoked Acts of Force Toward Others." *Developmental Science* 19: 1049–1057.

Dahl, A., M. Gingo, K. Uttich, and E. Turiel. Forthcoming. "Moral Reasoning about Human Welfare in Adolescents and Adults: Judging Conflicts Involving Sacrificing and Saving Lives." *Monographs of the Society for Research in Child Development.*

Dworkin, R. 1993. *Life's Dominion: An Argument about Abortion, Euthanasia, and Individual Freedom.* New York: Alfred A. Knopf.

Edmonds, D. 2013. *Would You Kill the Fat Man? The Trolley Problem and What Your Answer Tells Us about Right and Wrong.* Princeton: Princeton University Press.

Foot, P. 1967. "The Problem of Abortion and the Doctrine of the Double Effect." *Oxford Review* 5: 5–15.

Frankl, V. 1946 [1963]. *Man's Search for Meaning.* New York: Simon & Schuster.

Freeman, V. G., S. S. Rathore, K. P. Weinfurt, K. A. Schulman, and D. P. Sulmasy. 1999. "Lying for Patients: Physician Deception of Third-Party Payers." *Archives of Internal Medicine* 159: 2263–2270.

Greene, J. D., R. B. Sommerville, L. E. Nystrom, J. M. Darley, and J. D. Cohen. 2001. "An fMRI Investigation of Emotional Engagement in Moral Judgment." *Science* 293: 2105–2108.

Grinder, R. E. 1964. "Relations between Behavioral and Cognitive Dimensions of Conscience in Middle Childhood." *Child Development* 35: 881–891.

Haidt, J. 2001. "The Emotional Dog and Its Rational Tail: A Social Intuitionist Approach to Moral Judgment." *Psychological Review* 108: 814–834.

Hartshorne, H., and M. A. May. 1928–1930. *Studies in the Nature of Character, Vol. 1: Studies in Deceit; Vol. 2: Studies in Self-Control; Vol. 3: Studies in the Organization of Character.* New York: Macmillan.

Hay, D. F. 2006. "Yours and Mine: Toddlers' Talk about Possessions with Familiar Peers." *British Journal of Developmental Psychology* 24: 39–52.

Hoffman, M. L. 2000. *Empathy and Moral Development: Implications for Caring and Justice.* Cambridge: Cambridge University Press.

Kohlberg, L. 1971. "From Is to Ought: How to Commit the Naturalistic Fallacy and Get Away with It in the Study of Moral Development." In *Psychology and Genetic Epistemology*, edited by T. Mischel, 151–235. New York: Academic Press.

Lazarus, R.S. 1991. *Emotion and Adaptation*. New York: Oxford University Press.
Lee, K. 2013. "Little Liars: Development of Verbal Deception in Children." *Child Development Perspectives* 7: 91–96.
Liljenquist, K., C. B. Zhong, and A. D. Galinsky. 2010. "The Smell of Virtue: Clean Scents Promote Reciprocity and Charity." *Psychological Science* 21: 381–383.
Milgram, S. 1974. *Obedience to Authority*. New York: Harper & Row.
Neff, K. D. 2001. "Judgments of Personal Autonomy and Interpersonal Responsibility in the Context of Indian Spousal Relationships: An Examination of Young People's Reasoning in Mysore, India." *British Journal of Developmental Psychology* 19: 233–257.
Nucci, L. P., and M. S. Nucci. 1982. "Children's Responses to Moral and Social Conventional Transgressions in Free-Play Settings." *Child Development* 53: 1337–1342.
Nucci, L. P., and E. Turiel. 1978. "Social Interactions and the Development of Social Concepts in Preschool Children." *Child Development* 49: 400–407.
Nussbaum, M. C. 2000. *Women and Human Development: The Capabilities Approach*. Cambridge: Cambridge University Press.
Nussbaum, M. C. 2001. *Upheavals of Thought: The Intelligence of Emotions*. Cambridge: Cambridge University Press.
Nussbaum, M. C. 2006. "Human Capabilities, Female Human Beings." In *Theorizing Feminism*, edited by E. Hackett and S. Haslanger, 124–139. New York: Oxford University Press.
Perkins, S. A., and E. Turiel. 2007. "To Lie or Not to Lie: To Whom and under What Circumstances." *Child Development* 78: 609–621.
Piaget, J. 1932. *The Moral Judgment of the Child*. London: Routledge and Kegan Paul.
Pizarro, D., Y. Inbar, and C. Helion. 2011. "On Disgust and Moral Judgment." *Emotion Review* 3, no. 3: 267–268.
Rawls, J. 1971. *A Theory of Justice*. Cambridge: Harvard University Press.
Schnall, S., J. Haidt, G. L. Clore, and A. H. Jordan. 2008. "Disgust As Embodied Moral Judgment." *Personality and Social Psychology Bulletin* 34: 1096–1109.
Sen, A. 1999. *Development as Freedom*. New York: Alfred A. Knopf.
Smetana, J. G. 2006. "Social-Cognitive Domain Theory: Consistencies and Variations in Children's Moral and Social Judgments." In *Handbook of Moral Development*, edited by M. Killen and J. G. Smetana, 119–153. Mahwah: Lawrence Erlbaum Associates Publishers.
Sunstein, C. R. 2014. "How Do We Know What's Moral?" *New York Review of Books*, April 24. http://www.nybooks.com/articles/2014/04/24/how-do-we-know-whats-moral/
Thomson, J. J. 1976. "Killing, Letting Die, and the Trolley Problem." *The Monist* 59: 204–217.
Turiel, E. 1983. *The Development of Social Knowledge: Morality and Convention*. Cambridge: Cambridge University Press.

Turiel, E. 2002. *The Culture of Morality: Social Development, Context, and Conflict.* Cambridge: Cambridge University Press.

Turiel, E. 2008a. "Social Decisions, Social Interactions, and the Coordination of Diverse Judgments." In *Social Life, Social Knowledge: Toward a Process Account of Development,* edited by U. Mueller, J. I. Carpendale, N. Budwig, and B. Sokol, 255–276. Mahwah: Erlbaum.

Turiel, E. 2008b. "Thought about Actions in Social Domains: Morality, Social Conventions, and Social Interactions." *Cognitive Development* 23: 126–154.

Turiel, E. 2010. "The Relevance of Moral Epistemology and Psychology for Neuroscience." In *Developmental Social Cognitive Neuroscience,* edited by P. Zelazo, M. Chandler, and E. Crone, 313–331. New York: Taylor & Francis.

Turiel, E. 2015. "Moral Development." In *Handbook of Child Psychology, Vol. 1: Theory and Method,* 7th ed., edited by W. F. Overton and P. C. Molenaar, 484–522. Hoboken: John Wiley.

Turiel, E., and A. Dahl. Forthcoming. "The Development of Domains of Moral and Conventional Norms, Coordination in Decision-Making, and the Implications of Social Opposition." In *The Normative Animal: On the Anthropological Significance of Social, Moral, and Linguistic Norms,* edited by K. Bayertz and N. Roughley. Oxford: Oxford University Press.

Turiel, E., and M. Gingo. 2017. "Development in the Moral Domain: Coordination and the Need to Consider Other Domains of Social Reasoning." In *New Perspectives on Human Development,* edited by N. Budwig, E. Turiel, and P. Zelazo, 209–228. Cambridge: Cambridge University Press.

Turiel, E., and M. Killen. 2010. "Taking Emotions Seriously: The Role of Emotions in Moral Development." In *Emotions, Aggression, and Morality in Children: Bridging Development and Psychopathology,* edited by W. Arsenio and E. Lemerise, 33–52. Washington, D.C.: APA.

Turiel, E., C. Hildebrandt, and C. Wainryb. 1991. "Judging Social Issues: Difficulties, Inconsistencies and Consistencies." *Monographs of the Society for Research in Child Development* 56: 1–116.

Turiel, E., S. A. Perkins, and J. F. Mensing. 2009. "Judgments about Deception in Marital Relationships." Unpublished manuscript, University of California, Berkeley.

Vlastos, G. 1962. "Justice and Equality." In *Social Justice,* edited by R. B. Brandt, 31–72. Englewood Cliffs: Prentice-Hall.

Wainryb, C., and H. Recchia. 2012. "Emotion and the Moral Lives of Adolescents: Vagaries and Complexities in the Emotional Experience of Doing Harm." In *Adolescent Emotions: Development, Morality, and Adaptation,* edited by T. Malti, 13–26. *New Directions in Youth Development* 136: 13–26.

Wainryb, C., and E. Turiel. 1994. "Dominance, Subordination, and Concepts of Personal Entitlements in Cultural Contexts." *Child Development* 65: 1701–1722.

Wainryb, C., B. A. Brehl, and S. Matwin. 2005. "Being Hurt and Hurting Others: Children's Narrative Accounts and Moral Judgments of Their Own Interpersonal Conflicts." *Monographs of the Society for Research in Child Development* 70, no. 3: 1–122.

Walzer, M. 2007. *Thinking Politically: Essays in Political Theory*. New Haven: Yale University Press.

Wikan, U. 1996. *Tomorrow, God Willing: Self-Made Destinies in Cairo*. Chicago: University of Chicago Press.

Williams, B. 1973. "A Critique of Utilitarianism." In *Utilitarianism: For and Against*, edited by J. J. C. Smart and B. Williams, 77–149. Cambridge: Cambridge University Press.

Chapter 6

The Evolution of Justice

SARAH BROSNAN

Humans care deeply about justice and fairness.[1] We are upset by situations in which we are treated less well than others, situations in which we see others treated inappropriately, or even, in some cases, situations in which we are treated better than others. We also spend substantial amounts of time and energy rectifying wrongs related to unfairness or injustice. This appears to be a key feature of human psychology that is universally expressed.[2] But why do we do so? One school of thought is that this is cultural, a behavior that we teach to our children, either directly or indirectly, through our actions. Supporting this, there is substantial variation across countries in terms of how people respond to an "unfair" or "unjust" situation.[3] That being said, while there is certainly variation, every society tested thus far does have a norm of fairness that accords with its socioecology and culture. This ubiquity could indicate that the reaction to unfairness or injustice is something more basic in our biology. If so, this indicates that fairness is a biologically evolved behavior (albeit certainly with components that are culturally evolved or influenced) and that we should expect to see fairness, or, more specifically, elements related to fairness, in other species.

By studying these behaviors in other species, we learn about the sense of fairness in ourselves.[4]

Of course, we do not necessarily expect to see justice or fairness, in the full-blown "human" sense of the word, in other species. Justice is an abstract belief in how outcomes should be distributed, how procedures should be run, and how people should be treated, which as a whole cannot occur without the ability to consider what is fair, from both one's own and others' perspectives, and to agree, as a group or a culture, what those standards should be. This particular suite of behaviors does not, and, indeed, probably cannot, exist in other species because of the difference in cognitive ability between humans and other species. For example, these behaviors require abstract thinking that allows an individual to conceptualize a "fair" distribution outside of his or her immediate experience a theory of mind that allows the individual to consider how his or her actions may affect others or how others may feel, the development of norms around prescribed behavior, and language that allows the group to set, maintain, and promulgate the standards of the group.[5] While other species, and in particular other primates, have aspects of these characteristics, such as communication and theory of mind, they exist in less complex forms than in humans. Complex language, in particular, is a key feature that is present only in humans.[6] Therefore, it seems likely that even those species that have complex communication or aspects of theory of mind may still lack the suite of characteristics that allow them to fully develop fairness and justice.

Nonetheless, human behavior evolved just as our other features did, and we can learn about the roots of our own behavior by looking at related suites of behaviors in other species.[7] This tells us what behaviors and abilities were available as "raw materials" for natural selection as the sense of justice evolved and the contexts in which these behaviors may have been expressed. Such justice-related behaviors may be similar across species, or instead may represent precursors to the human sense of fairness that are not expressed in the same ways we see in humans.[8] We can also learn about the form of current behavior by considering the historical constraints that may have limited the evolutionary pathways available. Although in principle every pathway is possible, in reality behavior can only evolve from existing behavior; therefore, the future is constrained by the realities of the present. Understanding what those constraints were may help us to better understand situations in which the behavior does not manifest as we expect or wish for.[9]

Evidence gathered over the last dozen years indicates that responding negatively to perceived inequities is not a unique feature of humans.[10] Other species, in particular those that routinely cooperate, also respond poorly to being treated less well than another member of their social group. Moreover, and somewhat unexpectedly, there is some evidence that a few other species even appear to notice when they are *advantaged* as compared with their social partners.[11] This second feature is key; a full sense of fairness and justice must be other-regarding. It is not sufficient to care only when one is treated unfairly; this is a self-centered behavior that may benefit at times, but it isn't fairness.[12] Such an other-focused outlook is, as I discuss, more challenging, because despite there being a long-term benefit, it requires a short-term cost in order to achieve the longer-term gain.

In this chapter, I first present the data that have emerged regarding how other species respond to situations in which their outcomes differ from those of their social partners, both when they are disadvantaged relative to others and when they are advantaged. I then discuss how this response to inequity is related to the evolution of cooperation and, ultimately, what these data tell us about the evolution of the human sense of fairness. Overall, I make the case that if we want to fully understand the human sense of fairness, we need to look not just at our own species, but also at others.

STUDYING THE EVOLUTION OF BEHAVIOR

When biologists consider the evolution of any trait, there are two primary ways of evaluating it. First is in terms of the trait's evolutionary function (called the ultimate explanation), or what it characteristically does (or did) for individuals that manifest it. This includes the trait's evolutionary history and why and how it evolved, as well as whether the trait is still beneficial today. The second way is in terms of the trait's proximate mechanisms, or how the trait develops and is manifest within a specific individual. This includes the neural, hormonal, and cognitive pathways through which the behavior manifests, as well as how the trait develops across the life span and the degree to which and mechanisms by which it is learned. This distinction between the ultimate (evolutionary) and proximate explanations for a trait is particularly important when considering value-laden traits such as fairness or justice, in which we may see behaviors that function similarly to what we expect in humans but are underpinned by different mechanisms from those that are seen in humans. In this case, while the outcomes may be the same, care must be taken when drawing parallels with humans.[13] Likewise, the same mechanisms may lead to very different-looking behavioral outcomes, yet because of the shared mechanisms, they can nonetheless be relevant for understanding how the trait evolved.

Throughout this chapter, I use the comparative approach, which involves comparing species with one another in order to see whether and how behaviors are similar across species. There are two ways in which such phylogenetic comparisons can inform, and it is important to understand the differences between them.[14] First, comparisons can be made between closely related species to try to determine something about the time frame in which a behavior evolved. Traits, including behaviors, shared across a taxon because they evolved from a common ancestor are referred to as *homologies*, and the farther back on a phylogenetic tree the homology reaches, the longer ago (in the phylogenetic sense) the trait evolved. *Convergence,* on the other hand, occurs when two or more species that lack a common ancestor with the trait evolve similar characteristics, and it can be used to understand which ecological pressures selected for the trait in question. The emergence of multiple taxa that share a trait can help pin down which shared pressures may have led to the emergence of the given behavior.

Both convergence and homology are very important for understanding the evolution of behavior, emphasizing the importance of studying not just species that are closely related to us (e.g., the primates) but also more distantly related species that share relevant features in common. In fact, depending on one's interests, studying convergences might be more informative than studying homologies, as the former will highlight specific ecological pressures that led to selection for a trait. This approach is even more powerful as the number of comparisons increases. Moreover, this can happen even when the species involved are relatively closely related (i.e., are close on the phylogenetic tree); even within the same taxon, we may see convergences caused by what are presumably very recent changes in evolutionary pressure.[15]

HOW DO OTHER SPECIES RESPOND TO INEQUITY?

We cannot ask an animal how it feels about justice (and, arguably, humans do not always understand their own motivations, either). Therefore, to study a social ideal, such as fairness, we must first break the question down into tractable, empirically testable components. To do so, we consider what are the key elements and then design studies that address these elements. At its most basic, fairness is related to how one responds to receiving less than a social partner receives, which was therefore what we tested first.

When considering responses to unequal outcomes, researchers traditionally divide inequity into two components: disadvantageous inequity aversion and advantageous inequity aversion, also called overcompensation. The former is how an individual responds when it gets less than expected based on another's outcomes, while the latter is the individual's response when it gets more than expected based on the other's outcomes. It is also important to try to rule out other confounding factors. For instance, disadvantaged subjects may be forming expectations based on what their partners got (a social referent), but it might also be simply that there is a better reward visible (a nonsocial referent). This latter situation is called a *contrast effect* in psychology and is widespread across animals, so it is important to separate these nonsocial expectations from expectations based on what another individual actually received (inequity).[16]

Most studies of inequity in other species have followed the lead of the first such study (Brosnan and de Waal 2003). Subjects complete a task of some sort (often exchanging a token with a human experimenter), and we measure how the focal subject responds to the reward received for completing the task depending on whether the subject's partner gets the same outcome (control condition) or a more preferred outcome (the inequity condition). Additionally, there is typically a second control condition in which both individuals are shown the more preferred reward prior to completing the task for the less preferred reward (contrast control). In this latter case, both subjects have their attention drawn to the better reward, but both receive the less preferred one, so that there is equity in outcomes but a contrast with the evoked expectation. The dependent variable is the subjects' reactions to the less preferred reward. That is, do they participate in the interaction or refuse to do so, by refusing either to accept the token, return the token, or accept the food reward? Additionally, advantageous inequity aversion can be explored by adding conditions that allow us to compare how the subject responds to receiving the more preferred reward when the partner gets the same preferred outcome (high-value control) versus a less preferred outcome (advantageous inequity). Once these basic parameters have been established, we have enough baseline information to begin to ask more complex questions.

DISADVANTAGEOUS INEQUITY AVERSION

Indeed, such studies show that many nonhuman primates respond more negatively to receiving a less valuable outcome than a social partner receives than they do to receiving the same less preferred reward when the partner gets the same (less preferred) outcome. In the first such study, capuchin monkeys became quite upset if their partners received a better outcome than they did, refusing to participate in the interaction more than 40 percent of the time but refusing only about 10 percent of the time in the control condition. Further work has borne this out.[17] They also respond more strongly to inequity than to a contrast control, in which they (and their partners) initially see a preferred reward but ultimately receive the less preferred one, indicating that this response is specific to inequity.

Chimpanzees, too, respond negatively to inequity.[18] Because we have access to a greater number of subjects, we have been able to explore their reactions in more detail. For example, chimpanzees respond more strongly to inequity than they do to loss,[19] again indicating that while responses to contrast and to inequity are presumably driven by the same cognitive mechanism, a feeling of frustration engendered when the subject does not receive what is expected, they are distinct in the sense that the social context of inequity influences subjects' decision-making above and beyond a reaction to contrast.

Chimpanzees also show substantial individual variability in this response.[20] Initial studies implicated dominance, sex differences, and social group dynamics, but there was no consistent factor predicting responses.[21] We recently completed a large study to resolve this and found that relationship quality, as measured by the length of time the subjects had lived together in the same social group, determined which pairs were willing to voluntarily separate as a pair, but for the pairs that did so, personality predicted their responses.[22] We are now working to understand how these factors interact beyond dyadic encounters using an adapted paradigm that allows us to test the entire social group at the same time.[23]

CROSS-SPECIES COMPARISONS

As discussed earlier, the goal of a comparative research program is to explore the distribution of a behavior, in this case inequity, and whether it is either widely distributed across a taxon, indicating homology, or common descent, or patchily distributed, indicating convergence. In the latter case, a key question is what other features overlap with the given trait, as these are candidates to be among the factors that influenced the evolution of the trait. One existing hypothesis, derived from economics, is that fairness evolved to help individuals determine the relative value of cooperative partners. That is, if you are working with another individual who consistently takes more than his or her fair share, perhaps it is time to find another cooperative partner.[24] Indeed, this partner choice explanation is highly likely to apply to other species as well, as recognizing inequity need not be a cognitively complex task. It is likely that the response is an emotional reaction to persistent negative comparisons and does not require the animal (or the human) to either understand why he or she is upset or to recognize the utility of finding a new social partner.[25]

Work on capuchin monkeys and chimpanzees supports this hypothesis, as both species are highly cooperative in the lab and in the field.[26] Nonetheless, science requires attempts to falsify a hypothesis, and falsifying this hypothesis requires testing species that do not routinely cooperate. Additionally, capuchin monkeys and chimpanzees share more in common than simply their propensity to cooperate. Among other similarities, both are highly social, and both have large brain-to-body ratios, a measure that is argued to predict cognitive ability.[27] Finally, when looking at only two species, it is impossible to tell whether this is simply the result of a homology within the primates (or more broadly), or indicates convergence.

Thus far, data support the hypothesis that at the phylogenetic level, cooperation is linked to negative responses to inequity.[28] Homology is ruled out across the primates, as well as more narrowly, within the great apes.[29] Orangutans do not respond negatively to inequity,[30] nor do several species of New World monkeys, including callitrichids (tamarins and marmosets)[31], owl monkeys,[32] and squirrel monkeys.[33] Squirrel monkeys are perhaps the most interesting, as they and capuchin monkeys are part of the same phylogenetic family, the *Cebidae*, and are sympatric, occupying the same ecological niche in South and Central America. We can also rule out that either brain size or brain-to-body ratio is a key feature, because the orangutans do not respond and also because several species of macaques, an Old World monkey group that has a larger brain, but smaller brain-to-body ratio than capuchins, do show inequity responses.[34] Finally, we can rule out that the response to inequity is due solely to group size, as squirrel monkeys live in very large social groups but do not respond to inequity.

Supporting the cooperation hypothesis, both macaque species tested, rhesus macaques and long-tailed macaques, respond negatively to inequity. Although macaques do not cooperatively hunt, they engage in extensive coalitions and alliances, which requires a high level of coordination.[35] They also coordinate at very high rates when playing economic coordination games in the laboratory.[36] Finally, only a small sample of bonobos have been tested, but despite the fact that they did not reach statistical significance (likely a result of the small sample size), bonobos refused to participate about twice as often in the inequity condition as compared with the equity condition.[37] Like chimpanzees, bonobos are highly cooperative in the wild and in captivity.[38]

Data from nonprimate mammals also support this correlation between species that routinely cooperate and those that respond negatively to inequitable outcomes in experimental tests. Rats are also highly social mammals that show cooperation,[39] reciprocity,[40] empathy,[41] and prosocial preferences, preferring mutually rewarding options over those that reward only themselves.[42] In experimental tests, rats also show a negative response to inequity, and, like nonhuman primates, dominant animals are more sensitive to inequity than are subordinates.[43] Domestic dogs are cooperative in experimental studies[44] and are also sensitive to inequity.[45] Although the dogs only refused to participate when the reward was absent, they are both less tolerant in a subsequent food-sharing test with their partner and are later more likely to avoid both their partner and the experimenter if they were given a less preferred reward (as compared with equal-quality rewards).[46] Although initial work has focused on refusals, as refusals are very obvious outcomes that are easier to measure objectively, these results indicate that there may be responses to inequity that are not sufficiently strong for the animal to give up the less preferred reward (a very costly action) but may manifest behaviorally in other ways. Such behavioral changes may help to better understand which situations lead to a response to inequity. Lastly, this response extends beyond mammals; two species of corvids that are highly cooperative, ravens and crows, also respond negatively to inequity in experimental tasks.[47] Thus, the response to inequity appears to be sufficiently useful that it has evolved multiple times across multiple lineages. Future work in species that are not highly cooperative will be key in determining the robustness of this association between cooperation and inequity.

Finally, it is worth noting an interesting pattern among cooperative breeders. Cooperative breeders are species for whom both parents (biparental care) and older siblings are required to raise the offspring. Thus far, three cooperatively breeding or biparental-care species have been studied, tamarins and marmosets (both callitrichids) and owl monkeys. In none of these cases did subjects respond negatively to inequity.[48] On the surface, this seems contrary to the hypothesis, as cooperative breeding is indeed highly cooperative. However, the tested pairs were almost all mated pairs, mostly with offspring, so these individuals were highly dependent on their partners. If it is the case that the negative response to inequity is in part a trigger to let the subject know it is time to go find a new partner, this may require a much higher threshold in an interdependent partnership for which the costs of leaving are very high (i.e., having to find a new mate). Future work exploring the role of inequity during partnership formation would be very informative; I predict that subjects would be very sensitive to inequity during this period, because the costs of choosing poorly are particularly high but the costs of sampling are still relatively low, but would be less so once the bond is formed and offspring are involved because the costs of leaving the partner are so high.[49]

COOPERATION UNDER CONDITIONS OF INEQUITY

In the previous section, I considered the phylogenetic distribution of responding to inequity and argued that the current data best support a link between species that respond to inequity and those that cooperate with nonkin (outside the pair bond). This looked at a link at the species level, but one can also study whether inequitable situations lead to changes in *individual* decisions about whether or not to cooperate. Chimpanzees, for example, are very sensitive to the behavior of their partners. In a situation in which subjects could work together to obtain a food reward to be shared, subjects did best with a social partner who, in other contexts, shared tolerantly, and when given an option, they chose a more tolerant partner over a less tolerant one.[50] That being said, perhaps because of the challenges of working together, chimpanzees also prefer working alone to working collaboratively, unless there are gains that can only be achieved by working together.[51]

Capuchins, too, are sensitive to outcomes in cooperative tasks. In particular, they are sensitive to whether their partner helped them previously. In an early study of reciprocity, subjects were more likely to share food when their partner's help was required to obtain that food, and conversely, partners were more likely to continue helping to obtain food when the subject shared.[52] Similarly, capuchins were also more likely to choose an option that rewarded partners when their partner helped to obtain the food.[53] Capuchins also pay attention to the potential outcomes when choosing whether or not to cooperate. In most cooperation tasks, rewards are spaced out so that all individuals know what they are working for when they make the decision to participate. When rewards were clumped together, however, so that the subjects had to divide up the spoils after a success, cooperation plummetted.[54] Interestingly, it did so from the very first trial in the clumped condition, indicating that the subjects' knowledge of their partner's behavior from their daily interactions in their social group was sufficient to allow subjects to predict their partners' reactions in this novel experimental task. Moreover, this pattern was true for both unrelated subjects and mother-offspring pairs, indicating that kinship alone is not sufficient to promote either cooperation or tolerant food sharing.

In another task, subjects had to decide whether or not to work together for either the same rewards or different ones (the unequal condition; one reward was preferred by all subjects over the other).[55] We hypothesized that subjects would do better when rewards were the same and less well when rewards were different, but contrary to this, subjects were equally good regardless of the reward distribution. The key feature was instead the behavior of the partner. When members of the pair took turns working for the better outcome in the unequal condition, subjects continued to cooperate at very high rates in all conditions, despite the fact that in the unequal condition, subjects all received a less preferred reward than their partner half of the time. When one member of the pair dominated in the better outcome in the unequal condition, however, cooperation collapsed across all conditions, despite the fact that in the equal conditions, it was still the case that neither subject could do better than their partner. Subjects were apparently responding to the behavior of their partner, not to the outcomes, and were refusing to cooperate with subjects that had not behaved fairly even in situations in which there was no chance for unequal outcomes. This violates economic rationality (since the subject could do absolutely better without being any less well-off relatively by cooperating in the equal conditions) but makes sense if responses to inequity are emotional reactions aimed at determining whether the partner is a good cooperator.

Recent work has begun to consider in what cooperative contexts we should expect inequity responses.[56] When considering the different categories of cooperative behavior, evolutionary biologists break them down in terms of costs and benefits to each partner.[57] My colleague Redouan Bshary and I have argued that inequity should not be relevant in all of them. For example, in byproduct mutualism, in which one individual's self-serving actions benefit another individual, the equity (or lack thereof) is irrelevant, because there is no "cooperative partner" whose value one can assess; the "partner" is simply doing its own thing, and the recipient benefits incidentally. Inequity likely does make a difference in the context of reciprocity, in which individuals take turns benefiting, and in biological markets, in which partners exchange goods or services, with the rate depending on the trade-off between supply and demand.[58] Inequity may also be particularly relevant to reputational effects, or indirect reciprocity. In fact, the sophisticated inequity aversion seen in humans may help explain why indirect reciprocity is largely absent in other species; this requires both a system of values against which to judge another's behavior and an interest in helping fair individuals and punishing those who are not fair (i.e., third-party punishment, which is documented only in humans).[59]

Additionally, we argue that animals should be more focused on outcomes than on effort.[60] This is partly a result of the difficulty in judging whether another individual is failing to participate fully because of slacking or some other cause (injury, lesser ability, etc.).[61] Cheating by slacking should be under quite strong selective pressure; however, if subjects ignore effort and focus entirely on outcomes, cheating via slacking is still unlikely to evolve if individuals are sensitive to each subjects' inputs and invest in cooperation accordingly. Therefore, because of the challenges in assessing effort, especially as it relates to slacking versus other causes, it might be in subjects' best interests to ignore effort altogether. Indeed, work using the standard inequity paradigm indicates that primates are generally not sensitive to the amount of effort involved in the task,[62] although there are some contexts in which they do appear to show this sensitivity.[63] Humans may be better able to assess relative efforts involved in a cooperative endeavor, and may more commonly do so, although I expect that humans, too, often focus on outcomes rather than efforts.

WHERE DO WE SEE INEQUITY IN THE WILD?

All the data discussed up to this point regard experimental studies. A key question is how this behavior in the lab translates to natural behavior outside of experimental contexts. Some of the best work to date involves canid species, which play extensively and have very structured rules about play sessions. Observational work in the field indicates that when a canine violates these rules of engagement (i.e., plays unfairly), others stop interacting with the violator, refusing play invitations (e.g., play bows) and walking away if the violator attempts to join an ongoing play bout.[64] Moreover, among coyotes, juveniles that do not play fair are substantially more likely to leave the group at puberty, and the mortality rate for individuals that leave the group is much higher than for those that stay. In coyotes, then, there is a very real cost to failing to play fair.

Interest in inequity may appear in other contexts as well. Bonobos routinely scream after fights, and their screams after "fair" retaliation (i.e., when the caller was the initial aggressor who was then retaliated against) are acoustically distinct from those in fights after "unfair" retaliation (i.e., when the caller did nothing to instigate the aggressor's attack).[65] Additionally, these screams are individually identifiable, so it is at least possible that these apes are advertising that they were unfairly treated.

Of course, the social context is not the only one in which inequities occur. In particular, it will be key to look at situations in which animals work together and then must share an outcome or exchange goods and services.[66] Considering the first of these, inequity based violations may emerge after a group hunt, when individuals worked together to obtain a prey item, if the prey is not shared according to the standard expectations.[67] Inequalities may also play a role in decisions about group movements, for instance, when animals must decide, as a group, which food source to visit when one source is preferred by some members and another by others.[68] Future work will undoubtedly uncover additional circumstances in which inequity plays a role in decision-making and thereby help us to determine the situations in which inequities play the largest roles.

ADVANTAGEOUS INEQUITY

As mentioned at the beginning of this chapter, fairness involves two components: disadvantageous inequity aversion, which I have discussed up to this point, and advantageous inequity aversion, in which an individual responds if it is benefited relative to another. Humans show advantageous inequity aversion, although to a lesser extent than they show disadvantageous inequity aversion.[69] This is interesting to consider, because this imbalance between disadvantageous and advantageous inequity aversion seems counter to a sense of fairness, in which subjects are to care about both their own and others' outcomes. From an evolutionary perspective, however, this difference in preference is far less surprising, because of the imbalance in (at least short-term) benefits for responding to disadvantageous versus advantageous situations.

There is very little evidence for advantageous inequity aversion in other species. One notable exception is chimpanzees. Using the standard inequity paradigm, chimpanzees were more likely to refuse a preferred outcome if their partner got the less preferred one than if both chimpanzees got the more preferred outcome.[70] As with humans, this reaction was much less strong than the reaction to being disadvantaged.[71] It is also important to note that we do not know their underlying motivation. They never shared the preferred outcome, as might be expected if they were attempting to equalize outcomes, and may have primarily been concerned about future repercussions for acquiring a better outcome than their partner. Either way, however, this shows that the chimpanzees do notice when they receive more than a partner receives.

Another way to measure advantageous inequity aversion is with a game from experimental economics called the ultimatum game.[72] In the ultimatum game, one individual, the proposer, has the opportunity to split an outcome between himself or herself and a partner, the responder. If the responder likes the proposed split, he or she accepts it, and both individuals get their respective allocations. If, however, the proposer does not like the proposed split, he or she can refuse it, and neither player gets anything. Although there is substantial cross-cultural variation in this response,[73] in no society do individuals offer the minimum, which is the rational choice. In modern Western societies, proposers typically offer about half of the initial allocation, and responders tend to refuse anything less than about 30 percent of it.[74]

Although chimpanzees cannot be asked to freely split an allocation (which is quite difficult without language), they can participate in a so-called limited-form ultimatum game, in which the proposer chooses from between two initial allocation options. Chimpanzee responders failed to refuse unequal offers in any of the studies done thus far.[75] However, when we compared chimpanzees' choices when their partner had recourse versus when the partner did not, subjects overwhelmingly preferred the option that benefited them when the partner had no recourse, but switched their preference to the equally benefiting option when their partner did.[76] We repeated the task on children from the same class in a day care and saw the same pattern of results; the children never refused but showed a greater preference for the equal option when paired with a classmate.

While this lack of refusals may seem surprising in the context of human results using typical economic game paradigms, unlike in these typical games, the subjects in our version played face-to-face with known members of their social group, so they had recourse other than refusing to participate. In such a context, a wiser course of action than refusing to participate, and thereby ending all possibility of future gains, is to change the partner's behavior.[77] Indeed, we saw evidence of this, with subjects either directing banging or screaming at their partner (chimpanzees) or verbally expressing their dissatisfaction (children). Moreover, even in typical economic game setups, when human responders are given the option to communicate with the proposer, for instance, by writing a note, they take advantage of this option—and also accept much more unfair offers.[78] Overall, it seems that chimpanzees, at least, do recognize when their partners are disadvantaged and may alter their behavior in order to alleviate the inequality, at least when it is in their interests to do so. Although this behavior has not yet been seen outside of chimpanzees, it seems likely that a similar response will be found in other long-lived, highly social, large-brained species that routinely cooperate with one another.

WHAT DOES THIS TELL US ABOUT THE EVOLUTION OF FAIRNESS?

Some primates respond negatively to getting less than a social partner gets, and chimpanzees also notice when they are advantaged. What does this tell us about the evolution of fairness? First, it is clear that responses to receiving less than a partner receives, or disadvantageous inequity, are linked to cooperation, both at the phylogenetic level (i.e., cooperative species are more likely to show a response to inequity) and at the mechanistic level (i.e., cooperation falls apart within dyads if partners do not distribute outcomes equally). Frans de Waal and I have described this reaction as *first-order fairness*.[79] Essentially, when one individual is undercompensated, the individual protests, and if it continues, the individual is likely to explore other possible partnerships, ending the relationship.[80] This is an essential component to maintaining cooperation, because it allows individuals to recognize and avoid situations or partners that result in relative inequality, which is critical in the currency of natural selection. Indeed, while not a sense of fairness in and of itself, this supports the hypothesis that inequity responses evolved in the context of cooperation.

To be a sense of fairness, however, also requires what we refer to as *second-order fairness*. In this case, the initial conditions are the same; however, the advantaged individual forestalls the less advantaged partner's protest by equalizing the outcomes in some way. This may not mean creating exactly equal outcomes, but simply appeasing the protest so that the disadvantaged partner does not exercise his or her partner choice options. If done correctly, the protest disappears, and the cooperative relationship continues. Although this is certainly a short-term cost to the advantaged partner, the long-term benefits to the maintenance of a successful, beneficial cooperative relationship should outweigh the short-term costs.

Despite the potential benefit, thus far the only evidence for second-order fairness is found in humans and chimpanzees. This may not be surprising, given that second-order fairness requires substantial cognitive abilities that are not widespread in the animal kingdom. For instance, individuals must be able to delay gratification and inhibit the tendency to maximize outcomes immediately. They may also require some basic perspective taking, or theory of mind, in order to understand how a given outcome will affect their partner, as well as an ability to plan for the future and, potentially, understand how their actions now might provide benefit in the future. These abilities are not present in all species (but they are present, to at least some degree, in chimpanzees).[81]

One important caveat is needed here: second-order fairness does not necessarily require that the advantaged individual recognizes the need for amelioration or that it understands the reasons for its actions (the same is true for first-order fairness). Natural selection can promote behaviors that benefit the self with no understanding on the part of the organism about why. However, humans can understand the trade-off between a short-term cost now and a long-term goal, and have the ability to plan far into the future. Uniquely among animals, humans may be able to understand how an investment now will reap benefits for decades to come. This suite of abilities is likely the explanation for why humans have such a well-developed sense of fairness as compared with other species.

But again, while humans' sense of fairness is uniquely developed among animals, it evolved from the same roots. Understanding the origins of the sense of fairness helps us understand how cooperation and the sense of fairness are linked and why unfairness may impede cooperative decision-making differently across contexts. The knowledge that first-order fairness is much more common, and likely much easier to maintain, than second-order fairness reminds us why it is so much easier to be enraged by inequities one experiences than to develop the same sense of outrage at those experienced by others (particularly if we benefit). This is not just a personality failing on the part of a few people but a deeply ingrained trait that likely requires conscious effort to overcome.[82] By better understanding the evolutionary roots of the sense of fairness, we better understand ourselves and can better build institutions and rules to promote successful cooperation that will, in the long run, benefit each of us.

NOTES

1. In this chapter, I treat the two as more or less the same, although when I focus on fairness, as in most cases, I am talking about how an individual responds to a specific interaction rather than what individuals do (or do not) deserve. See other chapters in this volume (in particular Woodruff's chapter 1) for a discussion of how the two differ.
2. How it is expressed, however, varies substantially across cultures, in accordance with how each society is structured; see chapter 4 by Widlok in this volume.

3. See, e.g., Henrich et al. 2005; Gächter, Herrmann, and Thoni 2010; chapter 4 by Widlok in this volume.
4. Brosnan 2006; Brosnan and de Waal 2014. Of course, this is in contrast to some moral philosophers, who see justice as emerging after human specialties such as language or property (see chapter 2 by Hanley in this volume). As I describe below, I agree that we do not see justice in the "human" sense in animals, but I argue that we do see the roots of such justice in behaviors that we see in other species (perhaps related to what Woodruff refers to as the "sprouts" of justice that are present in humans). As such, I would disagree that justice emerged from any particularly human specialty, such as the development of property, but rather argue that the roots of justice-related behaviors were present in our biological heritage already and were expressed in these novel human specialties.
5. See chapter 3 by Wilson in this volume for the importance of language in how norms of justice emerge.
6. This is in accord with Aristotle's assertion in *Politics* 1 that humans are the only animal with speech because "nature does nothing in vain," and speech "serves to reveal the advantageous and the harmful and hence also the just and unjust"; note the very evolutionary language. However, as I argue, despite lacking language, other species are nonetheless able to reveal harm and distinguish between just and unjust, albeit in different and presumably less sophisticated ways. I, and others, would also disagree with Aristotle that humans are fundamentally more political than other animals; see de Waal 2007.
7. See Boehm 1999.
8. Brosnan 2014.
9. Konner 2002.
10. Brosnan 2013.
11. Brosnan and de Waal 2014.
12. See chapters by Woodruff, Wilson, and Hanley in this volume for more discussion of this distinction.
13. For a discussion of this issue with respect to the evolution of moral behavior, see Brosnan 2014.
14. See Brosnan, Newton-Fisher, and van Vugt 2009.
15. Brosnan 2011; Talbot et al. 2011.
16. Reynolds 1961; Freidin, Cuello, and Kacelnik 2009.
17. Brosnan and de Waal 2003; Fletcher 2008; van Wolkenten, Brosnan, and de Waal 2007. But see Silberberg et al. 2009; Dubreuil, Gentile, and Visalberghi 2006; McAuliffe et al. 2015 for differing results and a discussion of the variability in this response later in this chapter.
18. Brosnan et al. 2015; Brosnan, Schiff, and de Waal 2005; Brosnan et al. 2010; Hopper et al. 2014. But see Bräuer, Call, and Tomasello 2009; Bräuer, Call, and Tomasello 2006; Hopper et al. 2013a.

19. Hopper et al. 2014.
20. Price and Brosnan 2012.
21. Brosnan et al. 2010; Bräuer, Call, and Tomasello 2009; Hopper et al. 2014; Brosnan, Schiff, and de Waal 2005.
22. Brosnan et al. 2015.
23. Hall et al. 2015.
24. Fehr and Schmidt 1999; see also Brosnan 2011.
25. Brosnan 2006. See chapter 5 by Turiel, Dahl, Besirevic in this volume for a discussion of how emotions are involved in human decisions related to thinking about inequalities.
26. Boesch 1994; Mendres and de Waal 2000; Perry et al. 2003; Suchak et al. 2014.
27. Jerison 1985; Clutton-Brock and Harvey 1980; Rilling and Insel 1999. But see Deaner et al. 2007.
28. Brosnan 2013.
29. Brosnan 2013. This was a possibility given that the common ancestor to the great apes may have developed the behavior and passed it to all the great apes, even if their ecological constraints later diverged.
30. Bräuer, Call, and Tomasello 2009; Brosnan et al. 2011.
31. Freeman et al. 2013; Neiworth et al. 2009. Although see Mustoe et al. 2016.
32. Freeman et al. 2013.
33. Freeman et al. 2013; Talbot et al. 2011.
34. Hopper et al. 2013b; Massen et al. 2012.
35. Chapais 1991; Widdig, Streich, and Tembrock 2000.
36. Brosnan, Wilson, and Beran 2012.
37. Bräuer, Call, and Tomasello 2009.
38. Fruth and Hohmann 2002; Hare et al. 2007. But see Jaeggi, Stevens, and Van Schaik 2010.
39. Daniel 1943.
40. Rutte and Taborsky 2007.
41. Bartal, Decety, and Mason 2011.
42. Hernandez-Lallement et al. 2015.
43. Oberliessen et al. 2016.
44. Ostojić and Clayton 2013.
45. Range et al. 2009; Range, Leitner, and Virányi 2012. But see Horowitz 2012 for some limits on responses to inequity in dogs.
46. Brucks et al. 2016.
47. Massen, Ritter, and Bugnyar 2015; Asakawa-Haas et al. 2016; Wascher and Bugnyar 2013.
48. Freeman et al. 2013; Neiworth et al. 2009.
49. Brosnan 2013.
50. Melis, Hare, and Tomasello 2006a; 2006b. Ravens also prefer tolerant partners for cooperation; Asakawa-Haas et al. 2016.

51. Bullinger, Melis, and Tomasello 2011.
52. De Waal and Berger 2000.
53. Takimoto and Fujita 2011.
54. De Waal and Davis 2003.
55. Brosnan, Freeman, and de Waal 2006.
56. Brosnan and Bshary 2016.
57. Bshary and Bergmuller 2008.
58. Noe and Hammerstein 1995.
59. Fehr and Fischbacher 2004.
60. Brosnan and Bshary 2016.
61. Packer 1988.
62. Brosnan et al. 2011; Brosnan et al. 2010; van Wolkenten, Brosnan, and de Waal 2007.
63. Takimoto and Fujita 2011; de Waal and Berger 2000.
64. Bekoff 2009; Pierce and Bekoff 2012.
65. Clay et al. 2016.
66. Brosnan and Bshary 2016.
67. Boesch 1994.
68. Strandburg-Peshkin et al. 2015.
69. Blake et al. 2015; Loewenstein, Thompson, and Bazerman 1989.
70. Brosnan et al. 2010.
71. See Blake et al. 2015 for cross-cultural data comparing advantageous and disadvantageous inequity aversion in four- to fifteen-year-old children in seven societies.
72. Camerer 2003; Guth, Schmittberger, and Schwartze 1982.
73. Henrich et al. 2005.
74. Camerer 2003.
75. Jensen, Call, and Tomasello 2007; Jensen, Call, and Tomasello 2013; Proctor et al. 2013.
76. Proctor et al. 2013.
77. Milinski 2013; Proctor, Brosnan, and de Waal 2013.
78. Xiao and Houser 2005. Indeed, human proposers seem to expect this and make more fair offers when communication is possible; Xiao and Houser 2009.
79. Brosnan and de Waal 2014.
80. Note that this anthropormophic language does not imply intent or understanding on the part of the subject; the same can be accomplished with evolved tendencies independent of either understanding or intention.
81. See, for examples, Hare et al. 2000; Tecwyn, Thorpe, and Chappell 2013; Beran 2002.
82. See chapter 1 by Woodruff in this volume for a deeper discussion of the challenges of growing in justice.

WORKS CITED

Asakawa-Haas, Kenji, Martina Schiestl, Thomas Bugnyar, and Jorg J. M. Massen. 2016. "Partner Choice in Raven (Corvus Corax) Cooperation." *PLoS ONE* 11, no. 6: e0156962. doi:10.1371/journal.pone.0156962.

Bartal, I. B.-A., J. Decety, and P. Mason. 2011. "Empathy and Pro-Social Behavior in Rats." *Science* 334: 1427–1430.

Bekoff, Marc. 2009. *Wild Justice: The Moral Lives of Animals*. Chicago: University of Chicago Press.

Beran, M. J. 2002. "Maintenance of Self-Imposed Delay of Gratification by Four Chimpanzees (Pan Troglodytes) and an Orangutan (Pongo Pygmaeus)." *Journal of General Psychology* 129, no. 1: 49–66.

Blake, P. R., K. McAuliffe, J. Corbit, T. C. Callaghan, O. Barry, A. Bowie, L. Kleutsch, et al. 2015. "The Ontogeny of Fairness in Seven Societies." *Nature* 528, no. 7581: 258–261. doi:10.1038/nature15703.

Boehm, C. 1999. *Hierarchy in the Forest: The Evolution of Egalitarian Behavior*. Cambridge: Harvard University Press.

Boesch, C. 1994. "Cooperative Hunting in Wild Chimpanzees." *Animal Behavior* 48: 653–667.

Bräuer, J., J. Call, and M. Tomasello. 2006. "Are Apes Really Inequity Averse?" *Proceedings of the Royal Society B* 273, no. 1605: 3123–3128. doi:10.1098/rspb.2006.3693.

Bräuer, Juliane, Josep Call, and Michael Tomasello. 2009. "Are Apes Inequity Averse? New Data on the Token-Exchange Paradigm." *American Journal of Primatology* 71, no. 2: 175–181. doi:10.1002/ajp.20639.

Brosnan, S. F. 2006. "Nonhuman Species' Reactions to Inequity and Their Implications for Fairness." *Social Justice Research* 19: 153–185.

Brosnan, Sarah F. 2011. "A Hypothesis of the Co-Evolution of Cooperation and Responses to Inequity." *Frontiers in Neuroscience* 5: 43. doi:10.3389/fnins.2011.00043.

Brosnan, S. F. 2013. "Justice and Fairness Related Behaviors in Non-Human Primates." *Proceedings of the National Academy of Sciences* 110: 10416–10423.

Brosnan, S. F. 2014. "Why an Evolutionary Perspective Is Critical to Understanding Moral Behavior in Humans." In *Challenges to Moral and Religious Belief*, edited by M. Bergmann and P. Kain, 195–219. New York: Oxford University Press.

Brosnan, Sarah F., and Redouan Bshary. 2016. "On Potential Links between Inequity Aversion and the Structure of Interactions for the Evolution of Cooperation." *Behaviour* (March): 1267–1292. doi:10.1163/1568539X-00003355.

Brosnan, Sarah, and F. B. M. de Waal. 2003. "Monkeys Reject Unequal Pay." *Nature* 425 (6955): 297–299. doi:10.1038/nature01963.

Brosnan, S. F., and F. B. M. de Waal. 2014. "Evolution of Responses to (Un)fairness." *Science* (September): 1251776. doi:10.1126/science.1251776.

Brosnan, Sarah F., Timothy Flemming, Catherine F. Talbot, Laura Mayo, and Tara Stoinski. 2011. "Orangutans (Pongo Pygmaeus) Do Not Form Expectations Based on Their Partner's Outcomes." *Folia Primatologica* 82, no. 1: 56–70. doi:10.1159/000328142.

Brosnan, Sarah F., Cassiopeia Freeman, and Frans B. M. de Waal. 2006. "Partner's Behavior, Not Reward Distribution, Determines Success in an Unequal Cooperative Task in Capuchin Monkeys." *American Journal of Primatology* 68, no. 7: 713–724. doi:10.1002/ajp.20261.

Brosnan, S. F., L. M. Hopper, S. Richey, H. D. Freeman, C. F. Talbot, S. D. Gosling, S. P. Lambeth, and S. J. Schapiro. 2015. "Personality Influences Responses to Inequity and Contrast in Chimpanzees." *Animal Behavior* 101: 75–87. doi:10.1016/j.anbehav.2014.12.019.

Brosnan, S. F., N. E. Newton-Fisher, and M. van Vugt. 2009. "A Melding of the Minds: When Primatology Meets Personality and Social Psychology." *Personality and Social Psychology Review* 13, no. 2: 129–147. doi:10.1177/1088868309335127.

Brosnan, S. F., H. C. Schiff, and F. B. M. de Waal. 2005. "Tolerance for Inequity May Increase with Social Closeness in Chimpanzees." *Proceedings of the Royal Society B* 272, no. 1560: 253–258. doi:10.1098/rspb.2004.2947.

Brosnan, Sarah F., Catherine Talbot, Megan Ahlgren, Susan P. Lambeth, and Steven J. Schapiro. 2010. "Mechanisms Underlying Responses to Inequitable Outcomes in Chimpanzees, Pan Troglodytes." *Animal Behaviour* 79, no. 6: 1229–1237. doi:10.1016/j.anbehav.2010.02.019.

Brosnan, S. F., B. J. Wilson, and M. J. Beran. 2012. "Old World Monkeys Are More Similar to Humans Than New World Monkeys When Playing a Coordination Game." *Proceedings of the Royal Society B* 279, no. 1733: 1522–1530. doi:10.1098/rspb.2011.1781.

Brucks, Désirée, Jennifer L. Essler, Sarah Marshall-Pescini, and Friederike Range. 2016. "Inequity Aversion Negatively Affects Tolerance and Contact-Seeking Behaviours towards Partner and Experimenter." *PLOS ONE* 11, no. 4: e0153799. doi:10.1371/journal.pone.0153799.

Bshary, R., and R. Bergmuller. 2008. "Distinguishing Four Fundamental Approaches to the Evolution of Helping." *Journal of Evolutionary Biology*: 405–420. doi: 10.1111/ j.1420-9101.2007.01482.x.

Bullinger, A. F., A. P. Melis, and M. Tomasello. 2011. "Chimpanzees, Pan Troglodytes, Prefer Individual over Collaborative Strategies towards Goals." *Animal Behavior* 82: 1135–1141.

Camerer, C. F. F. 2003. *Behavioral Game Theory: Experiments in Strategic Interactions*. Roundtable Series in Behavioral Economics. Princeton: Princeton University Press.

Chapais, B. 1991. "Non-Kin Alliances, and the Stability of Matrilineal Dominance Relations in Japanese Macaques." *Animal Behaviour* 41: 481–491.

Clay, Zanna, Lucie Ravaux, Frans B. M. de Waal, and Klaus Zuberbühler. 2016. "Bonobos (Pan Paniscus) Vocally Protest against Violations of Social Expectations." *Journal of Comparative Psychology* 130, no. 1: 44–54. doi:10.1037/a0040088.

Clutton-Brock, T., and P. H. Harvey. 1980. "Primates, Brains, and Ecology." *Journal of Zoology* 190: 390–423.

Daniel, W. J. 1943. "Higher Order Cooperative Problem Solving in Rats." *Journal of Comparative Psychology* 35, no. 3: 297–305. doi:10.1037/h0056629.

Deaner, R. O., K. Isler, J. Burkart, and C. P. van Schaik. 2007. "Overall Brain Size, and Not Encephalization Quotient, Best Predicts Cognitive Ability across Non-Human Primates." *Brain, Behavior, and Evolution* 70: 115–124.

De Waal, Frans. 1982. *Chimpanzee Politics: Power and Sex among Apes*. New York: Harper & Row.

De Waal, F. B. M., and M. L. Berger. 2000. "Payment for Labour in Monkeys." *Nature* 404: 563.

De Waal, Frans, and Jason M. Davis. 2003. "Capuchin Cognitive Ecology: Cooperation Based on Projected Returns." *Neuropsychologia* 41, no. 2: 221–228.

Dubreuil, D., M. S. Gentile, and E. Visalberghi. 2006. "Are Capuchin Monkeys (Cebus Apella) Inequity Averse?" *Proceedings of the Royal Society B* 273: 1223–1228.

Fehr, Ernst, and Urs Fischbacher. 2004. "Third-Party Punishment and Social Norms." *Evolution and Human Behavior* 25, no. 2: 63–87. doi:10.1016/S1090-5138(04)00005-4.

Fehr, Ernst, and K. M. Schmidt. 1999. "A Theory of Fairness, Competition, and Cooperation." *Quarterly Journal of Economics* 114: 817–868.

Fletcher, G. E. 2008. "Attending to the Outcome of Others: Disadvantageous Inequity Aversion in Male Capuchin Monkeys (Cebus Apella)." *American Journal of Primatology* 70: 901–905.

Freeman, Hani D., Jennifer Sullivan, Lydia M. Hopper, Catherine F. Talbot, Andrea N. Holmes, Nancy Schultz-Darken, Lawrence E. Williams, and Sarah F. Brosnan. 2013. "Different Responses to Reward Comparisons by Three Primate Species." *PLOS ONE* 8, no. 10: e76297. doi:10.1371/journal.pone.0076297.

Freidin, Esteban, Marina I. Cuello, and Alex Kacelnik. 2009. "Successive Negative Contrast in a Bird: Starlings' Behaviour after Unpredictable Negative Changes in Food Quality." *Animal Behaviour* 77, no. 4: 857–865. doi:10.1016/j.anbehav.2008.12.010.

Fruth, B., and G. Hohmann. 2002. "How Bonobos Handle Hunts and Harvests: Food Sharing." In *Behavioural Diversity in Chimpanzees and Bonobos*, edited by C. Boesch, G. Hohmann, and L. F. Marchant, 231–243. Cambridge: Cambridge University Press.

Gächter, S., B. Herrmann, and C. Thoni. 2010. "Culture and Cooperation." *Philosophical Transactions of the Royal Society B* 365, no. 1553: 2651–2661. doi:10.1098/rstb.2010.0135.

Guth, W., R. Schmittberger, and B. Schwartze. 1982. "An Experimental Analysis of Ultimatum Bargaining." *Journal of Economic Behavior and Organization* 3: 367–388.

Hall, Katie, S. P. Lambeth, S. J. Schapiro, and S. F. Brosnan. 2015. "Chimpanzees Respond Differently to Inequity Based on Relative Food Values." *Abstracts of the 38th Annual Meeting of the American Society of Primatologists*: 84.

Hare, Brian, Josep Call, Bryan Agnetta, and Michael Tomasello. 2000. "Chimpanzees Know What Conspecifics Do and Do Not See." *Animal Behaviour* 59, no. 4: 771–785. doi:10.1006/anbe.1999.1377.

Hare, B., A. P. Melis, V. Woods, S. Hastings, and R. Wrangham. 2007. "Tolerance Allows Bonobos to Outperform Chimpanzees on a Cooperative Task." *Current Biology* 17: 619–623.

Henrich, Joseph, Robert Boyd, Samuel Bowles, Colin Camerer, Ernst Fehr, Herbert Gintis, Richard McElreath, Michael Alvard, Abigail Barr, and Jean Ensminger. 2005. "'Economic Man' in Cross-Cultural Perspective: Behavioral Experiments in 15 Small-Scale Societies." *Behavioral and Brain Sciences* 28, no. 6: 795–814.

Hernandez-Lallement, Julen, Marijn van Wingerden, Christine Marx, Milan Srejic, and Tobias Kalenscher. 2015. "Rats Prefer Mutual Rewards in a Prosocial Choice Task." *Frontiers in Neuroscience* 8 (January): 443. doi:10.3389/fnins.2014.00443.

Hopper, Lydia M., Susan P. Lambeth, Steven J. Schapiro, and Sarah F. Brosnan. 2013a. "When Given the Opportunity, Chimpanzees Maximize Personal Gain Rather Than 'Level the Playing Field.'" *PeerJ* 1 (September): e165. doi:10.7717/peerj.165.

Hopper, L. M., S. P. Lambeth, S. J. Schapiro, B. J. Bernacky, and S. F. Brosnan. 2013b. "The Ontogeny of Social Comparisons in Rhesus Macaques (Macaca Mulatta)." *Journal of Primatology* 2: 109. doi:10.4172/2167-6801.1000109.

Hopper, L. M., S. P. Lambeth, S. J. Schapiro, and S. F. Brosnan. 2014. "Social Comparison Mediates Chimpanzees' Responses to Loss, Not Frustration." *Animal Cognition* 17, no. 6: 1303–1311. doi:10.1007/s10071-014-0765-9.

Horowitz, Alexandra. 2012. "Fair Is Fine, but More Is Better: Limits to Inequity Aversion in the Domestic Dog." *Social Justice Research* 25, no. 2: 195–212. doi:10.1007/s11211-012-0158-7.

Jaeggi, Adrian V., Jeroen M. G. Stevens, and Carel P. Van Schaik. 2010. "Tolerant Food Sharing and Reciprocity Is Precluded by Despotism among Bonobos but Not Chimpanzees." *American Journal of Physical Anthropology* 143, no. 1: 41–51. doi:10.1002/ajpa.21288.

Jensen, K., J. Call, and M. Tomasello. 2007. "Chimpanzees Are Rational Maximizers in an Ultimatum Game." *Science* 318: 107–109.

Jensen, Keith, Josep Call, and Michael Tomasello. 2013. "Chimpanzee Responders Still Behave Like Rational Maximizers." *Proceedings of the National Academy of Sciences* 110, no. 20: E1837–E1837.

Jerison, H. J. 1985. "Animal Intelligence As Encephalization." *Philosophical Transactions of the Royal Society B* 308: 21–35.

Konner, Melvin. 2002. *The Tangled Wing: Biological Constraints on the Human Spirit*, 2nd ed. New York: Times Books.

Loewenstein, G. F., L. Thompson, and M. H. Bazerman. 1989. "Social Utility and Decision Making in Interpersonal Contexts." *Journal of Personality and Social Psychology* 57, no. 3: 426–441.

Massen, Jorg J. M., Caroline Ritter, and Thomas Bugnyar. 2015. "Tolerance and Reward Equity Predict Cooperation in Ravens (Corvus Corax)." *Scientific Reports* 5 (October): 15021. doi:10.1038/srep15021.

Massen, Jorg J. M., Lisette M. Van Den Berg, Berry M. Spruijt, and Elisabeth H. M. Sterck. 2012. "Inequity Aversion in Relation to Effort and Relationship Quality in Long-Tailed Macaques (Macaca Fascicularis): Inequity Aversion in Macaca Fascicularis." *American Journal of Primatology* 74, no. 2: 145–156. doi:10.1002/ajp.21014.

McAuliffe, Katherine, Linda W. Chang, Kristin L. Leimgruber, Rebecca Spaulding, Peter R. Blake, and Laurie R. Santos. 2015. "Capuchin Monkeys, Cebus Apella, Show No Evidence for Inequity Aversion in a Costly Choice Task." *Animal Behaviour* 103 (May): 65–74. doi:10.1016/j.anbehav.2015.02.014.

Melis, A. P., B. Hare, and M. Tomasello. 2006a. "Chimpanzees Recruit the Best Collaborators." *Science* 311: 1297–1300.

Melis, A. P., B. Hare, and M. Tomasello. 2006b. "Engineering Cooperation in Chimpanzees: Tolerance Constraints on Cooperation." *Animal Behavior* 72: 275–286.

Mendres, Kimberly A., and Frans B. M. de Waal. 2000. "Capuchins Do Cooperate: The Advantage of an Intuitive Task." *Animal Behaviour* 60, no. 4: 523–529. doi:10.1006/anbe.2000.1512.

Milinski, M. 2013. "Chimps Play Fair in the Ultimatum Game." *Proceedings of the National Academy of Sciences* 110, no. 6: 1978–1979. doi:10.1073/pnas.1222132110.

Mustoe, Aaryn C., April M. Harnisch, Benjamin Hochfelder, Jon Cavanaugh, and Jeffrey A. French. 2016. "Inequity Aversion Strategies between Marmosets Are Influenced by Partner Familiarity and Sex but Not by Oxytocin." *Animal Behaviour* 114 (April): 69–79. doi:10.1016/j.anbehav.2016.01.025.

Neiworth, Julie J., Elizabeth T. Johnson, Katherine Whillock, Julia Greenberg, and Vanessa Brown. 2009. "Is a Sense of Inequity an Ancestral Primate Trait? Testing Social Inequity in Cotton Top Tamarins (Saguinus Oedipus)." *Journal of Comparative Psychology* 123, no. 1: 10–17. doi:10.1037/a0012662.

Noe, R., and P. Hammerstein. 1995. "Biological Markets." *Trends in Ecology and Evolution* 10, no. 8: 336–339.

Oberliessen, Lina, Julen Hernandez-Lallement, Sandra Schäble, Marijn van Wingerden, Maayke Seinstra, and Tobias Kalenscher. 2016. "Inequity

Aversion in Rats, Rattus Norvegicus." *Animal Behaviour* 115 (May): 157–166. doi:10.1016/j.anbehav.2016.03.007.

Ostojić, Ljerka, and Nicola S. Clayton. 2013. "Behavioural Coordination of Dogs in a Cooperative Problem-Solving Task with a Conspecific and a Human Partner." *Animal Cognition* 17, no. 2: 445–459. doi:10.1007/s10071-013-0676-1.

Packer, Craig. 1988. "Constraints on the Evolution of Reciprocity: Lessons from Cooperative Hunting." *Ethology and Sociobiology* 9: 137–147.

Perry, S., J. H. Manson, G. Dower, and E. Wikbert. 2003. "White-Faced Capuchins Cooperate to Rescue a Groupmate from a Boa Constrictor." *Folia Primatologica* 74: 109–111. doi:10.1159/000070008.

Pierce, Jessica, and Marc Bekoff. 2012. "Wild Justice Redux: What We Know about Social Justice in Animals and Why It Matters." *Social Justice Research* 25, no. 2: 122–139. doi:10.1007/s11211-012-0154-y.

Price, Sara A., and Sarah F. Brosnan. 2012. "To Each According to His Need? Variability in the Responses to Inequity in Non-Human Primates." *Social Justice Research* 25, no. 2: 140–169. doi:10.1007/s11211-012-0153-z.

Proctor, Darby, Sarah F. Brosnan, and Frans B. M. de Waal. 2013. "How Fairly Do Chimpanzees Play the Ultimatum Game?" *Communicative and Integrative Biology* 6, no. 3: e23819. doi:10.4161/cib.23819.

Proctor, D., R. A. Williamson, F. B. M. de Waal, and S. F. Brosnan. 2013. "Chimpanzees Play the Ultimatum Game." *Proceedings of the National Academy of Sciences* 110, no. 6: 2070–2075. doi:10.1073/pnas.1220806110.

Range, Friederike, Lisa Horn, Zsófia Virányi, and Ludwig Huber. 2009. "The Absence of Reward Induces Inequity Aversion in Dogs." *Proceedings of the National Academy of Sciences* 106, no. 1: 340–345.

Range, Friederike, Karin Leitner, and Zsófia Virányi. 2012. "The Influence of the Relationship and Motivation on Inequity Aversion in Dogs." *Social Justice Research* 25, no. 2: 170–194. doi:10.1007/s11211-012-0155-x.

Reynolds, G. S. 1961. "Behavioral Contrast." *Journal of the Experimental Analysis of Behavior* 4: 441–466.

Rilling, J. K., and T. Insel. 1999. "The Primate Neocortex in Comparative Perspective Using Magnetic Resonance Imaging." *Journal of Human Evolution* 16: 191–233.

Rutte, Claudia, and Michael Taborsky. 2007. "The Influence of Social Experience on Cooperative Behaviour of Rats (Rattus Norvegicus): Direct vs. Generalised Reciprocity." *Behavioral Ecology and Sociobiology* 62, no. 4: 499–505. doi:10.1007/s00265-007-0474-3.

Silberberg, Alan, Lara Crescimbene, Elsa Addessi, James R. Anderson, and Elisabetta Visalberghi. 2009. "Does Inequity Aversion Depend on a Frustration Effect? A Test with Capuchin Monkeys (Cebus Apella)." *Animal Cognition* 12, no. 3: 505–509. doi:10.1007/s10071-009-0211-6.

Strandburg-Peshkin, Ariana, Damien R. Farine, Iain D. Couzin, and Margaret C. Crofoot. 2015. "Shared Decision-Making Drives Collective Movement in Wild Baboons." *Science* 348, no. 6241: 1358–1361. doi:10.1126/science.aaa5099.

Suchak, Malini, Timothy M. Eppley, Matthew W. Campbell, and Frans B. M. de Waal. 2014. "Ape Duos and Trios: Spontaneous Cooperation with Free Partner Choice in Chimpanzees." *PeerJ* 2 (June): e417. doi:10.7717/peerj.417.

Takimoto, A., and K. Fujita. 2011. "I Acknowledge Your Help: Capuchin Monkeys' Sensitivity to Others' Labor." *Animal Cognition*: 1–11.

Talbot, C. F., H. D. Freeman, L. E. Williams, and S. F. Brosnan. 2011. "Squirrel Monkeys' Response to Inequitable Outcomes Indicates a Behavioural Convergence within the Primates." *Biology Letters* 7, no. 5: 680–682. doi:10.1098/rsbl.2011.0211.

Tecwyn, Emma C., Susannah K. S. Thorpe, and Jackie Chappell. 2013. "A Novel Test of Planning Ability: Great Apes Can Plan Step-by-Step but Not in Advance of Action." *Behavioural Processes* (October): 174–184. doi:10.1016/j.beproc.2013.09.016.

Van Wolkenten, Megan, Sarah F. Brosnan, and Frans B. M. de Waal. 2007. "Inequity Responses of Monkeys Modified by Effort." *Proceedings of the National Academy of Sciences* 104, no. 47: 18854–18859.

Wascher, Claudia A. F., and Thomas Bugnyar. 2013. "Behavioral Responses to Inequity in Reward Distribution and Working Effort in Crows and Ravens." *PLOS ONE* 8, no. 2: e56885. doi:10.1371/journal.pone.0056885.

Widdig, Anja, Wolf Juergen Streich, and Guenter Tembrock. 2000. "Coalition Formation among Male Barbary Macaques (Macaca Sylvanus)." *American Journal of Primatology* 50, no. 1: 37–51.

Xiao, E., and D. Houser. 2005. "Emotional Expression in Human Punishment Behavior." *Proceedings of the National Academy of Sciences* 102, no. 20: 7398–7401.

Xiao, Erte, and Daniel Houser. 2009. "Avoiding the Sharp Tongue: Anticipated Written Messages Promote Fair Economic Exchange." *Journal of Economic Psychology* 30, no. 3: 393–404. doi:10.1016/j.joep.2008.12.002.

Chapter 7

The Dialectical Activity of Becoming Just

JON GARTHOFF

INTRODUCTION

In this chapter, I explicate connections between psychological theories of moral cognitive development and philosophical theories of virtue acquisition. More specifically, I discuss how resources from Lawrence Kohlberg's account of moral development (once suitably revised) augment our understanding of the acquisition of virtues; and I discuss how Talbot Brewer's explication of what he terms "dialectical activities" both brings out and enhances the appeal of moderately rationalist theories of moral development such as Kohlberg's. I close by showing how these interconnections help make sense of one of the more vexing questions of ethical theory, namely, how to think about ethics in nonideal circumstances. Throughout I use development of the individual virtue of justice as an example to illustrate these connections between cognitive development and acquisition of virtue.[1]

THE IDEA OF DEVELOPMENT IN COGNITIVE PSYCHOLOGY

There is a generic notion of development that denotes any change over time. As this idea was deployed in twentieth-century cognitive developmental psychology, however, it denoted the more specific phenomenon of progress through *stages*. This idea of development was distilled most clearly in the thought of Jean Piaget and his followers, notably including Lawrence Kohlberg and Carol Gilligan.[2] To use philosophers' categories, this tradition is modestly rationalist, in that it aspires to be empirically informed without claiming that empirical investigation is the only source of human knowledge. Members of this tradition often regard Jean-Jacques Rousseau and/or Immanuel Kant, themselves modest rationalists by this standard, as historical inspirations.[3] I use Kohlberg's account as the basis for exposition here.

First, there is the idea of progress. Progress is a kind of change; accordingly, it occurs only in temporally extended beings. Progress is not only change, however; it is change for the better. Thus, progress is possible only for beings subject to standards of evaluation. This includes at least all functionally organized individuals, since all such individuals may be evaluated relative to the standard of success in fulfillment of their function.[4] I refer to individuals subject to standards of evaluation as "entities." Living organisms are paradigm entities, as they are subject to biological standards of evaluation such as flourishing and Darwinian fitness. By contrast, fundamental physical particles are individuals but not entities, since they are neither functionally organized nor otherwise subject to standards of evaluation.

Not only is development a kind of progress, but it is also a normal kind. To say that development is normal is not to say that, as a statistical matter, most entities develop fully. Kohlberg claimed that most actual adults reached only stages two to four of his six-stage developmental scheme. But there are notions of normalcy compatible with statistical unlikelihood. It is normal for a sperm to fertilize an egg, for example, even though the vast majority of sperm do not do this. The relevant notion of normalcy is difficult to define precisely, but it consists roughly in success under ordinary—or perhaps sufficiently favorable—circumstances.[5]

Next is the idea of a stage, which is more complicated than it first appears. The relevant notion of a stage is discrete and sequential. Because stages are discrete, they are states that hang together with relative stasis. Thus, they at least approximate equilibrium states, which will not change unless subject to external influences. They also must have at least a minimal degree of stability—ability to retain or restore equilibrium under external influences—since they would otherwise not be sufficiently long-lived to qualify as discrete.[6] Stages contrast with the transitions between stages, which by contrast are characteristically transient. Accordingly, any developmental system is to some extent punctuated; it involves alternation between periods of relative stasis (the developmental stages) and periods of relative change (the transitions).

That stages are sequential subsumes several ideas. First, they are ordered, not mere collections or sets. This ordering, furthermore, is directional: there is a starting stage, and there are subsequent stages. One consequence is that it is not standardly possible to bypass stages: if an entity is to pass from the first stage to the third, it must do so by passing through the second. Conjoined with the idea of development as progress, a second consequence is that backsliding is not standardly possible: if an entity has passed from the first stage to the second, it will tend either to remain at the second or to pass to the third or beyond, but it will not characteristically return to the first. A third consequence is that transitions between stages are understood as a mixed state, not as an additional intervening stage. Also, mixed states are characteristically relatively unstable, in that those in them tend either to fall back into the previous stage or to advance to the next.

In Kohlberg's scheme, there are six stages of moral cognitive development, organized into three levels of two stages each. The first level he labels "pre-conventional," and it is characterized by a protomoral conception of norms as imposed by external authorities, with an imposed system of punishments and rewards serving as the principal inducement to conformity with these norms. The image of a very young child, almost entirely dependent on a parent for his or her ability to survive and flourish, suggests the spirit of this level. To the extent that these external authorities love the individual and manifest this love by attending to the individual's needs and interests, the individual will tend to progress toward the second level of development.[7] Some people never progress out of this level, and so they have adult conceptions of ethics characterized by subservience to legal or religious authorities or by the mutual manipulation of marketlike interactions.

The second level is labeled "conventional," since it is characterized by a conception of norms as socially given and corresponding to social roles.[8] The inducement to conformity with these norms is social approval for satisfying them and social disapproval for violating them. The image of a classroom of students or a group of teammates illustrates the spirit of this level, at least in its earliest incarnation. Children who have internalized the norms of these social groups, who want to be good students or teammates not only to satisfy authorities or earn rewards but also to live up to social expectations, have reached this level. As people mature, they become involved in increasingly broad and various social relations and roles, including most expansively citizenship, a social role whose adoption involves internalization of the overall societal system. When others within the social environment surrounding an individual live up to the expectations of their social roles, and when these social roles genuinely conduce to the good of the individual participant, it is expected that that individual will progress to the third level.[9]

The third level Kohlberg labels "post-conventional." At this level, an abstract conception of ethics is held, which transcends any actual social order and is used both to vindicate and to criticize individuals and social arrangements. It is expected that people will continue to progress toward and through this level if the individuals and social systems they live with treat them fairly, unless they reach the highest stage of development, at which point their moral conception becomes settled.

COGNITIVE DEVELOPMENT AND ACQUIRING JUSTICE

What has this account of moral cognitive development to do with acquisition of virtue? This is an underexplored issue, perhaps oddly so. After all, the two topics have much in common. Each concerns how human beings become better over time, combining claims about progress in human moral cognition with claims about how features of human psychology, including features of our psychology not constitutive of finite rational agency as such, both constrain and give rise to that progress.

No doubt there are many reasons these traditions have not been joined. One obstacle is that theories of moral cognitive development mainly grew out of work by psychologists, whereas theories of virtue grew mainly out of work by philosophers. In professional psychology, what I have characterized as modestly rationalist developmental psychology has fallen into disrepute, moreover, in part because of resistance to empirical research programs with remotely controversial moral presumptions. In philosophy, the culprit is exaggerated opposition between virtue theory, inspired by ancient Greek rationalism, and self-consciously modern rationalism descending from Rousseau and Kant. In this case, there are many important exceptions, notably including Barbara Herman.[10] These theorists combining ancient Greek and Kantian thought, however, tend not to relate their work to the developmental theories popular within the Kantian tradition a generation and a half ago.

This is partly for good reason. As controversial as the twentieth-century theories of moral cognitive development are, the idea that some suitably reformulated descendant of these theories will be correct remains plausible. A directly analogous account of individual virtue acquisition, by contrast, would not be plausible. The range of obstacles to intrastage improvement is too variegated and idiosyncratic to admit of a streamlined classification like Kohlberg's. It is also extremely unlikely, at this finer grain, that any single linearly ordered sequence of substages is adequate to encapsulate the variety of ways in which people improve.

Consider the obstacles to acquiring the virtue of justice described in Paul Woodruff's contribution to this volume.[11] Woodruff, following Plato, conceives of justice as giving individuals and groups their due, maintains that justice helps bind together communities of all sizes and scopes, and maintains further that there is mutual reinforcement between justice in the structure of a community and justice in the character of members of that community. One important example he cites of an obstacle to acquisition of justice is temptation: a person may be tempted to treat others unjustly by considering what he or she may gain by doing so, such as what occurs when a vacation is enabled by underreporting income on a tax form or when a promotion is achieved by spreading misleading rumors about a rival. There are too many distinct sources of temptation to classify readily, and these sources are too culturally local. Learning to resist or extirpate one type of temptation, moreover, may not greatly bolster the ability to resist or extirpate another type. What must be given up to live justly is often genuinely valuable, and successfully subordinating the value of a vacation to the value of justice may not bring with it success in subordinating the value of professional recognition to the value of justice.

Or consider another of Woodruff's obstacles: the absence of suitable models or coaches in the community.[12] The models or coaches an individual needs will at times be dependent on peculiarities of his or her situation. As a person changes jobs, for example, he or she will need models or coaches pertaining to just action in the new role, particularly if this new role is one of greater social power. Having children, which can generate progress toward justice when it liberates individuals from excessive selfishness, can also inhibit progress toward justice when unselfish but nevertheless self-oriented concern for children leads to making exceptions on their behalf. Furthermore, as individuals progress through stages of moral cognitive development, they need to find models or coaches appropriate to the distinctive challenges of their new stage. A civic-minded mentor emphasizing social over selfish goods may help develop justice in paying taxes if the temptation is a vacation for oneself but may not if the temptation is to give money to a charitable or religious institution.

A further reason to doubt that the fine-grained acquisition of excellences by individuals can be modeled in the same way as a coarse-grained account of moral cognitive development is that their subject matters, despite considerable similarity and overlap, are not the same. Kohlberg's theory does not assess individuals by virtue; it assesses, rather, the moral understanding that individuals have achieved.[13] In his investigations, Kohlberg did not attempt to discern how well his subjects treated people in their own lives. Nor did he attempt to discern how well people acted under experimental conditions, as is sometimes explored by work on the situation-specificity of action dispositions.[14] Rather, he and his team would provide anecdotal thought experiments and then seek to elicit the full range of considerations a subject took to be relevant to the anecdote presented. Often the anecdote was controversial, a difficult case for people at all stages of moral development. The actions recommended by experimental subjects in response to anecdotes were not used to classify subjects into developmental stages. The range of considerations appealed to by the subject as justification for those actions was instead what was deemed pertinent.

Thus, theories of virtue pertain in the first instance to moral character, whereas theories of moral cognition pertain in the first instance to moral understanding. While there are limits to this contrast, as both Kohlberg's developmental theory and Aristotelian virtue theory emphasize, there are at least two ways these can come apart in an individual's psychology. One is akrasia, where an individual understands how to act but is inadequately motivated by this understanding when making practical judgments.[15] The cases of unresisted temptation articulated earlier are examples of akrasia concerning justice. The other way is inverse akrasia, where an individual exercises good practical judgment notwithstanding his or her distorted moral understanding.[16] It is difficult to articulate an uncontroversial example of inverse akrasia, but the general idea (in the case of justice) is of someone who believes an unjust action should be done but who fails to act in accord with this belief, instead performing a just action with a guilty conscience.

Though he does not explicitly anticipate the category, Kohlberg's theory entails that there is little room for inverse akrasia. This is because he posits what he calls an "isomorphism" between philosophical understanding and psychological explanation: in Kohlberg's account, it is partly because an individual has a better understanding of morality that his or her moral cognition is more fully developed.[17] This claim may seem obvious, but much recent work in both philosophy and psychology has emphasized gaps between moral understanding and quality of moral cognition.[18]

Kohlberg likely overstates this connection, and he certainly pays insufficient heed to the distinction between reasons for which one acts and reasons that one can articulate. Indeed, there are two important distinctions there: between practical and theoretical understanding of what to do and between either of these and their articulation. Kohlberg's theory is not, however, blind to these distinctions. The need for patient interrogation of experimental subjects arises because he did not expect that all the reasons we think about in a circumstance of action are immediately or readily available.[19] While the claim is not crucial here, I doubt that the scope for inverse akrasia is large, and I suspect recent trends overstate prospects for more advanced moral cognition that arises from a source other than superior moral understanding.[20]

The scope of akrasia in human practical judgment, by contrast, is considerable. This is no objection to Kohlberg, since he does not purport to assess the quality of will or character. But it is a further obstacle—beyond fineness of grain and variegation of moves toward virtue—to using resources from moral cognitive development to illuminate virtue acquisition, or vice versa. In what follows, I introduce resources from Talbot Brewer to help confront these obstacles.

DIALECTICAL ACTIVITY AND ACQUIRING JUSTICE

An important resource for elaborating developmental cognitive psychology in the context of virtue acquisition is found in Brewer's work on what he calls "dialectical activity."[21] These are activities that tend to draw us back into engagement with them the more deeply we become engaged with them. Dialectical activities also tend to be more valuable for us the more deeply we engage them. For some dialectical activities, there is no end, in human conditions at least, to the prospects for reengaging with them.

Though Brewer does not himself present his idea this way, it may help to view dialectical activities as belonging to three broad (and nonexclusive) categories: creations, appreciations, and personal relationships. Creations include not only the intellectual creation of a philosopher or physicist but also the artistic creation of a painter or musician. Crafts can also exhibit creative dialectical activity, even where aesthetic ambition is limited by practical function. Appreciations involve engagement with any of these sorts of creations, such as when we become absorbed in observing a painting or listening to a piece of music. Personal relationships are various, of course, but they can involve dialectical activity almost without regard to the social relation involved, by virtue of the fact that people in general warrant sustained engagement and attention.[22]

A few features of dialectic activities in general are worth emphasizing. One is that they must be finally, which is to say noninstrumentally, good. They have this final value, moreover, independent of idiosyncratic attitudes we take toward them.[23] In music appreciation, for example, music is not good merely because we like it. Note that this is compatible with the claim that music is good because it is good for us, and we matter. The crucial point is not that the goodness of dialectical activities is wholly independent from us or from our nature. The crucial point is rather that the goodness for us of these activities does not depend on our taking an appropriate (or, indeed, any) interest in them.

Even so, our ability actually to enjoy the goodness of dialectical activities depends on our ability to take appropriate interest in them. As Brewer explains, we are characteristically ignorant of the precise nature of the value of these activities prior to extended engagement with them.[24] It is through engaging with them that we further disclose their value and so characteristically come to value them more deeply and perfectly. Without such sustained engagement, characterized by repeated occasions of absorbed attention, it is not possible either to realize the good of the activity or to appreciate fully what the good of the activity consists in. Brewer thinks these facts do not sit well with the hypothesis that their good depends on our idiosyncratic attitudes toward them, since these attitudes are so unspecific prior to our engagement.[25]

Sometimes dialectical activities run their course, so that their value for us is effectively exhausted. A child might become absorbed, for example, in the task of discovering an optimal strategy for playing tic-tac-toe. The child might return to this activity on multiple occasions, each time improving his or her understanding of different aspects of the game. Eventually, however, the game is solved, and at that point, thinking about the strategy of the game ceases to be of recurring interest, and the activities both of playing the game and of thinking about its strategy cease to be important sources of self-development. A simple game illustrates this point clearly, but it is not the only relevant example. A musical composition may be rich enough to reward repeated and sustained attention but not so rich as to support such interest indefinitely. In this example, there may continue to be enjoyment in hearing the music, but it will not be the dialectical activity of engaging with the composition or with the experience of hearing its performance.[26]

Crucially for both Brewer's purposes and ours, however, not all dialectical activities are similarly exhaustible. Certain intellectual activities, including but not limited to philosophy and mathematics, are like this. For beings like us, progress in these endeavors is possible no matter how much we already understand about the subject matter.[27] Relationships with other people can also be like this, especially when multiple parties to the relationship are mutually committed to developing themselves; we can continue to learn more about both ourselves and others, and this unfolding can stand in a positive feedback loop with maturation. As Brewer emphasizes, living well also has this feature. Though the ideal of living well can always be approached, it cannot be fully satisfied.[28] It is also a dialectical activity, since our initial grasp of the value of living well is vague and inchoate; the nature of this value becomes increasingly revealed to us the longer and more deeply we engage it. The last two examples here come together in what Brewer labels, following Aristotle, "character friendship": this is a relationship between people who both seek to improve themselves and live well and who are mutually committed to helping each other succeed in this activity.[29]

Brewer uses discussion of character friendship to help fill out the relationship between dialectical activity and acquisition of virtue. One of the most illuminating and distinctive aspects of Brewer's discussion is his emphasis on the shared history of friends. This shared history is crucial to why character friendship is necessary for acquisition of virtue. Brewer writes:

> When a friendship goes well, the parties to it find over and again that they are able to improvise mutually appealing ways of conversing and interacting. When they do, their history of successful improvisations both testifies to, and helps extend and refine, a shared evaluative sensibility. The rituals and repetitions of friends and lovers are never mere repetitions, because the memory of each prior enactment provides the next enactment with a subjective patina that increases its depth and resonance.[30]

He further characterizes the potentials for added meaning and texture in these relationships as "limitless."[31] In the remainder of this section, I expand on this idea in the context of acquiring the individual virtue of justice. The ideas of limitlessness and the irreplaceability of shared history in ongoing efforts to develop virtue also serve as themes for later sections of this chapter.

Notice immediately that the hypothesis that dialectical activity through engagement with character friendships is necessary to acquire the virtue of justice helps explain several features of this virtue. First, as Woodruff notes in chapter 1 of this volume, justice requires "a lifelong project requiring a serious commitment." This is characteristic of many dialectical activities. Second, Woodruff observes that acquiring and maintaining justice require "finding friends and companions who make similar commitments." This, too, agrees with Brewer's understanding of the development of virtue.

Both of these features can be illustrated with examples. Some dialectical activities are explicitly about justice, such as when union members meet to discuss their terms of employment and the actions needed to protect or improve those terms. If such meetings are mere discussions of strategy or tactics, structured only around the value of better terms for union members, then their potential for improving the individual justice of members is limited. But the meetings need not be limited in this way. They could involve a broader perspective on the justice or injustice of their treatment, including comparisons with historical examples. This perspective could involve criticism not only of management but also of leaders or those members who seek to advance union interests (or selfish interests) without regard to the justice of doing so. The shared nature of the relevant experiences and the concreteness of the discussion, together with the complexity and value of the enterprise, make this a prime candidate for dialectical activity. When a union proposal is rebuffed, for example, and a union leader proposes significant concessions, a number of questions arise. Was rejection of the proposal reasonable or unreasonable? Are the leaders sincerely advancing common interests in advising concessions? Would accepting concessions still constitute fair terms of employment? All this and more could be investigated by the union members, with new subtleties revealed during each round of discussion. If movement in the direction of justice is achieved, this can forge bonds of community both within the union and between the union and the broader society. It can also teach everyone involved more about what people are due, in this social circumstance, for their labor. Absent the concrete features of the scenario, there would be far stricter limits on the potential of the activity to enable its participants to become more just. A hypothetical discussion in a policy forum of structurally similar cases, while also of potential value, would be no substitute for lived engagement.

This example also brings out a third congruence between Brewer's account of dialectical activity and an account of virtue like Woodruff's: their common requirement of subjectivity. Brewer refers to the "subjective patina" of shared experience during the dialectical activities of character friendship as increasing "depth and resonance."[32] Woodruff advances what he calls a "subjective condition" on justice, which he glosses as a necessity that people *feel* they receive what they are due.[33] This is important partly because the disposition to act justly, even where this disposition helps constitute the virtue of justice, often depends reciprocally on the presence of a similar disposition in others. A disposition to pay taxes, to perform national service, or to refrain from littering may depend for its rationality on others having dispositions to do the same; it is important for justice to be seen and felt, thereby activating these reciprocal dispositions and entering a positive feedback loop with others. But this is not the only reason there are subjective conditions on justice. Absent engagement with others as one's own friends (or fellow citizens), it will be psychologically more difficult, and sometimes perhaps even impossible, to engage fully in the dialectical activities that help reveal the value of justice and accordingly help strengthen and extend dispositions and commitments to act justly.

DIALECTICAL ACTIVITY AND COGNITIVE DEVELOPMENT

Let us now return to the topic of moral cognitive development, reconsidered in light of the intervening discussion. Making use of Brewer's idea of dialectical activity, we can fill out our understanding of moral development within stages. More specifically, Brewer's idea helps us to see how it is possible for there to be indefinite progress toward a state that is antecedently only inchoately specified. We do not need a specific, antecedently articulated conception of morality in general, or of any virtue in particular, for this progress to occur.

Resources from developmental psychology also help us to fill out Brewer's account of virtue acquisition. As we learn more about the virtues by engaging in relationships with others, we not only better appreciate the good in them, but we also progressively achieve substages of development in the direction of virtue. Having achieved the virtuous disposition to pay taxes without regard to vacation, an individual is unlikely to fall back into his or her earlier disposition to cheat on taxes for this reason. These achievements are relatively resistant to backsliding. This relative resistance is likely less strong than the resistance of Kohlberg's stages, since less is involved in the relevant progress than wholesale reconfiguration of moral orientation. Movement toward acquisition of virtue will typically be more significantly contextualized, especially at the outset, reflecting in part whatever truth there is in situationism. But within these specific domains or relationships, a micro-level development through substages is realized.[34]

These observations reveal that—strictly speaking—stability of character is not what is characteristic of a virtuous human being. Stability entails stasis; it is the tendency of a state of equilibrium to restore itself despite external influences. Resilience also involves relative stasis, but it is stasis compatible with greater influence by new circumstances; it is the tendency of an equilibrium state either to restore itself or to move to a new, nearby equilibrium state.[35] One context in which the concept of resilience is important is environmental change. In view of the magnitude of social and economic changes that will be necessary to cope with global warming during the coming century, as well as the unprecedented pace of technological change, we will need theories of how to change with these changes without falling into dangerous disequilibrium.

In our context of virtue acquisition, it is not so much the rate of unavoidable change that generates the need for the flexibility of resilience. It is, instead, the conjunction of our limits with the way our understanding of ethics is generated by historical relationships. A generalized understanding of morality, such as that provided by Kant's Categorical Imperative, is of limited use in virtue acquisition even if it is correct. An important lesson of Gilligan's critique of Kohlberg, as well as of Herman's critique of starker forms of Kantianism, is that abstract principles such as these can be fully understood and fully incorporated into life only when they are made concrete through lived experience.[36] But given the limits of our cognitive and emotional capacities, and also the brevity of our life spans, this means that our understanding of what it is to realize an overarching principle like the Categorical Imperative is always extremely partial. We do not have advance understanding in meaningful detail of what the character of such an individual is like, since understanding that requires understanding all the social circumstances that the individual faces, and these change over time. To make sense of progress and development in such circumstances, we need to understand movement from one equilibrium to a related but distinct equilibrium.[37] Character resilience thus comes only with the flexibility of ongoing learning.

This relevance of context and history to development of moral understanding—a theme both of Gilligan's critique of Kohlberg and of Herman's Kantianism—*strengthens* the rationalist tradition of moral psychology in which Gilligan and Herman both participate. There is appreciation of this point, with respect to Herman's contributions. While there is dispute about whether she has understood Kant better than her predecessors, there is fairly widespread agreement that she has made Kantian ethics more appealing, since Herman's Kant is more flexible, less rigoristic, and more sensitive to context than earlier interpretations. Perhaps less appreciated is that the same is true of Gilligan. She is often known mainly as a critic of Kohlberg, but her positive view shares far more with Kohlberg than with radical postmodern views that exaggerate her critique.[38]

The earlier discussion of Brewer also helps explain how this is possible. Brewer shares with Gilligan and Herman an emphasis on the socially concrete and historically situated. But this is compatible with understanding that goods realized in this situated way are instantiations of broader, more general goods. Indeed, on Brewer's account, there must be such broader goods, for it is through engagement with these that we acquire a better understanding of the value of their concrete realizations. We better understand the value of friendship, for example, by engaging in activities with friends. Gilligan famously charged Kohlberg with seeing moral development as too closely akin to improved ability to solve math problems, as though a disengaged but plausible proposed resolution to a conflict between two people were as good as one worked out through conversation between them.[39] This concern is blunted if we reformulate Kohlberg's stages so that math problem frames do not count, on their own, as more developed. A child who approaches a schoolyard dispute as if it were a math problem fails to appreciate the relevance of the context of the dispute. A child who approaches a schoolyard dispute only by seeking to repair interpersonal relationships and assuage hurt feelings fails to appreciate the need for this repair to be premised on independent goods and conceptions of fairness. It is only when each of these aspects of moral understanding is integrated with the other that genuine progress in moral cognition occurs. This example helps explain affinities among Gilligan, Herman, and Brewer, in much the same way as the earlier example of the union meeting helped explain the affinities between Brewer and Woodruff.

This in turn shows that care must be taken when assessing charges that an ethical theory, or an account of moral cognition, is overly intellectualized. Such charges are sometimes appropriate, but it is easy also to understate the importance of intellectual engagement in a good human life. To claim that a certain degree of intellectual engagement is developmentally necessary for moral improvement is not to claim that the relevant improvement could be achieved merely through intellectual means.[40] Nor is it to claim that the good in question is closely akin to purely intellectual development, relevantly similar to better understanding mathematics. It is to say only that essential elements are missing when the specifically intellectual element of moral cognitive development is denied or downplayed.

BECOMING JUST IN NONIDEAL CONDITIONS

To this point, I have attempted to show how resources from Brewer's work on dialectical activity and virtue acquisition can be used to augment theories of moral cognitive development such as Kohlberg's, and vice versa. Some abstract structures of development theory (such as the discreteness of stages and the absence of backsliding) can be incorporated into an account of virtue acquisition. Some of the features of dialectical activities help to explain how moral development is possible, also how progress in appreciating a good that is at the outset valued only incipiently or inchoately can nevertheless be accomplished.

In the concluding section of this chapter, I consider how best to understand acquisition of virtue, including especially the individual virtue of justice, in nonideal conditions. This is not a topic taken up explicitly by Brewer or by prominent theorists of moral cognitive development.[41] I believe it is worth doing here, however, for the proposed integration of moral cognitive development with the theory of virtue helps make sense of this perplexing domain. Here again, resources from Brewer assist in the task.

It may help to distinguish three kinds of morally nonideal conditions. By morally nonideal conditions, I do not mean merely conditions that interfere with what would otherwise be morally obligatory or laudable aims, as when there are nonculpably insufficient quantities of vaccine available for a deadly disease. In such circumstances, the relevant nonideal condition is moral only in a derivative sense, as such conditions may obtain even when no individual, group, or institution exhibits a moral flaw of any kind.

By contrast with this sort of case, I am interested in nonideal conditions that are morally objectionable. The simplest such cases occur when one has acted wrongly. As a toy illustration, suppose I have culpably made incompatible promises, such as promises to meet two different individuals at different places at the same time. The only way to explain satisfactorily the wrong committed in such cases is to consider the agent as temporally extended, hence to deny that ethical theory can be complete if it is construed as exhausted by consideration of individuals or decisions at particular times.[42] If we locate the wrong (solely) at the moment when the second promise is made, we lose sight of the fact that failure to fulfill the promise is itself a wrong. If we locate the wrong (solely) at the moment when the promise goes unfulfilled, we lose sight of the fact that there is a sense in which a permissible course of action is available even in light of the conflicting promises. But this need to consider temporally extended features of agency is unsurprising if we frame the fault exhibited as lack of justice in an agent's character, since character and virtue are notions we understand only as long-term features of the exercise of agency.

These claims about permissibility stand in a relationship of mutual reinforcement with Brewer's emphasis on dialectical activity. Most obviously, this is because these views share an emphasis on individuals as temporally extended, but the affinities run deeper than that. A further affinity is found in Brewer's articulation of the importance of personal history to the acquisition of virtue. The need to apologize not only for making incompatible promises but also for failing to fulfill one of them is rendered intelligible by focus on the unfolding history of my relations with the person whom I wrong. To focus only on the error of making the promises betrays a failure to appreciate that the good of a concrete relationship partly underlies the error. Reengaging with that relationship, among other things by apologizing and making amends, is the way to become more just.

The relevant reengagement, moreover, cannot have as its aim making myself perfectly virtuous.[43] That is unachievable, for on a human timescale, perfect virtue is unachievable. Less obviously, it is also unachievable because (like everyone else) I have made errors and committed wrongs, and I am a temporally extended being whose history does not vanish when I become more virtuous or make amends. The impossibility of perfect virtue does not entail that justice and other virtues are inappropriate ideals for me. It entails only that I am not completely satisfactory when I assess myself against these ideals.[44]

The need to engage with a concrete good, if one is to become more just, is even clearer in the second class of nonideal circumstances: cases in which others have wronged one. It will not do to adopt a puritanical attitude toward one's friends and associates in such circumstances, for there is a significant cost to terminating a relationship, even when other, promising relationship candidates are available. Friendship and other relationships involve a shared history, and it is through this shared history that the good of the relationship is uncovered and explored. There is no substitute for that, and so it is a major cost, given the brevity of human life, to begin anew. Becoming more just requires not only improved understanding of right and wrong but also a sincere and sustained disposition to work toward relationship repair. This also helps explain why some of our most fraught relationships are those that lie at the boundaries of intimacy, such as relationships with coworkers or with extended family. In these cases, the absence of fuller intimacy may make repair more difficult to achieve, but repair is normally called for when these relationships become seriously damaged.

This point dovetails, moreover, with Brewer's emphasis on the good of the friend as part of what makes friendship a good for oneself. Here I do not mean what is good for the friend but rather the good of the friend as concrete instantiation of the kind *human being*, or perhaps *finitely rational being*. In all but the most extreme cases where we are wronged by our friends, that good should draw us back into the relationship rather than lead us to abandon it.

The third class of nonideal circumstances—injustice in the background conditions of society—is perhaps most challenging, since sincere and sustained efforts by concerned parties may not suffice to enable progress. This is part of why unjust societies are often devastating to human flourishing. The problem is not only that political injustices pose obstacles to success, cooperation, and fellow-feeling. The problem is also that one's relationships with other members of society may be damaged in a way that is beyond the power of the participants, understood apart from the broader social system, to put on the road to repair. These present some of the most challenging questions about what to do. How do I address problems of poverty and pollution, for example, when the society I live in lacks adequate institutions addressing these problems?[45]

But just as challenging, and even more disturbing, is the question of how to become more just in relation to others when no matter what I do, there are profound defects in these relationships. This exposes a third way in which we are impotent: not only can we not make ourselves immune to future error and not only can we not make our lives or characters ideal because of our past wrongs, but when facing certain obstacles, we may not even be able to move toward improvement. Unilateral or multilateral efforts may not suffice; a more properly social and political response may instead be required for genuine improvement to occur.

Recognizing these impotencies may encourage a dark view of human nature, according to which we are irredeemable. There is truth in that dark view, but our impotencies should also be viewed more positively. Satisfiability is not a constraint on applicable ideals, so there is space for ideals to apply to us even if no one can satisfy them. This exposes also that the satisfiability of ideals is not what characterizes the difference between ideal and nonideal conditions.[46] Even in ideal conditions, applicable moral ideals are not fully satisfiable. Thus, we need not be bothered by the fact that our past moral errors, or those of others, inevitably shape our future relationships. Even if there were no past mistakes, these would be morally imperfect. Similar observations hold for defects in social relationships in general, even where these are not attributable to those who stand in those relationships. Becoming just consists always in perfecting, not in perfection; the activity of becoming just is dialectical in Brewer's sense. Aspiration and exploration are marks of maturity, not defect. The absolutely perfect should not be the enemy of the more perfect.

There is dignity, moreover, simply in being normed by these ideals. Notwithstanding our impotence, we are not such that the ideals against which we find ourselves impotent fail to apply. That would be a truly contemptible state, but from that fate we are spared.

NOTES

I am extremely grateful to Kristina Gehrman, Mark LeBar, and especially Yannig Luthra for providing extensive comments on earlier drafts of this chapter, which have greatly improved it.

1. For an earlier discussion of the relationships between Kohlberg's developmental theory and Aristotelian virtue theory, see LeBar 2016.
2. See in particular Piaget 1932; Rawls 1971, chap. 8; Kohlberg 1973; Kohlberg 1981; Kohlberg 1984; Gilligan 1982.
3. See in particular Rousseau 1979; Kant 1996, 1997, 2015, part 2.
4. For a sophisticated account of natural functions, see Burge 2010, 292–315. Burge's account is influenced by Wright 1973.
5. For rich discussion, see Thompson 2008.
6. See Rawls 1971, part 3; Rawls 1993; Rawls 2001. For comments, see Hill 1994; Hill 2013; Krasnoff 1998; Freeman 2007; Weithman 2010; Garthoff 2016.
7. See Kohlberg 1973; see also Rawls 1971, 464–466.
8. Turiel, Dahl, and Besirevic, in chapter 5 of this volume, argue that Kohlberg's theory understates the critical engagement typically already present in children at this stage.
9. See Kohlberg 1973; see also Rawls 1971, 470–472.
10. Herman 1993 and 2007 in particular is worthy of note for her sophisticated incorporation of concrete social circumstances into contemporary Kantian ethics. Baron 1995 is another important contributor to that cause. From the Aristotelian side, Hursthouse 1999, Foot 2001, and LeBar 2009 and 2016 have resisted the tendency toward a facile opposition between these traditions. Also of note is Sherman 1997.
11. See chapter 1 in this volume.
12. See chapter 1 in this volume.
13. The relative permanence of understanding, by comparison with knowledge, explains why backsliding through stages must be rare.
14. This so-called situationist movement in social psychology was brought to the attention of philosophers by Harman 1998–1999 and Doris 2002. Kamtekar 2004 and Adams 2006 argue, in my view correctly, that Harman and Doris misunderstand the implications of this literature for ethical theory.
15. For the classic discussion, see Aristotle book 7 (2000 [c. 350 B.C.E.]).
16. Discussion of inverse akrasia descends from Bennett 1974 and is given fuller development in Arpaly 2003. For doubts about the extent of inverse akrasia, see Garthoff 2016 and Gehrman 2018.
17. Kohlberg 1973, 632–634.
18. Some relevant work is summarized in Kahneman 2011; also see Korsgaard 1986.

19. This in turn creates concerns about suggestion by the experimenters. Another complication is whether ability to articulate considerations suffices for understanding if the relative strength of those considerations is not appreciated.
20. Gerhman (2017) pushes back against this trend by exposing that some philosophers misread *Huckleberry Finn* in ways that undermine their claims about Huck's moral psychology.
21. Brewer (2009, chap. 2) explicates this notion, but discussion of the idea runs throughout that work.
22. The same is true, moreover, of relationships with the more sophisticated non-human animals.
23. Brewer (2009) emphasizes this point at every turn, and he uses "intrinsic value" in part to stress the distinctness of the value from the attitudes of any valuer. I avoid "intrinsic value" because I find that it admits too readily of an ambiguity between *noninstrumental value* and *value independent of anything else*. On this point, see Korsgaard 1983; Korsgaard also uses "intrinsic value" in her treatment, whereas I instead recommend eliminating that term in favor of "unconditional value" or "independent value."
24. Brewer (2009) elaborates on this idea in the first three chapters. For a discussion of how this idea relates to the stability of character traits, see "Rawlsian Stability in Ethical Theory," an unpublished essay by Jordan Baker.
25. I am sympathetic to Brewer's view of these matters, but I am unsure of the argumentative force of this point, as value could be constructed vaguely and then specified through engagement.
26. There may still be an interesting dialectical activity of engaging in creative interpretation of the composition, but that only reinforces the point.
27. I suspect this point can be developed to rebut Bernard Williams's suspicion that an endless human life must become unbearably tedious; see Williams 1973.
28. This point is made by Brewer (2001, 2002, and 2009). See also Garthoff 2015.
29. Brewer 2009, especially chap. 7; see also Brewer 2005.
30. Brewer 2009, 262.
31. Brewer 2009, 263.
32. Brewer 2009, 262.
33. Woodruff, chapter 1 in this volume. Though I concur with Woodruff that this is a constituent of justice, I doubt that it is most illuminating to understand it (as he does) as a condition separate from substantive conditions. In my judgment, a better approach integrates substantive and subjective conditions, claiming roughly that the subjective condition must be met *through* the substantive condition, by picking up on and responding well to substantive justice.
34. This is a departure from Woodruff's understanding of justice, since he repeatedly emphasizes the propensity of virtues to decay. See chapter 1 in this volume.

35. On the use of the concept of resilience in political philosophy, see Campbell forthcoming.
36. Again the most important texts are Gilligan 1982 and (Herman 1993 and 2007). For Kohlberg's revisions in light of the criticisms of Gilligan and others, see Kohlberg, Levine, and Hewer 1983.
37. This point may dovetail with Woodruff's titular metaphor "*Growing* toward Justice" (italics mine); see chapter 1 in this volume.
38. To some extent, this is Gilligan's own doing, since her rhetoric is perhaps more strident than necessary. Gilligan's (in my view questionable) separation of male and female development is also more in keeping with radical critics of rationalism than with Kohlberg's program.
39. See Gilligan 1982, especially chaps. 2–3.
40. Kohlberg 1973 already notes this, since he does not hold that explicit teaching or studying are principal mechanisms of moral development.
41. Though I do not discuss the issue here, in my view, it is a strength of theories of cognitive development that they view failure of progress later in life as the *stunting* of a capacity, which will differ from the as yet undeveloped capacity of a young person.
42. See Garthoff 2015, which draws on Herman 1993 and Herman 2007. For an earlier discussion of how these cases expose the limits of decision-procedure models of ethical theory, see Marcus 1980.
43. On this theme, see also chapter 1 by Woodruff in this volume.
44. In Garthoff 2015, I argue that this is compatible with the principle that ought implies can.
45. I explore this question in Garthoff 2004a and 2004b.
46. For a different view of how to understand virtue in nonideal circumstances, see chapter 8 by Alan Thomas in this volume.

WORKS CITED

Adams, Robert. 2006. *A Theory of Virtue*. New York: Oxford University Press.

Aristotle. 2000 [c. 350 B.C.E.] *Nicomachean Ethics*. Translated and edited by Roger Crisp. Cambridge: Cambridge University Press.

Arpaly, Nomy. 2003. *Unprincipled Virtue*. New York: Oxford University Press.

Baron, Marcia. 1995. *Kantian Ethics Almost without Apology*. Ithaca: Cornell University Press.

Bennett, Jonathan. 1974. "The Conscience of Huckleberry Finn." *Philosophy* 49: 123–134.

Brewer, Talbot. 2001. "Rethinking Our Maxims." *Ethical Theory and Moral Practice* 4: 219–230.

Brewer, Talbot. 2002. "Maxims and Virtues." *Philosophical Review* 111: 539–772.
Brewer, Talbot. 2005. "Virtues We Can Share: A Reading of Aristotle's Ethics." *Ethics* 115: 721–758.
Brewer, Talbot. 2009. *The Retrieval of Ethics*. New York: Oxford University Press.
Burge, Tyler. 2010. *Origins of Objectivity*. New York: Oxford University Press.
Campbell, Grace. Forthcoming. "Stability, Resilience, and Global Justice." Doctoral dissertation in progress, University of Tennessee.
Doris, John. 2002. *Lack of Character*. Cambridge: Cambridge University Press.
Foot, Philippa. 2001. *Natural Goodness*. New York: Oxford University Press.
Freeman, Samuel. 2007. *Rawls*. New York: Routledge.
Garthoff, Jon. 2004a. "The Embodiment Thesis." *Ethical Theory and Moral Practice* 7: 15–29.
Garthoff, Jon. 2004b. "Zarathustra's Dilemma and the Embodiment of Morality." *Philosophical Studies* 117: 259–274.
Garthoff, Jon. 2015. "The Salience of Moral Character." *Southern Journal of Philosophy*: 178–195.
Garthoff, Jon. 2016. "Rawlsian Stability." *Res Publica* 22: 285–299.
Gehrman, Kristina. Forthcoming 2018. "The Character of Huckleberry Finn." *Philosophy and Literature* 42.
Gilligan, Carol. 1982. *In a Different Voice*. Cambridge: Harvard University Press.
Harman, Gilbert. 1998–1999. "Moral Philosophy Meets Social Psychology." *Proceedings of the Aristotelian Society*: 315–331.
Herman, Barbara. 1993. *The Practice of Moral Judgment*. Cambridge: Harvard University Press.
Herman, Barbara. 2007. *Moral Literacy*. Cambridge: Harvard University Press.
Hill, Thomas E. Jr. 1994. "The Problem of Stability in Political Liberalism." *Pacific Philosophical Quarterly* 75: 333–352.
Hill, Thomas E. Jr. 2013. "Stability, a Sense of Justice, and Self-Respect." In *A Companion to Rawls*, edited by Jon Mandle and David A. Reidy, 200–215. Hoboken: Wiley-Blackwell.
Hursthouse, Rosalind. 1999. *On Virtue Ethics*. New York: Oxford University Press.
Kahneman, Daniel. 2011. *Thinking, Fast and Slow*. New York: Farrar, Straus and Giroux.
Kamtekar, Rachana. 2004. "Situationism and Virtue Ethics on the Content of Our Character." *Ethics* 114: 458–491.
Kant, Immanuel. 1996 [1797]. *The Metaphysics of Morals*. Translated by Mary Gregor. Cambridge: Cambridge University Press.
Kant, Immanuel. 1997 [1785]. *Groundwork of the Metaphysics of Morals*. Translated by Mary Gregor. Cambridge: Cambridge University Press.
Kant, Immanuel. 2015 [1788]. *Critique of Practical Reason*. Translated by Mary Gregor. Cambridge: Cambridge University Press.
Kohlberg, Lawrence. 1973. "The Claim to Moral Adequacy of a Highest Stage of Moral Development." *Journal of Philosophy* 70: 630–646.

Kohlberg, Lawrence. 1981. *The Philosophy of Moral Development*. New York: Harper & Row.

Kohlberg, Lawrence. 1984. *The Psychology of Moral Development*. New York: Harper & Row.

Kohlberg, Lawrence, C. Levine, and A. Hewer. 1983. *Moral Stages: A Current Formulation and a Response to Critics*. Berlin: Karger.

Korsgaard, Christine. 1983. "Two Distinctions in Goodness." *Philosophical Review* 92: 169–195.

Korsgaard, Christine. 1986. "Aristotle on Function and Virtue." *History of Philosophy Quarterly* 3: 259–279.

Krasnoff, Larry. 1998. "Consensus, Stability, and Normativity in Rawls's Political Liberalism." *Journal of Philosophy* 95: 269–292.

LeBar, Mark. 2009. "Virtue Ethics and Deontic Constraints." *Ethics* 119: 642–671.

LeBar, Mark. 2016. "Norms of Justice in Development." In *Developing the Virtues*, edited by Julia Annas, Darcia Narvaez, and Nancy E. Snow, 273–294. New York: Oxford University Press.

Marcus, Ruth Barcan. 1980. "Moral Dilemmas and Consistency." *Journal of Philosophy* 77: 121–136.

Piaget, Jean. 1932 [1966]. *The Moral Judgment of the Child*. Translated by Marjorie Gabain. New York: Free Press.

Rawls, John. 1971. *A Theory of Justice*. Cambridge: Harvard University Press.

Rawls, John. 1993. *Political Liberalism*. New York: Columbia University Press.

Rawls, John. 2001. *Justice as Fairness: A Restatement*. Cambridge: Harvard University Press.

Rousseau, Jean-Jacques. 1978 [1762]. *On the Social Contract*. Translated by Judith R. Masters. Edited by Roger D. Masters. New York: St. Martin's Press.

Rousseau, Jean-Jacques. 1979 [1762]. *Emile*. Translated by Allan Bloom. New York: Basic Books.

Sherman, Nancy. 1997. *Making a Necessity of Virtue*. Cambridge: Cambridge University Press.

Thompson, Michael. 2008. *Life and Action*. Cambridge: Harvard University Press.

Weithman, Paul. 2010. *Why Political Liberalism? On John Rawls's Political Turn*. New York: Oxford University Press.

Williams, Bernard. 1973. "The Makropulos Case: Reflections on the Tedium of Immortality." In *Problems of the Self*, 82–100. Cambridge: Cambridge University Press.

Wright, Larry. 1973. "Functions." *Philosophical Review* 82: 139–168.

Chapter 8

Should Epistemic Injustices Be Redressed by the "Corrective Virtues"?

ALAN THOMAS

This chapter considers whether or not so-called epistemic injustices are to be remedied either by the cultivation of individual virtues of redress or via the capacities of the state.[1] As British philosopher Bernard Williams once remarked, the word *virtue* has acquired "comic or other undesirable associations," and no one but philosophers use it.[2] Yet, as Williams also remarked, since the revival of virtue ethics, the concept now seems indispensable. Philosophers have put the concept to work not only in thinking about the features of ethically admirable people but also in other domains of philosophy. In particular, the theory of knowledge has found an important role for the concept of a virtuous knower in the development of virtue epistemology, a discipline that has shadowed its ethical counterpart. In her groundbreaking book *Epistemic Injustice: Ethics and the Power of Knowing*, Miranda Fricker took this epistemic discussion in a novel and fruitful direction by asking about everyday cases of the injustices that we impose on each other *as* knowers.[3] This completed the circle; it brought the discussion in epistemology back into connection with the discussions in ethics and politics where the term *virtue* has its home.

In this chapter, I focus on a particular aspect of Fricker's treatment of the class of cases that she calls instances of "epistemic injustice," namely, her claim that the way to redress such injustice is by cultivating what she calls "corrective virtues." Fricker believes that the two virtues of hermeneutic and testimonial justice are necessary in order to redress the injustices that she has identified.[4] This aspect of her view has been criticized in two of the most thoughtful responses to her book: if the origin of these injustices is structural, then how can an individualistic response centered on the virtues—given that the latter are primarily properties of individuals—be our most effective response?[5]

There is certainly some pressure toward the conclusion that corrective virtue is not enough. However, there is a counterpressure, too: given the connection between knowing and asserting, we are discussing a phenomenon that is pervasive in human life and regulated by social norms that are often informal and beyond the scope of direct legal regulation. Certainly, we would prefer to be in a social world where no one was derogated or silenced, but how can a liberal democratic state legislate to bring about such a world without constant and ongoing intrusion into the micro-interactions of daily life?[6] This is not a pragmatic issue about scope or scale; rather, it is centered on the constraints that can reasonably be placed on the liberal right of privacy. These constraints are overridden in what Corey Brettschneider has called an "Invasive State":

> The dystopia of the Invasive State evokes the liberal fear of a government that seeks to promote equality at any expense, with no respect for the boundary between the public and the private.

> The Invasive State would spy on the family and civil society, intervening whenever it would be necessary to protect an ideal of equality.[7]

How do we address epistemic injustice, given its constitutive involvement in assertoric speech, without invoking the invasive state—the liberal, secular equivalent of a confessional society that exemplifies "one of the most effective forms of invasion of privacy—the demand that everyone stand up and be counted"?[8] Answering this question is part of a broader attempt to understand what it is to become just in our dealings with one another as thinkers, speakers, and testifiers who are bound up, in all kinds of ways, with the concept of knowledge. I will begin with a very basic question: what is epistemic injustice supposed to be?

The first section of this chapter sets out Fricker's conception of epistemic injustice. The second section addresses the question of how, in this context, one distinguishes injustices from the broader class of ways in which we can wrong one another. The third section examines what I take to be a basic case of epistemic injustice, namely, the attempt to disqualify a person from the status of knower. The fourth section explains this kind of injustice as a species of expressive injury through speech. The conclusion is that the redress for such injustices lies in the state's promotion of a democratic ethos—political speech that the state engages in in its own right.

THE IDEA OF EPISTEMIC INJUSTICE

Fricker claimed that as thinkers and speakers concerned with identifying those who know, and who rely heavily on testimony from others, we can identify certain kinds of wrongs that we do to one another that are sufficiently serious to count as injustices.[9] Those wrongs bear on our capacity to engage in these activities: to speak knowledgeably and to rely on the testimony of others. As social animals, this latter kind of dependence is both extensive and deep. We know, from Solomon Asch's famous conformity experiment in psychology, that a third of experimental subjects will override the evidence of their own visual perception to conform with the judgments of a peer group.[10] Such conformity can, in some contexts, be a vice, but it is a tacit acknowledgment of the virtue of knowing when to defer to group judgment and the importance of the latter in the social acquisition and use of knowledge.[11]

Fricker divided this class of wrongs into two types: in cases of *hermeneutic injustice,* a social group is cut off from the interpretative resources that it needs in order even to conceptualize the harms imposed on it. Fricker gives the example of a woman in the late 1960s who is unable to conceive of her experience as sexual harassment as she lacks the concepts to do so.[12]

In cases of *testimonial injustice,* people receive either too much or too little credit for what they say because of an identity prejudice grounded on their membership in a certain group. An apposite example is the African American female doctor who was one of three who volunteered to help a fellow passenger on an airline flight in the United States in 2016.[13] Her offer to help was at first dismissed; later, her credentials were checked before she was permitted to approach the patient. In the meantime, a white male doctor who presented himself at the same time was allowed to treat the sick person, with no checking of his credentials.

The stereotypes that we rely on in our reasoning as "quick and dirty" heuristics carry hidden dangers of stereotyping: the white male who presented himself on the flight met a stereotype of a "typical doctor," while the African American female did not. Once again, a recognition of the importance of stereotypes and other heuristics in our reasoning acknowledges that our reasonableness is embedded in an ecology; but that which typically helps us to be more effective decision makers in the face of potentially overwhelming informational complexity carries its own risks of error.[14]

I will restrict myself to three questions about Fricker's account of epistemic injustice. First, if it is true that we can wrong one another as knowers, then what merits calling these wrongings of individuals injustices? (Do we need to look more deeply into the nature of justice and, for that matter, the nature of epistemology to answer this question?)

The second question follows naturally from the first. If these are cases of injustice, how do we separate their identification and correction from the domain of state action? (If in a liberal society such action is limited by privacy rights, then how ought we to address epistemic injustices if we have agreed that such injustices can occur?)

This allows us to formulate the third, summative question, from which I began. In suggesting that the appropriate response to these cases is the cultivation by the individual of corrective virtues, is Fricker guilty of a misplaced individualism, of attempting to solve problems caused by structural power with an appeal to individual virtues?

WRONGINGS VERSUS INJUSTICES

In thinking about knowledge, it is undoubtedly insightful to think about the characteristics of admirable people in this domain, just as the virtue ethicist does in the domain of morality. Fricker's insight was that it is equally insightful to think about ways in which we act unjustly in this domain. But why, of all the critical terms of appraisal to which she could have appealed, did Fricker use *injustice* as her central term? I focus here on this question solely in regard to testimonial injustice, setting aside hermeneutical injustice for another occasion.

We need an example to fix ideas. Suppose that one of Thomas Jefferson's female slaves, Isabel Hern, tells Jefferson not to go into the woodshed because he risks being bitten by a snake hidden there. Failing to take this testimony seriously, Jefferson goes into the woodshed and is promptly bitten by the snake. Fricker is explicit that we are not to construe the situation this way: that Jefferson comes to an assignment of the credibility of the speaker, an assignment of probability to the claim, and then revises down his first judgment of speaker credibility because he is talking to a slave (and a woman). Jefferson's judgment is, indeed, a judgment of the trustworthiness of his interlocutor across the two dimensions of sincerity and competence. However, a social stereotype affects the determination of this credibility directly: the work of prejudice is not that it lowers a *prior* estimate of credibility.

So Hern is the subject of a derogatory judgment in the way in which Jefferson fails to take her testimony seriously, tracking her across a range of social situations. This is because this derogation is rooted in a social stereotype operative among a dominant group and imposed on a dominated group. Fricker wants to say more, that these judgments harm a person in the dominated group in her capacity as a knower. Hern is simply, by virtue of her identity, not taken to be credible, in a way that constitutes a harm to her. It will prove important in what follows to ask what significance attaches to the word *capacity* in this diagnosis. It seems to me that a "one-off" case of injustice cannot remove a capacity. That is why we are to see this stereotype as tracking an individual across a range of situations, such that a capacity is diminished or damaged. In what way can repeatedly being silenced or ignored result in this outcome?

Fricker suggests three separate explanations that need not, it seems to me, be mutually exclusive. The first simply appeals to repeated derogation itself, a repeated wronging of a person in his or her role as an epistemic agent.[15] The second appeals to the way in which being repeatedly subject to such treatment leads to the person thus derogated losing confidence in his or her ability to participate in our ordinary practices surrounding knowledge. The third, most ambitious explanation is taken from Bernard Williams: that sociability does not simply enter into the stabilization of the dispositions involved in knowledge but serves also to stabilize the very idea of the mental state that is appropriately the expression of knowledge.

Williams claims that in testimonial exchange, our interlocutor must have sufficient diachronic continuity of character to allow us to apply a distinction between changes in the evidence shared between us and changes in the dispositions that make up that person's character. Sociability, in the guise of epistemic virtue, helps to stabilize the very idea of an individual character. Williams takes as his central example the protagonist of Denis Diderot's *Rameau's Nephew*. He is committed to the idea of total transparency in his epistemic dealings with others while, unfortunately, he presents himself under the guise of a different person every time we encounter him. He is a conversational "shape shifter." An equally appropriate literary example is the eponymous character—or characters—who reappears throughout Herman Melville's suggestively titled *The Confidence Man*. Is there one confidence man or many? Williams concludes that stability of character is mutually interdependent with the idea of generalized social trust of the kind essential to the social relations of a modern commercial republic.[16] So sociability enters not only into the stabilization of knowledge but also into whether we are dealing with knowledge at all, as opposed to fantasy or wishful thinking.

Like Fricker, I am most drawn to the truth of this third explanation, but I will also parallel her own discussion by not treating it at any length. This is for two reasons. The first is that I have discussed Williams's explanation—and tried to make a case for its truth—elsewhere.[17] The second is that making it the primary explanation of epistemic injustice makes the latter a hostage to fortune. The ambitiousness of Williams's claim makes it inherently controversial—more controversial, one might think, than the clear instances of epistemic injustice that ground it. I therefore restrict my focus in this chapter to a consideration of Fricker's first two explanations and look at the advantages and disadvantages of each.

The first explanation, then, is that people very often suffer from testimonial injustice when they are either given too little or too much epistemic credit. One advantage of this explanation—which Fricker emphasizes—is that it makes epistemic injustice widespread. People are pervasively interrupted, ignored, or silenced, and this treatment is grounded on identity prejudice. But I do not think this is, in fact, the better explanation of epistemic injustice, for two reasons.

I concede that we could use the word *justice* very broadly, as John Stuart Mill does, basically to apply to any very serious wrong to an individual that gives rise to strong feelings of disapprobation—differentiated by some further features of the case.[18] Any such example can be brought within the domain of justice in this broad use of the term. But this capacious use makes it difficult to see why these are cases of injustice as opposed to, simply, very widespread and repeated wrongings of a person. It also makes it hard to see the function of the word *capacity* in Fricker's diagnosis that we are wronging one another in our *capacity* as knowers. This seems to mean only that in every exercise of this capacity, there is the opportunity for being wronged—instance by instance, as it were. So the mention of the capacity is redundant in explaining what distinctive kind of harm this is to the agent.

We gain the pervasiveness of epistemic injustice, then, at the cost of a loss of distinctiveness. It is not clear, if we do not follow Mill's capacious use of the terms *justice* and *injustice*, why these are injustices at all. However, I concede that this point can be addressed by examining an ambiguity inherent in our use of the term *justice*. All parties agree that we are not in this discussion directly appealing to socioeconomic justice or injustice; assigning credibility to an interlocutor is not a scarce good that we need to distribute to one person with a weather eye on its availability to any other person of some designated class. If this epistemic issue is a matter of justice, then it is a matter of what Joel Feinberg called "noncomparative justice."[19]

We might describe both comparative and noncomparative justice as instances of giving each person his or her due. However, in the case of comparative justice, we must treat an individual as a member of a class defined for the relevant project of justice; distributing child benefits, for example, is sensitive to the recipient having childcare responsibilities. By contrast, in the case of noncomparative justice, we give each person his or her due without regard for how we treat others in the relevant class in the same way; there is no such relevant comparator class.[20]

Which of these two conceptions of the concept of justice does Fricker have in mind? Take the basic case of refusing to take you to *be* someone who knows something, as in the Jefferson/Hern case—a case prior to judging whether to accept testimony from you. In such a case, there would be a refusal to grant you credit: the credit owed to you as a person who had exercised epistemic virtues in a creditworthy way.[21] I would argue that this refusal to grant you credit is a form of derogatory judgment, one of the characteristic vices of noncomparative injustice.

Consider now an extension to the testimonial case: in normal cases, epistemically responsible belief on the part of the person getting told is to accept an assurance from the teller in a context marked by an appropriate degree of interpersonal trust. There is a transfer of credit. By contrast, derogatory judgment involves a refusal to accept such a transfer from a person of a certain social kind. So the broader class of epistemic wrongs is also a form of derogatory judgment.

If we draw this distinction, then we can vindicate Fricker's appeal to the concept of justice; we can interpret her as referring to noncomparative justice. (She does not use the term, but it is a natural further specification of her position.) This isolates, from within the very broad class of wrongings of a person as an epistemic agent, one very specific way in which an injustice is done to someone. It is a denial of epistemic credit that is due to the person. This is wholly separate from any appeal to socioeconomic justice, because epistemic credit is an indivisible good: by handing out some, I do not reduce its availability for anyone else. (Relatedly, there is no properly defined class of recipients.) But I have noted that a problem remains with this explanation: Fricker's reference to a *capacity* is still redundant. Repeated denials of credit may or may not remove a capacity to know.[22] This is for several reasons, each of which is of independent interest.

First, there is the complexity of social identity. A range of categories and associated identifications can reinforce or counteract one another. For example, novelist Virginia Woolf was discriminated against as a woman, but she was both upper-class and wealthy and enjoyed a degree of social privilege in light of these latter facts (something of which she was entirely self-aware). By contrast, the slave on Jefferson's plantation is discriminated against as a woman, as a slave, as poor, and as uneducated. If Woolf is disbelieved by a person whom she takes to be of lower social standing, will she subsequently lose her confidence or her intellectual courage? Perhaps—or perhaps not; she has other resources to resist being "silenced" that prevent a series of derogatory judgments leading to a loss of a capacity.

The second problem for the "loss of confidence" explanation is related to the first. David Owen has noted that if one's social setting can either reinforce or undermine one's confidence, it is also true that one's social setting can be real or imaginary.[23] Imagined communities can play a role in bolstering a person's confidence; consider a deep-seated religious identification with a transcendent community that bolsters one's confidence in the face of a hostile social environment. Once again, the point is that a person may be able to draw on compensatory social resources to counteract identity-based prejudice.

A third problem for the confidence/courage explanation is what we mean in this context by a capacity for knowledge. As Michael Williams has pointed out, the idea of such a capacity is ambivalent between two distinct phenomena that Wilfrid Sellars labeled "actions" and "acts":

> Actions are done on purpose . . . acts are actualizations of a capacity. . . . [S]eeing—which is a way of knowing—is a mental act, not an action. Seeing that there is, say, a rabbit in the garden, involves the actualization of a trained recognitional capacity which means that seeing is not the sort of thing one does "on purpose" . . . lots of ordinary knowledge depends only on the unself-conscious exercise of basic cognitive abilities.[24]

If this is an insight, and I believe it is, then it would seriously limit the potential scope of Fricker's explanation that a loss of confidence will see the loss of a capacity for knowledge. Michael Williams and Sellars are reminding us that for a broad swathe of knowledge, it is not clear that a loss of confidence, or loss of intellectual courage, could undermine our claims to know. That is precisely because such claims are the product of Sellarsian "acts" as opposed to "actions" that are by their nature immune to being undermined in this kind of way.[25] It is true that a range of background conditions have to hold for any given exercise of a capacity for knowledge to be successful. However, it is not clear how an agent's loss of confidence, or intellectual courage, could undermine such fundamental kinds of knowledge as perceptual or memory-based beliefs. This is particularly pertinent to Fricker's cases of testimonial injustice if, in the tradition inaugurated by Thomas Reid, our a priori entitlement to take testimony at face value is of the same generic class as our a priori entitlement to take perception and memory at face value.[26]

I have canvassed two explanations of what Fricker could mean by epistemic injustice. The first is very broad and can be called an injustice of a noncomparative kind, but it seems to make Fricker's mention of one's capacities as a knower redundant. The second mentions a capacity and appeals to a loss of confidence in explaining the loss of this capacity, but this explanation can, I think, take one only so far. My concern is that it greatly restricts the class of cases.

Perhaps we do not need to choose here. I noted that these diagnoses of epistemic injustice need not be mutually exclusive. Fricker's book was path-breaking and open to both interpretation and further development; perhaps both classes of cases ought to be conjoined to acknowledge a broad class of epistemic wrongs and some cases where epistemic capacity is diminished. I am sympathetic to this argument but would like to explore one more explanation of why epistemic injustice marks off an important and distinctive kind of case. The proposal is that epistemic injustice is to be viewed as putative *disqualification* from epistemic status. I purport, by how I treat you, to deny you epistemic credit in a special sense, namely, by implying that you were never in a position to receive it in the first place.

THE IDEA OF STATUS AND ITS "DENIAL"

There is at least one sense of the term *egalitarian* in which we are all egalitarians now, which makes it an effort of historical imagination to recapture what the Haitian, French, and American revolutions signified in the history of the modern West.[27] It is the task of this section to specify this sense while also solving a further problem: that it is difficult to understand the nature of epistemic injustice, as we find it difficult to believe that the unjust can, in this case, really mean what they say.

In trying to specify the sense of the term *egalitarian* at issue, we can begin with a historical example to fix ideas. French historian and political theorist Pierre Rosanvallon cites a document that the Abbé Sieyès appended to his "Essai sur les privilèges."[28] Under the ancien régime, society was "represented" by three estates: the clergy, the nobility, and representatives of the common people. Representation is a very thin notion here, given that the deliberations of all three estates had a merely advisory role for the monarch and no independent legislative power. The document, titled "A Petition to the King," is a response from the French nobility in 1614 to the request that the third estate's deputies be treated with more respect by the aristocratic deputies of the second, as if they were brothers. The tone of the aristocratic response, as it appeals to the monarch, is one of outrage and scorn:

> I am ashamed, Sire, to tell you of the offensive terms in which we have once again been addressed. They compare your state to a family consisting of three brothers. . . . How can the nobility have been linked with the vulgar in the closest society that exists among men, which is brotherhood. . . . Render judgement, Sire, and in a declaration steeped in your justice remind them of their duty and order them to recognize what we are, what difference exists between us, and tell them *that they can in no way compare themselves to us.*[29]

We are resistant even to trying imaginatively to occupy a world view in which the human species is divided into stratified classes, not all of whose members count as fully human. To be an egalitarian in the modern sense, then, is to be unable to take this claim seriously in one particular way, namely, by taking it literally.

One cannot really imagine that inegalitarians of the past literally believed that their conspecifics were not all members of the species *Homo sapiens*. Indeed, if we take the language of "dehumanization" literally, then we inadvertently exonerate inegalitarian treatment from the perspective of the perpetrator. If the wrongdoer literally believes that there exists a categorical difference between himself and a social inferior—as if the latter were indeed vermin of a different species—then treating people as vermin may be morally outrageous from our perspective but nonculpably ignorant from the perpetrator's perspective. That does seem a very undesirable diagnosis of the error involved.

David Owen tries to resolve this interpretative puzzle by appealing to Stanley Cavell's notion of "soul blindness."[30] Cavell interprets the thoughts of a slave owner who claims that his slaves are "not human beings":

> This is a definite state of mind. He means, indefinitely, that they are not purely human. He means, indefinitely, that *there are kinds of humans*. . . . He means, indefinitely, that slaves are different, primarily different from him, secondarily perhaps different from you and me. . . . In the end he will appeal to history, to a form, or rather to a way, of life: this is what he does. . . . It could be said that what he denies is that the slave is "other," i.e., other to his one. They are, as it were, merely other; not simply separate, but different. It could also be said that he takes himself to be private with respect to them, in the end unknowable by them.[31]

Cavell is directing us to a better interpretation of inegalitarian claims from the past: they are an attempt to reinsert categorical difference into the category of equal status. Equality of status turns out to be, for the inegalitarian, an internally differentiated idea grounded on a class-based categorization of "forms of life." (I do not restrict the term *class* to socioeconomic class but rather extend it to gender, sexual orientation, and race.) In his own work, Owen further connects epistemic injustice to the class of what he calls "dignitary harms." They do not simply impinge on one's rights; they target the very status that underpins them:

> We can come at the same point in a slightly different way by distinguishing what Michael Rosen calls "respect as observance" and "respect as respectfulness." The former denotes simply observing your human or civic rights. So we may say that I recognize the dignity of your person by not breaching these rights. The second refers to an attitude with which I interact with you. Thus we may say that I acknowledge the dignity in your person by engaging respectfully with you.[32]

Epistemic injustices, on this account, turn out to be one way to attack a person's status as free and equal: by an attack on his or her dignity that is detachable from a breach of that person's rights. I think this is an insightful diagnosis of the paradigmatic case of epistemic injustice as opposed to a broader class of epistemic wronging of a person. In this interpretation, the epistemically unjust have the putative aim of disqualifying a person from epistemic status, but the actual expressive content of their action is subtly different. After all, they have no power to disqualify from status, but by acting as if they do, they purport to introduce segregation of rank into epistemic status. Some people need not be listened to because, to use the language of the seventeenth-century aristocrat, "they can in no way compare themselves to us."

One might wonder, at this point, how I can be less enthusiastic about an explanation of epistemic injustice that appeals to a loss of confidence as eroding a person's capacity to know yet more enthusiastic about a view in which a speaker attempts the impossible by speaking falsely. You cannot really, by your words, disqualify a person as a knower; you cannot really mean, if you imply that a person has less than fully human status, that they do. Why is this, then, a better explanation of epistemic injustice?

It is a better explanation because it does not focus on the effect of speech as action—that which it seeks to bring about—as does the "loss of capacity" explanation. Instead, it focuses on the expressive injury *in* what is said, not what one aims to bring about by saying it, its illocutionary effect, not its perlocutionary effect.[33] The putative expression of a disqualification from status is itself injurious because of the kind of speech that it is. It may not secure what it seeks to bring about, but the very attempt expresses an attitude of contemptuous indifference toward another person. Epistemic silencing need not, of course, be speech; this is a case of expressive inaction just as Jefferson's failure to take the testimony of a female slave seriously is an expressive inaction. Not taking a person seriously can be an expression of a contemptuous attitude toward him or her.

Furthermore, the agent who silences another *may* succeed in recruiting others to his or her cause: if the agent implies that you are a person not to be taken seriously, maybe others will follow in that belief. What is being invoked here is the power of social ostracism, an attempt to sever the connections of mutual acknowledgment. Once again turning to the historical example, the radical inegalitarians of the past were interested not merely in classifying people in stratified classes—like rearranging a butterfly collection—but in grounding rights to dominate and a correlative obligation to obey on this stratification in "forms of life." Categorization is at the service of domination.

As I have noted, perhaps a range of wrongs fall under the heading of epistemic injustices. But is the correction of any of the wrongs I have identified the business of the state? I think this point about the expressive wrongs involved in this third, paradigmatic case of epistemic injustice helps us to approach this issue.

EPISTEMIC INJUSTICE AND THE LIMITS OF STATE ACTION

How can Fricker discuss justice and injustice when it comes to knowledge while not placing these issues within the domain of action by the liberal state? If we are dealing with the everyday norms of knowledge in thought and speech, do not structural causes call for structural remedies and not, as Fricker implies, the exercise of corrective virtue by individuals?[34] Both Elizabeth Anderson (2012) and James Bohman (2012) share this concern about Fricker's individualistic, virtue-focused approach to correcting for testimonial injustice. Their concern is that this remedy fails to address the structural sources in the nature of social power of the plausible cases of individual domination that Fricker captures so well in her examples. How could the remedy *not* lie in state action?

My own view is that both parties to this dispute can claim part of the truth. Fricker is right that an important class of cases falls outside the remedial action of the state; this is so even if such a state has fully implemented the principles of justice to produce a society well ordered by justice. However, Anderson and Bohman are also right that these cases of epistemic injustice are also cases of domination. How can both views be partly true?

My answer is that any liberal view has to assign three kinds of normative status to people. There is the liberty to express the values that constitute your personal point of view (an "option"). There are the rights that both constrain you in your ability to block the expression of other people's points of view and hence to constrain their ability to constrain you (a "constraint"). Then there is an important third category, an ethos that enjoins you not to exploit the nuisance value of your own protected status—a status protected by the first two kinds of rights.

I take the concept of nuisance from the theory of private tort—civil wrongs—but my aim here is to apply it more broadly as an ethical category. You need not be acting illegally, but you may be acting immorally, when you exploit the fact that while acting within your rights, you may still impinge on the legitimate interests of others. Any ethical outlook that accommodates rights has to concede that this third category of interference exists. When we are protected by a moral right, our freedom of action is impinged upon by the compossibility constraint, namely, that all others have received the same protection as we have. Yet we also expose ourselves to a further potential impingement on our interests, namely, that others can interfere with us by creating a nuisance while acting within their rights. To adapt an example suggested by Thomas Christiano, suppose you and a group of friends want to play a competitive game of cards—bridge or poker—but one of the players keeps flouting the rules in trivial ways that nevertheless ruin the game for everyone. A shared project has been subject to vexatious interference—a nuisance.

Extending this analogy, both Christiano and David Estlund have argued that the authority of democratic legislation places individuals under a moral obligation to respect majoritarian decisions that do not violate constitutional rights (provided that doing so is not excessively burdensome to the person concerned).[35] Christiano has also extended this account to address the question of whether a person who is fully entitled to a greater share of legitimately assigned social power can use that power to frustrate the ends of democratic legislation by interfering with those ends so as to reduce the class of feasible goals? Note the use of the word *interfering*: such a person is fully within his or her legal and moral rights but is exploiting the nuisance value of his or her protected status. Christiano's insightful answer is that any stable liberal state is going to require a democratic ethos to constrain such behavior. If it is not unduly burdensome, this person ought to exercise restraint, not exploit his or her nuisance value, and comply with the obligation to respect the will of the majority.

I think there are interesting structural analogies between this kind of case and cases of epistemic injustice. I have diagnosed a core case of epistemic injustice as when a dominating agent behaves *as if* another person has been disqualified from the status of knower. Since we are dealing here with an essential role for epistemic community in sustaining this status by mutual recognition, it is, of course, not up to an individual to withdraw status in this way; but that person proceeds as though he or she can. If successful, the individual may recruit others to the cause, including the person who is silenced—and henceforth silences himself or herself. But once again, we can see two aspects to this domination: (1) an obstruction of a persons' legitimate right to speak by (2) the expressive injury of the implication that they are not properly members of the class entitled to be heard. I would argue that these kinds of injustice, too, require an ethos to constrain them in a manner that strictly parallels the role that Christiano has identified; hence Fricker's emphasis on the role of corrective virtues located outside the formal ambit of the state.

My basic point, then, is that on *any* liberal view of justice or domination, the limitations of state action have to be complemented by a democratic ethos sustained by democratic virtues. So Fricker need not appeal to any idea to which we are not already committed as liberals. This ethos forms part of the bundle of liberties attached to the status of citizen. Beyond the application of the principles of justice to the basic structure of society, there are cases where domination can nevertheless arise unless citizens not only respect others but also positively refrain from exploiting their own liberty to interfere with the legitimate projects of others. Located within this range, cases of epistemic injustice are indeed properly both viewed as instances of domination *and* as the focus for a corrective exercise of virtue.

I noted that liberal states operate with some conception of fairness, yet they are also regarded as aiming to be neutral among different, controversial ideals about how people ought to lead their lives. Does a democratic ethos violate this ideal of neutrality? I do not believe it does, because the liberal democratic state has its own values.[36] It can promote *those* without violating neutrality. I do not mean that any state, no matter how objectionable, will seek to preserve itself (even though that seems true). Liberal democratic states seek to preserve themselves in the right ways and for the right reasons, by transmitting their democratic values through all the expressive means at their disposal. For example, in his discussion of how the liberal state ought to approach hate speech, Brettschneider has argued:

> the state should actively pursue democratic persuasion, given the problem of complicity that can accompany neutralist protections for free speech. . . . By criticizing hate groups and promoting the ideal of free and equal citizenship, the state can clarify that its protection of groups from coercive intervention is not tantamount to approval of their message.[37]

There are clear differences between cases of epistemic injustice and cases of hate speech; my aim is not to assimilate them but merely to point out that similar issues arise when we consider how to deal with them in either case.

As I have also noted, the expressive injury of testimonial injustice is not the same as hate speech, as it can be a form of action—even inaction—that expresses a contemptuous attitude toward another person's status as free and equal. It need not be speech, and the attitude it expresses is not hate (though it does not follow that it need be less injurious). What matters here is not the expressed emotion but the belief that it presupposes, as in Brettschneider's distinction between the emotion of hate and "hateful viewpoints."[38] The latter are beliefs: "expressing an idea or ideology that opposes free and equal citizenship."[39] Here, too, I think in our response to epistemic injustices, we ought to develop a parallel to Brettschneider's response to hateful viewpoints, developed in the service of his own "value democracy." In his proposal, we do not coercively ban hate speech, but we use the expressive resources of the state—as "educator, speaker and spender"—to match it with more and better nonhate speech that undercuts the effects of hate speech by subjecting it to relentless criticism.[40]

In my view, Brettschneider's proposal maps onto the trichotomy among liberties, constraints, and an ethos of restraint. (Brettschneider at one point characterizes his view as appealing to "an ethos in liberal democracy.")[41] His discussion is solely concerned with hate speech; many liberal societies take a very different approach to such speech from that of US First Amendment jurisprudence. Such societies remove the right to free expression so that we do not even reach the stage of asking proponents of hate speech to refrain from speaking that way; they are coercively required not to do so. In Brettschneider's alternative approach, we concede the right to express hateful viewpoints but are not complicit with it. That is because our collective agent, the liberal state, is not neutral in its advocacy of the values of free and equal citizenship themselves (neither need individuals abstain from such advocacy). The state is under a positive obligation to bring about an ethos of democracy.[42]

How would this work in the analogous case of epistemic justice? There is at least one direct connection running from the idea of democratic persuasion to epistemic justice, namely, that the former places demands on the education system, including the demand not to use epistemic injustice as one of its own methods. Brettschneider's example is that teachers challenging hateful viewpoints expressed by students ought not simply silence them.[43] What Brettschneider calls "democratic persuasion" itself, then, is constrained by epistemic justice. But does the analogy run more deeply?

I believe it does. In seeking to counter those who would derogate others in the strongest sense—by purporting to disqualify them from epistemic status—a corrective ethos of restraint, centered on individual corrective virtue, is reinforced by the expressive capacity of the state. We cannot expect state intervention in every case, at the level of informal social norms, of testimonial injustice between individuals.[44] But we can expect the public resources of our social world—via the education system, the informal regulation of truthfulness in speech, or norms of respect in public institutions and civic discourse—to seek to drown out testimonial injustice with examples of more and better testimonial justice. We are not relying solely on faith in the idea that "good speech always drives out the bad" in some "free" marketplace of ideas; on this issue, the state is not neutral.

Thus, we can agree both with Fricker and with Anderson, noting in the latter case that there is no incompatibility between corrective virtue and political policy per se. Anderson is explicit that her focus on the structural basis of domination is complementary to the corrective virtues, aimed at putting in place background conditions that "enable individual virtue to work."[45] These background conditions are the responsibility of the liberal democratic state even if what they enable must necessarily fall beyond this domain. Public reinforcement of the norms of epistemic justice can reasonably be expected to have pervasive effects beyond the necessarily limited site of their implementation.[46]

CONCLUSION

In this chapter, I addressed the question of what it is to become a virtuous thinker and speaker who participates in our ordinary practices of knowledge justly as opposed to unjustly. Fricker invites us to take up a perspective from which each of us cultivates corrective virtues to provide redress for the everyday epistemic injustices represented by hermeneutic and testimonial injustice. Her critics point instead to the need to challenge the structural sources of such domination. I suggest that both parties capture part of the truth. I agree with Fricker that there are certain identifiable wrongs of a hybrid ethical and epistemological nature that are sufficiently serious to count as forms of epistemic injustice. In seeking to redress them, the liberal state plays an enabling role for corrective virtue. That is because the neutrality characteristic of liberal societies when it comes to comprehensive views of how people ought to live does not extend to the honoring of those very values which makes a liberal society possible. In its expressive dimension, a liberal democratic state can act so as to facilitate the exercise of corrective virtue on the part of individuals who seek to become just in their epistemic dealings with others.[47]

NOTES

1. Fricker 2007.
2. Williams 1985, 9.
3. Fricker 2007.
4. Fricker 2007, chaps. 4 and 7.
5. Anderson 2012; Bohman 2012.
6. Nagel 1998; Brettschneider 2012, 10–11.
7. Brettschneider 2012, 168.
8. Nagel 1998, 24.
9. The target notion, then, as Chris Hookway helpfully puts it, is "distinctive forms of personal wrong that are both epistemological and an injustice." Hookway 2010, 151.
10. Asch 1951.
11. Welbourne 1986; Morton 2012.
12. Fricker 2007, 148–150.
13. Hauser 2016. Cited also by Owen 2016.

14. Gigerenzer and Selten 2001. Specifically, in the case of stereotypes, the risk is that they will be assumed to be representative in the absence of knowledge of the prior probabilities that underpin this representativeness.
15. Mark LeBar has suggested to me a fourth, alternative line of explanation: that the harm to Isabel Hern is not epistemic but an undermining judgment regarding her authority to speak. This diagnosis of the case requires a fuller response than I can give here. I would note, however, that one might reasonably treat cases of testimonial authority as grounded on a prior entitlement to that authority. Further, in this kind of case, one might ground an authority to speak on a track record of reliability in getting things right (of the kind that is at the kernel of David Estlund's theory of democratic authority in which the moral authority of democratic legislation presupposes the answer to a prior epistemic question of reliability). So in any appeal to authority, an epistemic question is deferred but not wholly avoided. Estlund 2009.
16. Williams 2002, chap. 8.
17. Thomas 2015.
18. Specifically, in the case of Millian rights, that they be assignable to a specific individual and that the responsibility for rectifying breaches of rights has broad scope and is applicable to anyone.
19. Feinberg 1974.
20. Thomas 2012.
21. Greco 2003; Greco 2008.
22. For a very interesting analysis of cases where it does, see Jones 2012.
23. Owen 2016.
24. Williams 2009, 12. Williams continues: "To be sure, the normative rules in play cannot, in the first instance, be imperatival in form: they cannot be what Sellars calls 'ought-to-do' rules. But not all rules are 'ought to do.' "
25. Williams, following Sellars, argues that the former are subject to "ought to be" not "ought to do" rules: they can be challenged in such a way that the default entitlement that they establish can be undermined. "Default entitlements only accrue to accredited epistemic subjects. The status of epistemic subject, along with that of moral agent, is earned through training and acculturation" (Williams 2009, 13). They are subject to what Williams calls "external authorizing conditions" (2009, 16), and some of these may be enablers and not reasons, considerations that allow other considerations to play the reason-giving role (2009, 17).
26. Burge 1993; Stevenson 1993.
27. Rosanvallon 2013, 10–11.
28. Rosanvallon 2013, 12–13.
29. Sieyès 1982, 26; emphasis added.
30. Owen 2016.
31. Cavell 1999, 376–377; emphasis added.

32. Owen 2016; Rosen 2012, 57–58.
33. Austin 1962.
34. For some of the relevant complexities in the appeal to "structure" here, see Pettit 2012, 43–44, 63; Hayward 2011, 484–487.
35. Estlund 2009; Christiano 2010; Thomas 2017, chap. 12.
36. Brettschneider 2012.
37. Brettschneider 2012, 109.
38. Brettschneider 2012, 75. In Brettschneider's account, they are at the limit of a broader class of "discriminatory viewpoints" that "oppose or are inconsistent with the ideal of free and equal citizenship" (2012, 4).
39. Brettschneider 2012, 1.
40. Brettschneider 2012, 7, 22. In the light of values that are, reflexively, justified as public reasons (Brettschneider, 2012, 14.) Another noteworthy aspect of Brettschneider's account of "democratic persuasion" is that it is intended to go beyond presenting counterarguments and actually to win them.
41. Brettschneider 2012, 45.
42. Brettschneider's view (2012, 47) is that this is most effectively brought about by promulgating the reasons for rights, namely, the ideal of freedom and equality itself.
43. Brettschneider 2012, 101.
44. Brettschneider calls this the illiberal dystopia of an invasive state but focused on defending not a state's illiberal values but liberal values; it uses "coercion to enforce the values of free and equal citizenship" with no further constraints on that intervention (2012, 10–11).
45. Anderson 2012, 168.
46. Thomas 2017, chap. 3.
47. For very helpful comments on this chapter, I am grateful to Kathryn Brown, Machteld Geuskens, and Mark LeBar.

WORKS CITED

Anderson, Elizabeth. 2012. "Epistemic Justice As a Virtue of Social Institutions." *Social Epistemology* 26, no. 2: 163–173.

Asch, Solomon. 1955. "Opinions and Social Pressure." *Scientific American* 193, no. 5: 31–35.

Austin, J. L. 1962. *How to Do Things with Words*. Oxford and New York: Oxford University Press.

Bohman, James. 2012. "Domination, Epistemic Injustice and Republican Epistemology." *Social Epistemology* 26, no. 2: 175–187.

Brettschneider, Corey. 2012. *When the State Speaks, What Should It Say?* Princeton: Princeton University Press.

Burge, Tyler. 1993. "Content Preservation." *Philosophical Review* 102, no. 4: 457–488.

Cavell, Stanley. 1999 [1979]. *The Claim of Reason: Wittgenstein, Skepticism, Morality, and Tragedy*. Oxford and New York: Oxford University Press.

Christiano, Thomas. 2010. "The Uneasy Relationship between Democracy and Capital." *Social Philosophy and Policy* 27, no. 1: 195–217.

Estlund, David. 2009. *Democratic Authority: A Philosophical Framework*. Princeton: Princeton University Press.

Feinberg, Joel. 1974. "Noncomparative Justice." *Philosophical Review* 83, no. 3: 297–338.

Fricker, Miranda. 2007. *Epistemic Injustice: Power and the Ethics of Knowing*. New York: Oxford University Press.

Gigerenzer, Gerd, and Richard Selten, eds. 2001. *Bounded Rationality: The Adaptive Toolbox*. Cambridge: MIT Press.

Greco, John. 2003. "Knowledge As Credit for True Belief." In *Intellectual Virtue: Perspectives from Ethics and Epistemology*, edited by Michael DePaul and Linda Zagzebski, 111–134. New York: Oxford University Press.

Greco, John. 2008. "What's Wrong with Contextualism?" *Philosophical Quarterly* 58, no. 232: 416–436.

Hauser, Christine. 2016. "Black Doctor Says Delta Flight Attendant Rejected Her; Sought 'Actual Physician.'" *New York Times*, October 14. http://www.nytimes.com/2016/10/15/us/black-doctor-says-delta-flight-attendant-brushed-her-aside-in-search-of-an-actual-physician.html?_r=0.

Hayward, Clarissa Rile. 2011. "What Can Political Freedom Mean in a Multicultural Democracy? On Deliberation, Difference and Democratic Government." *Political Theory* 39, no. 4: 468–497.

Hookway, Christopher. 2010. "Some Varieties of Epistemic Injustice: Reflections on Fricker." *Episteme* 7, no. 2: 151–163.

Jones, Karen. 2012. "The Politics of Intellectual Self-Trust." *Social Epistemology* 26, no. 2: 237–251.

Morton, Adam. 2012. *Bounded Thinking: Intellectual Virtues for Limited Agents*. Oxford: Oxford University Press.

Nagel, Thomas. 1998. "Concealment and Exposure." *Philosophy and Public Affairs* 27, no. 1: 3–30.

Owen, David. 2016. "Epistemic Dignity and Racial Justice." Seminar paper, University of Alabama.

Rosen, Michael. 2012. *Dignity: Its History and Meaning*. Cambridge: Harvard University Press.

Sieyès, Abbé. 1982 [1788]. "Essai sur les privilèges." In *Qu'est-ce que le tiers état?*, edited by Abbé Sieyès, 1. Paris: Presses Universitaires de France.

Stevenson, Leslie. 1993. "Why Believe What People Say?" *Synthese* 94: 429–451.

Thomas, Alan. 2012. "Giving Each Person Her Due: Taurek Cases and Non-Comparative Justice." *Ethical Theory and Moral Practice* 15, no. 5: 661–676.

Thomas, Alan. 2015. "Williams on Integrity, Ground Projects and Reasons to Be Moral." In *Why Be Moral?* edited by Robert B. Louden and B. Himmelmann, 249–272. Berlin: De Gruyter.

Thomas, Alan. 2017. *Republic of Equals: Predistribution and Property-Owning Democracy*. New York: Oxford University Press.

Welbourne, Michael. 1986. *The Community of Knowledge*. Aberdeen: Aberdeen University Press.

Williams, Bernard. 2002. *Truth and Truthfulness*. Princeton: Princeton University Press.

Williams, Michael. 2009. "Responsibility and Reliability." *Philosophical Papers* 37, no. 1: 1–26.

Chapter 9

Confucian Values and Resources for Justice

MAY SIM

INTRODUCTION

Some commentators maintain that the historical content and context of Confucian relations that are based on familial and hierarchical kinships prohibit Confucianism from offering a general account of relationships and virtues that can be extended to equals and strangers beyond the family, that is, righteousness or justice. I challenge such an account by showing that even though the Confucian virtues are cultivated first in the family, they transcend the family hierarchy and apply to everyone else. Apart from the universal applicability of the Confucian virtues, I show how self-determination is inseparable from the exercise of justice in Confucianism, since one must be capable of freely choosing one's action in order to be a moral agent. Accordingly, I explore the familial, social, and political resources for self-determination in Confucianism.

Jiwei Ci is a contemporary commentator who is skeptical that Confucianism has the resources for a "general insight into the social or relational character of person," that is, justice.[1] There is not a single Chinese term in classical Confucianism that is the translation of *justice*.

If justice is construed as a moral virtue that enables someone to relate or act well toward other human beings (as Plato and Aristotle understand it; see chapter 1 by Woodruff in this volume), then the Confucian virtue of *yi* (義, sometimes translated as *righteousness, justice,* or *appropriateness*) is a functional equivalent. Just as Plato's account of justice in the *Republic* presupposes other moral virtues such as wisdom, courage, and temperance, and Aristotle's account of general justice in the *Nicomachean Ethics* presupposes all the character virtues (e.g., temperance, truthfulness, courage, honor, generosity, friendliness, etc.), the Confucian virtue of righteousness (*yi*) also requires other virtues such as truthfulness, reciprocity, courage, fairness, and so on. Accordingly, when Ci talks about how a Confucian account of kinship is not general enough to include the virtues of relating to strangers, he is referring to its impotence as the virtue of justice. Ci disagrees with rival interpreters who maintain that Confucianism's communitarian understanding of human relations is superior to liberalism's extreme individualist perspective, while maintaining that both of these perspectives are problematic. Contrary to Ci's understanding of Confucianism, I show how Confucianism not only can account for justice or righteousness but can also offer resources for justifying self-determination, a prerequisite for exercising justice. In showing the Confucian resources for self-determination, I am also responding to Ci's claim that China lacks "the value of freedom" because "freedom is not available as a moral resource . . . and as a right."[2]

THE SHORTCOMING OF MODELING THE STATE ON THE FAMILIAL HIERARCHY ACCORDING TO CI

In "The Confucian Relation Concept of the Person and Its Modern Predicament," Ci argues against the possibility of deriving "a general Confucian relational concept of the person from its historical content and context."[3] He starts by showing that Confucian relationships are historically based on "the five primary relations between father and son, ruler and minister, husband and wife, older and younger [brothers], and friend and friend."[4] Ci maintains that the most important of these is the hierarchical father-son relation, while the "most dispensable" is friendship, which is also the only relation accessible to equals. He explains that the father-son relation embodies both the natural hierarchy and affection (of father for son) in Confucianism, so that the virtue of filial piety, of which brotherly piety is a variant, is the ultimate basis of humaneness or benevolence. In Confucianism, the virtue of filial piety (*xiao*, 孝) is the love, respect, and obedience that children have toward their parents, and brotherly piety (*di*, 弟) refers to the love and deference that a younger brother accords to his elder brother. Humaneness or benevolence (*ren*, 仁) is the highest virtue in which one's familial love is extended, in a graduated manner, to the broader community. More important for Ci, the father-son relation is the model "of a more general principle that governs all hierarchical relations," namely, the principle that the superior is morally obligated to the inferior.[5] Just as the father is morally obligated to care for his son, the ruler is obligated to care for his people.

More elaborately, Ci observes that the affection in the father-son relation is not merely a one-sided obligation that the father owes the son but is also the natural basis for "the general principle of reciprocity," which shows up in the virtue of *yi* (righteousness or justice), which governs the ruler-ruled relation.[6] Just as filial piety (i.e., respect and conformity) is due from a son to a father, a ruled person owes righteousness (*yi*) to the ruler; that is, the ruled honors and defers to the ruler because of the ruler's superior moral character. Despite the hierarchy in these familial and state relations, in which the subordinate owes the superior respect and obedience, the natural love a father has for his son offers the reciprocity that tempers this natural father-son hierarchy and other hierarchical relations for Ci. The result is a reciprocity between the two hierarchies: the highest virtue of *ren* that a ruler has for his people (by extending his familial love to everyone under his rule in the state) is reciprocated by the virtue of righteousness (*yi*), that is, the appropriate behavior of obedience and conformity that the people exhibit toward the ruler (cultivated by their extension of filial piety in the family to obedience in the state). As Ci puts it, "The family, then, through its cultivation of the flexible virtue of filial piety, serves as the training ground for loyal obedience (*zhong*) in the hierarchical relation between the ruler and his subjects. The result is the ruling of the state on the model of the family."[7]

In spite of the fact that ruling a state is modeled on the family, Ci argues that this model is limited to the family and the clan and is impotent in nonhierarchical relations in the state. Granting that the family model works for the relationship between ruler and subjects, in that the ruler acts as a father to the subjects in a state, which is just a larger or extended family, and the subjects in turn extend the virtues of filial and fraternal piety to the ruler, Ci questions whether the subjects know how to relate to one another as they move beyond their clans, because he claims that they know how to behave only in hierarchical relationships but not in relationships between equals:

> Although the subjects know how to relate to the ruler (by knowing how to relate to the father), they still do not know how to relate to each other when they move beyond the boundary of the clan. There the customary relations of "natural" hierarchy-reciprocity end, and they know not what to do . . . they do not know how to relate to others except on the basis of family and kinship ties.[8]

Thus, Ci thinks that the traditional familial hierarchy-reciprocity virtues cannot be extended to nonhierarchical modern relations between strangers. Stressing that equality is increasingly significant in both familial and intimate relations, as well as in relations among strangers, Ci says, "It is only when individuals relate to one another as equals that it is possible for them to relate to all potential strangers."[9]

I think that Ci's misunderstanding of the Confucian virtues led him to limit them to the traditional Chinese society. I argue that beyond the hierarchical familial and political relations, a proper understanding of the Confucian virtues can not only provide general insights for relating to strangers in a modern society but also justify a certain degree of freedom and self-determination that is required for a democracy.[10]

INDISPENSABILITY OF FRIENDSHIP AMONG THE FIVE PRIMARY RELATIONSHIPS

To begin, I think that Ci downplays the significance of the relationship between friends when he characterizes it as the "most dispensable" of the five primary relationships. Not surprisingly, dispensing with the relationship between equals comes hand in glove with Ci's claim that Confucianism does not have the resources for nonhierarchical relations between strangers who are equals. Contrary to Ci, friendship is key to Confucianism. Consider Confucius's assertion: "To have friends [*peng* 朋] come from distant quarters—is this not a source of enjoyment?" (1.1).[11] *Peng*, as Ames and Rosemont explained, refers to students who share the same teacher and hence are equals.[12] In this context, *peng* refers to how these students of Confucius originate from states separated by great distance, showing that strangers can not only relate to one another as friends but also give joy to one another. The joy comes from the fact that one could learn much more from a stranger, and learning (*xue*, 學) is a virtue that Confucius emphasizes, as it enables one to cultivate all the Confucian virtues.[13]

Friendship is significant, too, because it is the relationship in which the virtue of trust or truthfulness (*xin*, 信) is cultivated. Truthfulness is such a key virtue that Confucius wonders if one who is not truthful or who does not live up to one's words can be a person (2.22, *ren er wu xin*, 人而無信). By this, he means that trust is such a key part of personhood that unless one has this virtue of living up to one's words, one lacks the essential function of a person, that is, one who stands by what he says. Put otherwise, if someone utters words to which he does not adhere, he cannot relate well to others or have any dealings with them. Imagine a constant liar in whom no one trusts. Given Confucius's emphasis on human relations in everything we do and as prerequisites for the cultivation of virtues (including the virtue of *yi*, righteousness), culminating in the highest virtue of *ren*, humaneness, it follows that one cannot even be regarded as a person without trust. This is because someone who lacks the trust of others would be isolated and would be incapable of perfecting his humaneness, which virtue is definitive of one's humanity for Confucius.[14] The character of *xin*, 信 illustrates this well, for it is composed of the radical for *person* (*ren*, 人) next to the radical for *speech* (*yan*, 言), showing that a trustworthy person is one who stands by his speech.

More elaborately, one of Confucius's disciples, Zengzi, includes under his daily self-examination of three items the following: "In my interaction with friends [*peng you*, 朋友], have I not been truthful/trustworthy?"[15] Self-examination or reflection is one way of cultivating oneself, and that friendship helps one to cultivate the virtues is evident when Confucius insists that one ought not to befriend another who is not as good as oneself (1.8). In this same analect, he also advocates that one who is cultivating oneself to become an exemplary person (*junzi*, 君子), who necessarily possesses the virtues of *yi* (justice) and *ren* (humaneness), among others,[16] should focus on the significance of being truthful (*xin*). The implication is that choosing a friend who is one's equal in goodness is key to cultivating the virtue of *xin* that is a prerequisite for being a person and for becoming a *junzi*. Put otherwise, if friends are not mutually trustworthy or truthful to each other, they cannot alert each other about their weaknesses, which knowledge is required for cultivating the virtues. In contrast to Ci's view that friendship is dispensable, Confucius's *Analects* shows that befriending one's equal is vital to one's personhood, learning, cultivating the virtues of truthfulness, and becoming an exemplary person.[17] Far from not knowing how to relate to strangers or equals, befriending them entails a choice of whom one befriends, learning from each other, being truthful, and reflecting on one's friendship to cultivate oneself.

THE SIGNIFICANCE OF FRIENDSHIP AS A BRIDGE BETWEEN THE FAMILY AND THE STATE FOR MENCIUS

Not only is the relationship between friends indispensable among the five primary relations for Confucius, but a look at Mencius's philosophy will show how it also bridges the familial and hierarchical relations in the state by being the only relation that can reflect the basis of, and what is common to, all these relations. More specifically, Mencius asserts that someone cannot bring order to the people unless he gains the confidence of his superiors (4A 12.1).[18] An instance of such ineffectiveness in bringing order to the people could be a government official's inability to rule the people unless he has the confidence of the ministers. For someone to gain the confidence of his superiors, Mencius claims, he must gain the trust of his friends, which cannot be obtained unless he serves his parents in a way that makes them happy. In turn, someone cannot make his parents happy unless he finds, upon examining himself, that he is sincere. To be sincere, Mencius maintains that one must be enlightened about the good (*shan*, 善). Being enlightened about the good or sincerity is, for Mencius, the Way of Heaven. Mencius goes on to explain that to reflect on sincerity is the human Way, which, for him, necessarily inspires others (4A 12.1).

Given that the human Way is dependent on the Way of Heaven for knowing the good or sincerity, an elaboration of the Way of Heaven is in order. Mencius believes that Heaven produced everything in the world, humankind and things included, with the principles or laws of nature that govern them (6A 6.8).[19] Mencius quotes the *Odes*:

> Heaven gives birth to the teeming people.
> If there is a thing, there is a norm.
> This is the constant people cleave to.
> They are fond of this beautiful Virtue. (6A 6.8)

More specifically, Mencius holds that all human beings are born with the four incipient virtues of humaneness/benevolence (*ren*, 仁), righteousness/justice, propriety, and wisdom; "they are not welded to us externally" (6A 6.7). Accordingly, he claims that all we need is to reflect with our Heaven-endowed heart/mind (*xin*, 心) to know our nature and the virtues that govern us, as well as the norms that govern all things.[20] Because of Mencius's belief that "in general, things of the same kind are all similar" (6A 7.3), and he holds that "We and the sage are of the same kind" (7.4),[21] he also thinks that our hearts take pleasure in the same virtues, namely, order (*li*, 理) and righteousness/justice (*yi*, 義), just as all human mouths take pleasure in eating meat (6A 7.8).

Mencius's analysis of sincerity (or being enlightened about the good) shows that it is the sameness rather than the difference in human nature and human virtues that serves both the private and the public good. Rather than a move from filial piety to obedience and conformity to the ruler in the state, that is, the hierarchical relations that Ci stresses, the basis of both familial and state relations is an understanding of human nature and the human good and virtues that are the same for all human beings. Contrary to the hierarchical relations in the family and the state, the relation of friendship and the virtue of truthfulness or trust best capture the human Way of reflecting on one's enlightenment about the good, because we are all equal in our ability to be sincere. Put otherwise, only among friends is someone most free to speak the truth, uncensored by the ritual proprieties that govern filial relations with parents or obedience and conformity to rulers.

As Mencius puts it, "People have a common saying: 'The world, the state, the family.' The root of the world lies in the state; the root of the state lies in the family; the root of the family lies in oneself."[22] For Mencius, the individual is the ultimate foundation of order in the family, the state, and the world. This is because all individuals are alike in their human nature by having the incipient virtues of *ren* (humaneness) and *yi* (justice), along with the virtues of ritual propriety and wisdom. Since human nature already comes with these sprouts of virtue, Mencius holds that human beings are not only good by nature, by being inclined toward the virtues, but they can also know their nature and virtues such as humaneness and justice. Relations between friends (i.e., individuals) are not only indispensable but key for adjudicating other relations, because they transcend any cultural parochialism of families and states by being based on the universality of human nature.

Far from being dispensable, then, friendship is crucial to realizing the sameness of our human nature and virtues. Human nature sets our norm as the human Way of reflecting on our sincerity, or serving Heaven by completing our nature and the natures of all things produced by Heaven.[23] One way for there to be trust between friends is if they could see each other exercise the virtue of filial piety (that is, the ritual propriety of love, respect, and obedience toward parents), because they are alike in having this incipient virtue, as well as take delight in watching the same exercise of virtue. This is why it is important in Confucianism to choose a friend who is as good as oneself. Having the trust of one's friends can lead to having the trust of one's superiors, because the obedience and deference toward one's parents in the home (which is the basis of trust in friendship) is also the root of the virtue of righteousness (*yi*) in relating to one's superiors. Put otherwise, just as it is right to obey and defer to one's parents because it realizes filial piety, it is just or righteous to obey and honor one's superiors because of their moral goodness.

Contrary to Ci, there is not a gap between familial and nonfamilial, hierarchical and equal, because the same human nature exists in everyone; everyone relates to others who are kin and nonkin. Perfecting these relationships, that is, justice, stems from perfecting one's own nature, which already contains the sprouts of humaneness, righteousness, ritual propriety, and wisdom, which nature is universally shared by all human beings.

THE VIRTUE OF RECIPROCITY IN EQUALIZING RELATIONSHIPS

Another way in which Ci misunderstands Confucianism is in his restriction of the virtue of reciprocity (*shu*, 恕) to hierarchical relations, coining the term "hierarchy reciprocity" to capture the reciprocal virtues between fathers and sons as well as rulers and ruled. More elaborately, Ci's understanding of hierarchy reciprocity is different from the virtue of reciprocity per se in Confucianism, because whereas different actions are expected in the former, in which unequals are engaged in reciprocity, the same action is expected in the latter, in which equals are engaged in reciprocity. For instance, in a hierarchy reciprocity between fathers and sons, fathers are to love and care for their sons, while sons are to obey and defer to their fathers. In contrast to Ci's hierarchy reciprocity between unequals, reciprocity in Confucianism is primarily a relationship between equals that is best captured by the "silver rule": "Don't do to another what you don't want done to you."

Reciprocity (*shu*) is also included as a virtue that is prerequisite to *ren* (humaneness). For instance, responding to Zhonggong's inquiry about how to become humane (*ren*), Confucius says, "Do not impose upon others what you yourself do not want, and you will not incur personal or political ill will" (12.2). Again, when asked (by Zigong) about the one saying that captures how someone should act in his entire life, Confucius says, "There is *shu* [恕]: do not impose on others what you yourself do not want."[24] I think that for the Confucians, to put oneself in another person's place in reciprocity is an act of equality rather than one of hierarchy. What is reciprocated is the act of not imposing on another the *same* action that you do not want him to impose on you. This is not the case in Ci's proposed concept of hierarchy reciprocity, in which *different* actions are due from the people in hierarchical relations. For Ci, whereas a ruler behaves with humaneness toward the ruled, the ruled behaves with obedience and conformity to the ruler, that is, righteousness or justice. In contrast to Ci's account, I think that even when reciprocity is exercised in hierarchical relations, what is emphasized is the sameness between agent and patient, so that the same action that one does not desire is not imposed on another.

Consider Mencius's remark: "Losing the people is due to losing their hearts. . . . There is a Way for getting their hearts: that which you desire, share with them in accumulating, and that which you dislike, do not inflict on them" (4A 9.1). Reciprocity provides a measure for being a virtuous ruler: he is to use his own likes and dislikes to act toward his people, sharing the former and refraining from the latter. Again, the ruler does this by equalizing himself with the people rather than behaving as if he were separate from and superior to them. If equalizing himself with his people is the right thing for the ruler to do, then the act of reciprocity between a virtuous ruler and the ruled is necessarily one that is also just (*yi*).[25] The ruler is not trying to accord himself more in terms of profits, for instance. Thus, justice in the distribution of goods is achieved.

Misinterpreting the Confucian view of reciprocity also meant that Ci missed yet another key equalizing aspect in this ethical tradition, just as he missed the resources for relating equals in friendship. This is another reason he denies that Confucianism could provide the resources for relating to strangers or people who are equals. In other words, Ci is charging Confucianism with lacking the resources for righteousness or justice because he neglects the primary meaning of reciprocity (*shu*), which is a virtue that relates people who are equals, substituting hierarchy reciprocity, which relates unequals for it instead.

JUSTICE (*YI*) AS A VIRTUE IN HUMAN RELATIONSHIPS

Another Confucian virtue that is salient for navigating relations with strangers, one that I touched on earlier, is *yi* (義, righteousness/justice/appropriateness).[26] Like the virtues of truthfulness, reciprocity, and sincerity, *yi* is a virtue for achieving the highest virtue of humaneness (*ren*). As such, it is a virtue that is required for everyone's perfection regardless of one's role. This is because *yi* is about doing what is just or appropriate rather than being partial.

Confucius says, "Exemplary persons [*junzi* 君子] in making their way in the world are neither bent on nor against anything; rather, they go with what is appropriate [*yi* 義]" (4.10). More elaborately, *yi* concerns those things or situations that could benefit one at the expense of another and thus tempt one to do what is inappropriate or unrighteous, such as situations involving profit, protecting one's own safety, or not living up to one's words. Confucius asserts: "If on seeing a chance to profit, they think of *yi*, on seeing danger they are ready to give their lives, and when long in desperate straits, they still do not forget the words they live by—such persons can also be said to be complete" (14.12). *Yi* is the virtue that enables someone to do the right thing, for instance, by being fair in the distribution of goods and being courageous or truthful, regardless of the benefits to oneself that wrongdoing may bring.

As I've explained elsewhere:

> Just as justice for Aristotle is the crown of our other-regarding virtues, *yi* for Confucius sums up the abilities that allow one to act correctly toward others. The *phronimos* with the fullness of virtue necessarily possesses justice and self-regarding virtues such as courage, temperance, and self-love. Similarly, the one with *ren*, for Confucius, is disposed to *yi* and so extends himself to doing what is good for human beings in general.[27]

More elaborately, I explained that there are three senses of *yi* that enable Confucius's exemplary person to act justly in any circumstances.[28] The three senses of *yi* are (1) the *junzi*'s virtue or cultivated disposition to act justly, for example, with truthfulness and courage; (2) the *junzi*'s actual act of justice, which realizes his disposition or virtue of justice, such as his act of fairness in distributing goods or courage in times of danger; and (3) the *junzi*'s knowledge of "the *kind* of action that is just (i.e., a universal standard shared by the community conversant with *li* [ritual propriety]," for instance, that "equitable actions are just and stealing is unjust."[29]

Mencius would agree with Confucius that someone who behaves with *yi* (義) is complete in his virtues, because Mencius holds that *yi* is the way (*dao*, 道) or path to the ultimate virtue of humaneness. He says, "Humaneness is one's home and *yi* is one's way [*dao*]" (仁家義道, 4A 10.2–10.3; my translation). The lesson from Mencius's analysis is that *yi*, as a Confucian virtue, is not limited to the family or hierarchical relations, as Ci would have it. Rather, like the other Confucian virtues, *yi*, Mencius maintains, is a virtue that is to be fully achieved by everyone. This is because *yi* is one of the four incipient virtues in human nature and is also the necessary path to human perfection. Mencius says, "There are things [i.e., *yi*, 義, righteousness] one desires more than life, and there are also things one hates more than death. It is not the case that only the worthy person has this heart. All humans have it. The worthy person simply never loses it" (6A 10.5). Put otherwise, for Mencius, the feeling of shame or disdain is innate in everyone and is the sprout of *yi*. Feeling shame when one does something that is morally wrong is what spurs one on to improve oneself. He says, "Shame is indeed important for people! . . . If one is not ashamed of not being as good as others, how will one ever be as good as others?" (7A 7.1–7.3).

Apart from being one of the four innate virtues, *yi* for Mencius is also the way (*dao*) to reach the highest virtue of *ren*. Since *ren* is the ultimate goal for all human beings, *yi*, as the way to *ren*, is not restricted to only certain groups, say, those who are superior in hierarchical relations as opposed to those who are inferior in status. Consider the generality of Mencius's remarks about humaneness (*ren*) and righteousness/justice (*yi*):

> People all have things that they will not bear. To extend this reaction to that which they will bear is *ren*. People all have things that they will not do. To extend this reaction to that which they will do is *yi*. If people can fill out the heart that does not desire to harm others, their benevolence will be inexhaustible. If people can fill out the heart that will not trespass, their righteousness will be inexhaustible. (7B 31.1–31.2)

Starting from the innate virtues in every person's natural feelings, reaching the highest Confucian virtue is a matter of extending one's natural compassion, and a heart that is ashamed of immoral acts toward one's own family, to others who are not one's kin. In other words, if human beings naturally do not desire to harm or be unrighteous toward their kin, extending such a desire to others who are not their kin, be they equals or superiors, is precisely what Confucianism teaches.

It is important to note here that even though all human beings are born with compassion, for Mencius, this feeling is only the sprout of the virtue of humaneness. To achieve the full virtue of humaneness, one must cultivate this feeling so that it extends from one's own family to others who are not one's kin in the larger community. The same requirement of cultivating one's feeling of shame that begins with one's unrighteous or immoral acts in the family context so that this feeling of shame is extended to unjust acts outside one's familial relations, that is, to strangers, is the way to achieve the full virtue of justice.[30] The reason Confucianism can provide resources for relations between equals, even though its virtues are first cultivated in the familial hierarchical relations, is that the moral norms are general standards for all human beings. Being righteous or acting with appropriateness is required in all relationships.[31]

What this closer examination of the virtue of *yi* or justice in Confucianism shows is that, like the other virtues (e.g., learning, truthfulness, sincerity, and reciprocity) *yi*, too, is a way for one to relate to others regardless of whether they are in a hierarchical or equal relationship to one. To refrain from taking something to which one is not entitled (7A 33.3), that is, to exercise *yi*, is not only correct in one's interactions with family relations. Rather, it is the general norm for interacting with anyone, strangers and equals alike. To fail to extend such righteousness to others because they are strangers or equals is precisely to fail in being humane (*ren*), to fail to extend one's love for one's own family to others in the wider world.

HUMANENESS (*REN*) AS THE ULTIMATE CONFUCIAN VIRTUE IN ALL HUMAN RELATIONSHIPS

Thus far, we have seen that *ren* is the ultimate virtue for Confucianism, which one begins cultivating in familial relationships and which is gradually extended to others in the community regardless of whether they are equal or hierarchically related to one.[32] The virtues that are required to become *ren* are continuous with those required in a family, because virtues such as truthfulness, sincerity, reciprocity, and justice/righteousness are required in all situations, without which someone cannot be moral or perfect his human nature. More specifically, these are virtues of character, which an exemplary person (*junzi*, 君子) does not discard, because they are stable qualities that make him who he is.

If Ci has raised any doubts that Confucian virtues are extended to all human beings, strangers and equals alike, Confucius's remark that *ren* is to love human beings (*ai ren*, 爱人) and that knowledge is to know human beings (*zhi ren*, 知人) should dispel them (12.22). That such love leads to reciprocal actions is evident in Confucius's claim that "those who are *ren* establish others when desiring to establish themselves; promote others when desiring to reach their goals" (6.30; my translation). Put otherwise, what is good for an individual is not in conflict with what is good for others in the wider community. By helping others achieve their good, one is also helping one's own goodness. For instance, by helping others to become just, one is also exercising the virtue of justice by acting in an other-regarding manner that is virtuous. When others in one's community are just, they in turn enhance the goodness of the community within which one lives and hence further realize the virtue of justice that one desires.

RESOURCES FOR SELF-DETERMINATION IN CONFUCIANISM

Having shown how the Confucian virtues are resources for dealing with others who are equals or strangers, the most important of these virtues being that of humaneness (*ren*), which cannot be achieved without the others I've discussed, namely, truthfulness, sincerity, reciprocity, and justice (*yi*), I turn now to sketch how they can provide the resources for the sort of "exercise of initiative and choice . . . of self-making," or a "moral resource," that Ci finds lacking in "Chinese moral culture, both past and present."[33] In other words, I want to argue that if self-determination, or what Ci calls "self-making," is valued in this ethical tradition, the conditions to freely determine oneself ought to be protected in this tradition.[34]

That self-determination is essential to Confucianism can be shown by its indispensability in family relations, as well as in one's relationships with teachers and rulers. Despite the fact that the Confucian virtues are cultivated by following ritual proprieties in the family, such as the rituals of behaving with love, obedience, and respect toward one's parents and elders, Confucius enjoins one to remonstrate with one's parents in a certain way (4.18). For instance, we can imagine how a younger person with more knowledge about climate change might try to persuade his older parents to be more environmentally conscious in their daily lives. This assumes that obedience and respect for someone's elders is not blind and that someone is responsible for his elders' moral behavior. By trying to change his parents' behavior so that they are not using up more resources in the natural world than others or not destroying the environment more than what is unavoidable, this person is exercising the virtue of justice by working for a fair distribution of natural resources.

Confucius's stance against blind obedience extends to relationships with teachers beyond the family: "In striving to be *ren*, do not yield even to your teachers" (15.36). This means that even the virtue of learning demands the exercise of freedom, the freedom to differ from one's teachers if what they teach does not lead to justice or humaneness in as inclusive or as effective a way as possible. Self-determination here means that one should creatively and critically explore one's teacher's views so that one can expand on the virtue of humaneness.

Furthermore, the continuity between the family and the state also means that self-determination is extended to the state too. Confucius urges someone to withdraw from serving in a corrupt state, saying: "It is a disgrace to remain poor and without rank when the way [*dao*] prevails in the state; it is a disgrace to be wealthy and of noble rank when it does not" (8.13). If this sounds too passive as political self-determination, consider Mencius's more radical view asserting that a ruler who mutilates *ren* and righteousness cannot be called a "ruler" but instead, a "mere fellow," and one would be right to execute him (1B 8.3). Here again, the virtue of justice is key to one's actions as a citizen. Justice is not only one of the measures of good government but also the justification for the action one takes.

This analysis reveals that self-determination and justice guide one's familial, pedagogical, and political relations. This freedom is in turn based on the Confucian virtues, especially righteousness and humaneness (*ren*), which require the exercise of freedom and initiative in one's actions, rather than mere conformity and obedience. My argument about Confucianism and its resources for democracy is this: if *ren* and the other Confucian virtues require the freedom of choice (consider how friends are chosen, how choice is required in the virtues of reciprocity and righteousness, etc.), one could claim that the ability to choose one's actions, that is, to determine oneself, is a condition for the realization of the Confucian virtues. For instance, consider that someone cannot be *ren* unless he is able to choose to act with righteousness or reciprocity. Thus, a self-identified Confucian state, such as China, is one that is philosophically based on self-determination, regardless of whether such self-determination is being realized, for instance, the freedom to hold certain religious or political beliefs, without which its citizens cannot achieve their virtues.[35]

Moreover, if Confucianism enjoins someone to withdraw from a corrupt state or to remove someone who violates humaneness (*ren*) and justice (*yi*) from ruling, then it ought to endorse the self-determination or freedom to participate in government or to vote for one's rulers. Additionally, if truthfulness is a key virtue for Confucian personhood, then the freedom of speech is a condition for the realization of truthfulness in this ethical tradition. That a genuinely Confucian state that is striving for humaneness and righteousness or justice would advocate freedom of speech, freedom of thought, and freedom to participate in government follows from Confucianism as a moral theory, because these acts of freedom make possible the conditions for self-determination, without which none of the Confucian virtues is achievable.[36] Confucius's assertions that "Becoming *ren* is self-originating—how could it originate with others?" (12.1) and "It is the person who is able to broaden the way, not the way that broadens the person" (15.29) capture the role that self-determination plays in this tradition.

CONCLUSION

In contrast to Ci, I argue that the historical content and context of Confucian relations do not prohibit Confucianism from offering a general account of relationships that can be extended to equals and strangers beyond the family and hierarchical kinships and hence do not prevent it from offering resources for justice. This is because the Confucian virtues, though cultivated first in the family, transcend the family and hierarchy and apply to everyone else. Apart from the universal applicability of the Confucian virtues, I show how self-determination is inseparable from the exercise of these virtues. Accordingly, Confucianism can offer the resources for endorsing the freedom of speech, thought, and political participation, in short, democratic values, because these are the conditions that make possible the self-determination that is a prerequisite for the Confucian virtues, especially justice.

NOTES

1. Ci 2001, 163. Other commentators who are skeptical about the applicability of familial kinships to relationships within the state include Fukuyama 1995 and King 1985.
2. Ci 2014, 44–45.
3. Ci 2001, 149.
4. Ci 2001, 152.
5. Ci 2001, 153.
6. Ci 2001, 154.

7. Ci 2001, 155.
8. Ci 2001, 155.
9. Ci 2001, 156.
10. For my account of how Confucianism can justify both the first-generation civil and political rights as well as the second-generation economic, social, and cultural rights, see Sim 2010 and Sim 2011.
11. For all citations from Confucius's *Analects*, with my modifications, see Ames and Rosemont 1999.
12. Ames and Rosemont 1999, 230.
13. See 1.14 for Confucius's emphasis on the love of learning, as well as the significance of continuous learning for the cultivation of other virtues (2.4, 2.15, 17.8). See also 12.24, in which Zengzi says, "The exemplary person [*junzi*, 君子] attracts friends through culture [*wen*, 文], and through friendship promotes *ren*" (my modifications).
14. In prioritizing the community over the individual for human perfection, Confucius agrees with Aristotle's priority of the *polis* over the individual, since a solitary individual is incapable of perfecting his virtues. See Sim 2007a, chap. 6, esp. 175, for an elaborate discussion of this issue.
15. My translation of 1.4. See 1.7 for a similar remark; the difference is that truthfulness in 1.7 refers to one's speech, whereas 1.4 refers to the trustworthiness of one's actions and that a friend could be relied on for support. More elaborately, 1.7 emphasizes that one should live up to one's words in interactions with friends. And 5.26 has Confucius asserting that having trust in friendship is one of the things he most desires.
16. Confucius's exemplary person (*junzi*) is comparable to Aristotle's *phronimos*, who possesses all the virtues of character. See Sim 2007a, chap. 1, where I compare these authors' paradigmatic individuals by elaborating on how Confucius's *junzi* is a just person who "possesses the appropriate self and other-regarding virtues and the skill to accomplish the moral ends he sets out before him" (26) and contrast him with Thrasymachus in Plato's *Republic*, who would only act "justly" for his own gain.
17. See Sim 2007a, chap. 7, for details on how there are friendships between equals and unequals for Confucius and how both are essential to the cultivation of virtues.
18. For all references to and quotations from Mencius, with my modifications, see Van Norden 2009.
19. For the implications on self-determination of Mencius's account of heaven's relation to human nature, see Sim forthcoming 2019.
20. "The function of the heart is to reflect. If it reflects, then it will get it. If it does not reflect, then it will not get it. This is what Heaven has given us" (6A 15.2).
21. A detailed analysis of this is provided in Sim 2018.
22. 4A 5.1, 天下之本在國，國之本在家，家之本在身。.

23. See 7A 1.1–1.3, "To understand one's nature is to understand Heaven. To preserve one's heart and nourish one's nature is the way to serve Heaven"; and 7A 4.1, "The ten thousand things are all brought to completion by us." For details on how human nature is bound up with heaven's nature in Confucianism, see Sim 2007a, chap. 4; and Sim forthcoming 2019.
24. 15.24. See also 5.12, in which Zigong aspires to *shu*, and 4.15, in which Zengzi explains that "putting oneself in the other's place [*shu*, 恕], nothing more," captures the one thread that unites Confucius's *dao* (Way). For a detailed discussion of *shu*, see Sim 2007a, 42–45.
25. For a discussion of how both *shu* and *yi* are required for virtuous actions, see Sim 2007a, 156.
26. See Sim 2007a, 32–33, 156, for more details on Confucius's concept of *yi*.
27. Sim 2007a, 33.
28. I elaborate on the comparability between the concept of *ren* (humaneness) for Confucius and "general justice" for Aristotle (the possession of complete virtue toward another so that one always pursues the good or benefit of another) and between Confucius's *yi* (righteousness) and Aristotle's "special justice" (where one is just in a certain way, i.e., in situations concerning wealth, honor, or safety) in Sim 2010, 200–201. Since a *junzi* possesses *ren* (i.e., all of the moral virtues), he would also *always* act with *yi* (justice).
29. Sim 2007a, 32, 33 n.18.
30. Aristotle would disagree with Confucius that the sort of *yi* (righteousness or justice) cultivated in the home is the same as political justice. This is because political justice for Aristotle is between people who are proportionately or numerically equal and are in pursuit of a life that is self-sufficient and directed toward the common good. In contrast, Aristotle would maintain that neither equality nor self-sufficiency is available to familial relations. See Sim 2007a, 175, for details on this disagreement between the two thinkers. Ci's account that Confucian familial relations are impotent in providing resources for justice among strangers is closer to Aristotle's view.
31. For a discussion of how righteousness is required in a variety of life situations, such as humaneness and ritual propriety, see Sim 2007a, 156.
32. For more on my understanding of *ren*, see Sim 2012; Sim 2015.
33. Ci 2014, 45, 51.
34. For more on this argument, see Sim 2004; Sim 2007b. See also Sim 2007a, 156, where I discuss how the Confucian self must be able to make judgments and choices in order to act with virtue.
35. Consider the assertions by President Xi Jinping at the 2,565th commemoration of the day of Confucius's birth: "The ideology and culture of today's China . . . is a continuation and sublimation of traditional Chinese ideology and culture." And "Confucianism . . . is key to understanding the national

characteristics of the Chinese as well as the historical roots of the spiritual world of the present-day Chinese." Quoted in Gardels 2014.

36. It is important to note that even though Confucianism would endorse the civil and political rights I mention here, it would not tolerate the freedom to say, think, or do anything an individual wishes without any regard for the common good. Rather, the freedom it endorses would always be the freedom to pursue or carry out some virtue. See Sim 2013 for details on which sorts of rights are supported by Confucian values.

WORKS CITED

Ames, Roger T., and Henry Rosemont Jr. 1999. *The Analects of Confucius: A Philosophical Translation*. New York: Ballantine.

Ci, Jiwei. 2001. "The Confucian Relation Concept of the Person and Its Modern Predicament." In *Personhood and Health Care*, edited by D. C. Thomasma, D. N. Weisstub, and C. Herve, 149–164. Dordrecht: Kluwer Academic.

Ci, Jiwei. 2014. *Moral China in the Age of Reform*. New York: Cambridge University Press.

Fukuyama, Francis. 1995. "Confucianism and Democracy." *Journal of Democracy* 6, no. 2: 20–33.

Gardels, Nathan. 2014. "Xi Launches Cultural Counter-Revolution to Restore Confucianism as China's Ideology." *Huffington Post*. http://www.huffingtonpost.com/nathan-gardels/xi-jinping-confucianism_b_5897680.html.

King, Ambrose Y. C. 1985. "The Individual and Group in Confucianism: A Relational Perspective." In *Individualism and Holism: Studies in Confucian and Taoist Values*, edited by Donald Munro, 57–70. Ann Arbor: University of Michigan Press.

Sim, May. 2004. "A Confucian Approach to Human Rights." *History of Philosophy Quarterly* 21, no. 4 (October): 337–356.

Sim, May. 2007a. *Remastering Morals with Aristotle and Confucius*. New York: Cambridge University Press.

Sim, May. 2007b. "Virtue-Oriented Politics: Confucius and Aristotle." In *Aristotle's Politics Today*, edited by Lenn E. Goodman and Robert Talisse, 53–75. Albany: SUNY Press.

Sim, May. 2010. "Rethinking Virtue Ethics and Social Justice with Aristotle and Confucius." *Asian Philosophy* 20, no. 2: 195–213.

Sim, May. 2011. "Rival Confucian Rights: Left or Right Confucianism?" *International Philosophical Quarterly* 51, no. 1 (March): 5–22.

Sim, May. 2012. "Defining *Ren* for Confucius: Review of Roger Ames' *Confucian Role Ethics: A Vocabulary*." *Frontiers of Philosophy in China* 7, no. 4: 616–621.

Sim, May. 2013. "Confucian Values and Human Rights." *Review of Metaphysics* (September): 3–27.

Sim, May. 2015. "Why Confucius's Ethics Is a Virtue Ethics." In *The Routledge Companion to Virtue Ethics*, edited by Michael Slote and Lorraine Besser-Jones, 63–76. New York and London: Routledge.

Sim, May. 2018. "The *Phronimos* and the Sage." In *The Oxford Handbook of Virtue*, edited by Nancy E. Snow, 190–205. New York: Oxford University Press.

Sim, May. Forthcoming 2019. "Self-Determination and the Metaphysics of Human Nature in Aristotle and Mencius." In *Dao Companion to the Philosophy of Mencius*, edited by Yang Xiao. Netherlands: Springer.

Van Norden, Bryan W., trans. 2009. *The Essential Mengzi*. Cambridge: Hackett.

Chapter 10

Legislating the Personal Virtue of Justice

MATTHEW A. EDWARDS

INTRODUCTION

This chapter addresses the prospect of using law as a tool to inculcate the personal or individual virtue of justice. Such a project arguably falls under the rubric of "virtue jurisprudence," so my first task in this chapter is to situate the emerging virtue jurisprudence within the landscape of normative legal theory. After doing so, I discuss some of the major challenges that face any efforts to use the law to make people just—most notably the claim that the legislative virtue inculcation project might violate our shared liberal commitments to autonomy. Finally, the chapter highlights some of the ways we can conceptualize the legislative virtue inculcation project to make it less objectionable to possible critics.

THREE FORMS OF NORMATIVE LEGAL THEORY

The Dominant Forms of Normative Legal Theory

An understanding of virtue jurisprudence requires some basic knowledge of the current state of normative legal theory.[1] In contrast to work that primarily seeks to explain the content and contours of legal doctrine, "the ultimate goal of all normative legal theories is to justify final recommendations about what the law should be, all things considered, insofar as the state of the art permits."[2] To accomplish these aims, one of the core missions of normative legal theory is setting standards for the principled evaluation of existing or proposed legal rules, practices, and institutions.[3] Because law (arguably) lacks a significant normative core of its own,[4] the normative principles against which existing or proposed legal rules are judged largely come from outside law itself. Normative legal theory thus necessarily becomes parasitic, to some extent, upon the three prevailing schools of normative moral and ethical theory: consequentialism, deontology, and virtue ethics.[5]

The two dominant forms of normative legal theory are closely linked to consequentialism and deontology in moral or ethical theory. First, many scholars who are engaged in normative legal theorizing take a pragmatic stance; they focus on whether existing or proposed legal rules produce good outcomes (however "good" is defined) or achieve certain stipulated public policy objectives, which are assumed or separately demonstrated to be normatively desirable.[6] The law and economics movement, with its decidedly utilitarian flavor, is the prevailing example of this consequentialist school of thought in legal academia.[7] From this consequentialist perspective, legal rules are typically judged to be praiseworthy if they produce economically efficient or welfare-maximizing results.[8] In fact, some prominent law and economics scholars have argued forcefully that lawmakers should eschew completely any concerns unrelated to welfare in policy formulation.[9]

Obviously, such pragmatic reasoning raises a host of complex empirical issues as scholars and regulators settle on the proper metrics to measure the effects of a law (happiness, wealth, utility, efficiency, and so on) and show that the relevant legal rules or practices actually cause the desired beneficial effects. In this world view, normative legal theory largely becomes empirical, as policymakers and scholars draw on all of the tools of social science to figure out the path the law should take to maximize social welfare.[10] In terms of judicial decision-making (as distinguished from legislation or administrative rule-making), this pragmatic turn raises a host of issues related to the judicial role and rule of law, as judges move from their purported area of expertise (interpreting the meaning of authoritative legal texts) into the realm of social science and policymaking.[11]

Just as consequentialism in moral theory has its objectors—people who think that innocent fat men should not be pushed in front of trolleys[12]—some legal theorists eschew efficiency-based evaluation of legal rules grounded in utilitarian calculations or welfare economics in favor of the application of deontological principles to legal questions. These theorists focus their attention on whether law or legal institutions protect individual rights, liberty, and autonomy.[13] For example, when Michael Bloomberg was the mayor of New York City, his administration famously (and unsuccessfully) sought to limit portion sizes for soda sales in the city.[14] Ultimately, New York's highest court determined that the NYC Board of Health's administrative rules exceeded the scope of its regulatory authority and the plan was struck down.[15] But public objections to the plan had little to do with legal niceties concerning separation of powers or whether the regulatory scheme was likely to achieve its stated health goals. Instead, "[a]utonomy concerns about the portion rule dominated the public discourse. . . ."[16] Admittedly, the Bloomberg soda law might seem a bit of a minor issue in the annals of autonomy and choice. (An op-ed piece in the *New York Times* even chided: "Large cups of soda as symbols of human dignity? Really?")[17] But the soda issue illustrates how deontological arguments about law fundamentally differ from consequentialist arguments.

As a further illustration of deontological perspectives on legal regulation, Yofi Tirosh recently wrote a provocative article in support of a "right to be fat." According to Tirosh:

> A legal system that fails both to appreciate the uniqueness of literally every body and to allow its subjects the freedom to live their lives with their own, special, intimate bodily texture (which is both a product of who they are and makes them who they are) is a legal system that cannot claim to be based on the liberal premise of respect for basic liberty, autonomy, and dignity.[18]

Whether or not the law should recognize a right to be fat, this example illustrates the distinction between the two dominant forms of normative legal theory. Tirosh is quite careful to make clear that he is not relying on empirical data on obesity, which "serves primarily utilitarian, instrumentalist arguments." Instead, he is making a deontological, rights-based claim by asserting, that "Our concept of liberty should be broadened to include an appreciation of body size . . . as an important locus of freedom, autonomy, and dignity."[19]

Virtue Jurisprudence: The Third Path in Normative Legal Theory

Normative legal theory is dominated by consequentialist and deontological approaches;[20] most scholars explicitly or implicitly judge legal rules based on whether they produce good consequences or protect individual rights or liberties. More recently, however, a third path has emerged in normative legal theory, a path that is indebted to the resurgence of virtue ethics in modern moral theory. Just as it is hard to proffer a concise, cogent, and uncontroversial version of virtue ethics, it would take an entire book to explain what virtue jurisprudence entails and to argue why it is normatively superior to its consequentialist and deontological rivals. For our purposes, it is enough to note that those writing in the field of virtue jurisprudence accept the centrality of character, virtue, and authentic human flourishing (eudaimonia) in moral, ethical, and legal discourse.[21] Lawrence Solum states: "For virtue jurisprudence, the end of law is not to maximize preference satisfaction or to protect some set of rights and privileges: the goal or telos of law is to promote human flourishing—to enable individuals and to lead lives that express human excellence or virtue."[22] The basic thrust becomes clearer—and potentially much more controversial—when Solum explicates a virtue theory of legislation (as opposed to judging):[23] "Writ large, virtue jurisprudence is the view that the proper aim of legislation is the promotion of human flourishing through creation of the conditions for the development of human excellence—the distinctively human virtues and vices."[24] Virtue jurisprudence thus seems to be endorsing a central tenet of classic forms of virtue ethics: the notion that the law, along with other social institutions, should be used as a tool to inculcate individual virtues and promote authentic human flourishing:[25]

> As Aristotle and Augustine rightly held, a community's laws will inevitably play an important educative role in the life of the community. They can powerfully reinforce, or fail to reinforce, the teachings of parents and families, teachers and schools, religious leaders and communities, and other persons and institutions who have the leading roles in the moral formation of each generation.[26]

Thus far, there is very little virtue jurisprudence scholarship devoted specifically to virtue legislation, so we cannot be sure exactly what such a project might entail.[27] Nevertheless, the next section anticipates and discusses two major challenges to using the law to inculcate virtues such as justice.[28]

TWO MAJOR CHALLENGES TO LEGISLATIVE VIRTUE INCULCATION

Does Legislative Virtue Inculcation Violate Our Autonomy?

Many scholars have argued that the use of the law to promote virtue conflicts with our deep liberal commitments to individual autonomy.[29] The question is not whether law *can* change our character or make us virtuous; the question is whether using the law in such a way is morally permissible or unduly paternalistic.[30] This is "one of the great questions of political philosophy," as Michael Sandel states: "Does a just society seek to promote the virtue of its citizens? Or, should law be neutral among competing conceptions of virtue, so that citizens can be free to choose for themselves the best way to live?"[31]

Not surprisingly, debate over this subject largely concerns the use of criminal law to promote virtue and punish vice. For his part, Kyron Huigens has argued that "the inculcation and maintenance of the capacity for sound practical reasoning (virtue in its correct, technical sense) is a prominent objective of punishment that can justify punishment."[32] In opposition, Ekow Yankah has asserted that "a law dedicated to instilling virtue brushes aside our deepest liberal commitments," as it denies "to others their choice in building an authentic life of their own devising."[33] The conflict over the use of criminal law to inculcate virtue recalls the classic 1960s Hart-Devlin debate over the propriety of "morals legislation," including criminal laws prohibiting consensual homosexual relations.[34] The conventional wisdom is that those arguing against the legal regulation of personal morality decisively triumphed in this debate,[35] thus enshrining some version of Mill's harm principle[36] as a foundational value in legal discourse.[37]

The harm principle has even become an animating value in US constitutional law, much to the dismay of conservative Supreme Court justices. A case in point is *Obergefell v. Hodges*, the recent landmark gay marriage case, in which the Supreme Court explicitly held that same-sex couples have a fundamental right to marry that must be recognized in all states. Justice Anthony Kennedy, writing for the Court, found it "appropriate to observe these cases involve only the rights of two consenting adults whose marriages would pose no risk of harm to themselves or third parties."[38] Even though Kennedy's majority opinion in *Obergefell v. Hodges* made no mention of Mill, several conservative justices saw the harm principle at work.[39] Chief Justice John Roberts (joined by Justices Antonin Scalia and Clarence Thomas) wrote in dissent: "The elevation of the fullest individual self-realization over the constraints that society has expressed in law may or may not be attractive moral philosophy," but "the Fourteenth Amendment does not enact John Stuart Mill's *On Liberty*."[40]

The history of the debate over "legal moralism," the voluminous legal literature invoking Mill's harm principle as a core (though debated) tenet of modern legal thought, and recent Supreme Court jurisprudence on gay rights make it fairly certain that any legislative efforts to inculcate moral virtues will be met with a good deal of skepticism.[41] At the very least, Katrina Wyman is correct that "advocates of using law to promote virtue with the ultimate goal of achieving human flourishing need to acknowledge and discuss the potential inconsistency between their project and liberal commitments to encouraging individuals to pursue their own conceptions of the good life."[42]

Can Virtue Be Imposed by Law?

Even if we accept that it would be good for the law to inculcate virtue, we are faced with the question of whether the law can alter our character in such a way. Does law truly have such power? First, let us begin with what is arguably a less controversial proposition: law can affect behavior through a variety of regulatory mechanisms; an obvious, key feature of the law is its coercive nature.[43] At its essence, "Law makes us do things that we do not want to do."[44] More than a century ago, Holmes famously wrote about the "bad man," explaining, "A man who cares nothing for an ethical rule which is believed and practised by his neighbors is likely nevertheless to care a good deal to avoid being made to pay money, and will want to keep out of jail if he can."[45] Second, even beyond the directly coercive force of law, expressive theories of the law have explored the ways in which law can alter behavior and even change preferences independent of sanctions.[46] Accordingly, at the very least, most observers would agree that "law and regulation can do a good job of compelling people to mimic virtuous behavior,"[47] though they might vigorously debate exactly *how* law is working to achieve its ends and the optimal mix of regulatory methods to achieve particular social goals.[48]

But using sanctions and other regulatory tools to make people behave as if they possess virtue is quite different from making them truly virtuous. This is a recurring theme in Robert George's writings:

> coercing people to do the right thing, even when it is successful, does not make them morally better; it does nothing more than produce external conformity to moral norms. Morality . . . is above all an internal matter, a matter in rectitude in choosing: one

> becomes morally good precisely, and only, by doing the right thing *for the right reason.* . . . So, someone is not "just and noble" for doing merely out of fear of punishment something that would truly be just and noble if done for the sake of what is good and right. If the legal enforcement of moral obligations does nothing more for the masses than present them with subrational motives for outward conformity with what morality requires it does nothing toward making men moral.[49]

In other words, a person would not be virtuous if he acted as a just person would act simply to avoid criminal, civil, or social sanctions. Putting aside sanctions, even following the law as a *model* for virtuous behavior would raise what Kimberley Brownlee calls the "emulation problem":

> We cannot aim to do as the law models in order thereby to act virtuously because to do so would undermine the virtuousness of the act. Virtue cannot be indirectly pursued in our individual choices. This means that, even though the law can model virtue for us, we will not act virtuously if we emulate the law in order to act virtuously.[50]

Brownlee's point is connected to the very nature of virtue, as the term is used in modern virtue ethics: "Virtues do not consist simply of acquired dispositions to engage in certain external actions. They are far deeper character traits that, in addition to manifesting themselves in specific actions, are bound up with a person's reasons for taking a particular action as well as her emotional state as she does so."[51] Put another way, virtuous people do the right thing for the right reason.[52] Doing the right thing alone is not enough. Julia Annas gives us a useful example:

> Having a virtue isn't just a matter of acting in a certain way. I could sit down and write a large cheque for a good cause, but this might not be out of generosity. I might want to impress someone, or to avoid tax, or to relieve feelings of guilt about something. Someone observing me might well say that that was a generous thing to do, but they wouldn't be well-advised to infer from this that I was generous. Generosity is a matter of character—it's a matter of the kind of person I am.[53]

The causal complexity of this inquiry is daunting. When we see the person making the charitable donation in Annas's example, we cannot tell whether her apparent generosity is evidence of virtue or something else. I am suggesting not that these vexing causation issues mean that the law cannot play a role in shaping character but rather that it will often be difficult to know whether the external manifestations of virtue indeed reflect virtue as the term is understood by virtue ethicists or instead represent mere compliance with law or social norms to avoid legal and nonlegal sanctions (or habit, which may or may not be virtuous).

THE PATH FORWARD: "NUDGING" TOWARD THE VIRTUE OF JUSTICE

This chapter points to two formidable challenges to using the law to inculcate virtues such as justice. First, we have the argument that it may be improper to use the law to inculcate virtue because this tactic would violate our liberal commitment to autonomy. Second, it is not clear whether the use of the law to inculcate virtue will work. After all, mere compliance with legal rules is unlikely to be considered virtuous, at least as the term *virtue* is used in much of modern virtue ethics. Accordingly, we have to ask how, exactly, legislation can fruitfully contribute to the character-forming, virtue-inculcating mission served by other social institutions.

Furthermore, it is unclear whether a legislative program of justice inculcation can ever really be made palatable to staunch antipaternalists who are aghast at the prospect of government bureaucrats defining "the good life" for us in a way that is disconnected from more conventional understandings of happiness.[54] To gauge the strength of this antipaternalist strain in US politics, one only needs to consider the recent public policy debate over the "nudge" agenda promoted by behavioral economics scholars.[55] Cass Sunstein, the scholar most closely associated with nudging and "libertarian paternalism,"[56] carefully emphasizes that nudging is geared primarily toward *means* paternalism, not *ends* paternalism.[57] Moreover, for the most part, Sunstein's behaviorally informed regulation emphasizes soft rather than hard forms of paternalism (hence the term nudging).[58] Despite these two major concessions, libertarian paternalism remains quite controversial, suggesting that antipaternalists who find Sunstein's nudge agenda objectionable are going to have strong negative reactions to a robust program of aretaic legislation aimed at making us more virtuous or just.

Nevertheless, I do not want to suggest that the legislative virtue inculcation project is futile. Accordingly, in the final part of this chapter, I suggest some ways we can think about using the law to inculcate an individual virtue of justice to make this mission more plausible and palatable, at least to some critics. To my mind, such a plan requires either taking the following steps or explaining why such actions would be unwise assuming a philosophical commitment to virtue ethics:

1. The individual virtue of justice needs to be defined with a level of specificity and thickness to make it of use to legislators and regulators.

2. If the ultimate end of law is human flourishing, this concept needs to be reconceptualized in a way that alleviates antipaternalism concerns (unless virtue jurisprudence wishes to adopt proudly the mantle of paternalism).
3. Virtue ethicists need to consider whether they want to forswear the use of criminal law to punish vice, either as a matter of strategy (to appease antipaternalists) or as a matter of principle.

I address each of these points briefly. But first, I must acknowledge that my focus in the remainder of this chapter will be limited to paternalism objections to virtue legislation. This chapter does not directly address the related questions of whether (1) virtue (however defined) can ever be inculcated by law and (2) even if law can inculcate virtue, how scholars and regulators can know, as an empirical matter, whether law deserves the credit for the presence of virtue. Resolving these thorny issues is beyond my scope here and my capabilities. I will leave it to others to determine whether law can truly change character and, when character is altered or formed, how we can be sure that it was law and not innumerable other social forces that deserve the credit for this change.

Defining the Individual Virtue of Justice

As a threshold matter, any project that entails the legislative promotion of an individual virtue of justice requires us to define this particular virtue with sufficient thickness to make it of use as a guiding principle for regulatory action.[59] Or perhaps, as some have suggested, it would be sufficient to have, at least, a firm grasp on the nature of *injustice* to inform this virtue legislation project.[60] In either case, absent a clear sense of what this virtue entails, we will be left with a rather useless exhortation to use law to make people just or to fight injustice, without any sense of what, exactly, this entails and what legislative tools are likely to achieve these ends. Donald Kochan makes this point well: "If virtue is contextual as some contend, or is otherwise difficult to define then broad-based, universally applicable legislation may not be the best place for virtue analysis."[61]

Some of the philosophically sophisticated scholars in this volume have begun the formidable project of defining the individual virtue of justice.[62] A key component of this individual virtue of justice appears to be how we take account of what is due to others with whom we interact in society. Paul Woodruff states rather elegantly: "Justice, as a virtue of the individual soul, would then require the wisdom to judge what is due to the people with whom we have dealings; such wisdom would regulate our natural capacity to be angry at those who violate justice (including ourselves)."[63] In a similar vein, May Sim, who writes about Confucian values, explains that the virtue of *yi* "enables someone to do the right thing, for instance, by being fair in the distribution of goods and being courageous or truthful, regardless of the benefits to oneself that wrongdoing may bring."[64]

Further building on this theme, Ryan P. Hanley explores how three key Enlightenment figures—Jean-Jacques Rousseau, Adam Smith, and Immanuel Kant—all see "a key role for the other-directed sentiments in the process of becoming just."[65] For example, Hanley explains how Smith draws a key distinction between legitimate self-interest (which underlies much of Smith's economic theory) and "pernicious selfishness that devalues others and their ends." Hanley later notes that Kant, like Smith, also proffers an understanding of sympathy that "enables us to transcend our individual self-preference, to recognize our equality with others, and ultimately to develop the concept of justice itself." This ends up sounding quite similar to what May Sim explains about Confucian virtues:

> what is good for an individual is not in conflict with what is good for others in the wider community. By helping others achieve their good, one is also helping one's own goodness. For instance, by helping others to become just, one is also exercising the virtue of justice by acting in an other-regarding manner that is virtuous. When others in one's community are just, they in turn enhance the goodness of the community within which one lives and hence further realize the virtue of justice that one desires.

The legal regulation of business is an ideal environment for thinking about this individual virtue of justice. After all, the business world is filled with innumerable contractual and fiduciary relationships that are the subject of pervasive legal regulation. A virtue ethicist likely would believe that virtuous people take account (in some manner) of what is due to others when they interact as employers and employees, lenders and borrowers, buyers and sellers, or principals and agents. I recognize that this is only a starting point; the open question is whether virtue theory provides helpful, practical guidance for determining what, exactly, to use Woodruff's phrase, is "due to the people with whom we have dealings" in these disparate business contexts. How do just and virtuous employers or employees behave? How do just and virtuous mortgage lenders or borrowers behave? How do just and virtuous vendors or suppliers behave? Does virtue in such relationships go beyond mere compliance with the law? These are the types of questions we would begin to ask as we endeavor to examine various business relationships with the individual virtue of justice in mind.

Human Flourishing in Virtue Jurisprudence

A law and economics scholar who promotes the idea that ideal legal rules should maximize efficiency will need to provide a sense of what he or she means by efficiency, just as legal scholars who support deontological approaches must explain what they mean by autonomy, rights, and duties. Similarly, scholars who press the case for eudaimonistic versions of neo-Aristotelian virtue ethics must advance some notion of what is meant by authentic human flourishing or happiness. Gregory Alexander and Eduardo Peñalver, whose approach is explicitly inspired by Amartya Sen and Martha Nussbaum, claim:

> any adequate account of human flourishing must stress two characteristics. First, human beings develop the capacities necessary for a well-lived, and distinctly human life only in society with, indeed, dependent upon, other human beings. To put the point even more directly, living within a particular sort of society, a particular web of social relationships, is a necessary condition for humans to develop the distinctively human capacities that allow us to flourish. The second characteristic of human flourishing to be stressed is that human flourishing must include at least the capacity to make meaningful choices among alternative life horizons, to discern the salient differences among them, and to deliberate deeply about what is valuable within those available alternative choices. This is what authentic, robust freedom must involve.[66]

Alexander and Peñalver then identify the following four capabilities they "regard as crucial components of human flourishing":

> (1) *life*, a good [that includes] . . . subsidiary goods such as health and security; (2) *freedom*, which includes identity and self-knowledge; (3) *practical reason*, which Aristotle defined as "the capacity of deliberating well about what is good and advantageous for oneself"; and (4) what Nussbaum calls "*affiliation*," a good that encompasses subsidiary goods such as social participation, self-respect, and friendship.[67]

We need not decide here whether this conception of human flourishing is ideal. I have little doubt that it would be subject to intense philosophical debate.[68] My point here is simply that a capacious, more "liberal" conception of eudaimonia or human flourishing (to use the term *liberal* imprecisely), which emphasizes freedom and the creation of the conditions for making worthwhile choices in life may have broader appeal than versions of eudaimonia more closely linked to traditional virtue ethics.

Virtue Jurisprudence and the Punishment of Vice

Obviously, critics of paternalism are concerned not only with how well-being is defined but also with how the state chooses to promote virtue. It thus seems reasonable to assume that the legislative promotion of virtue may be more palatable to critics if criminal sanctions for the punishment of vice are largely removed from the virtue ethicist's toolbox. Lawrence Solum, a leader in the virtue jurisprudence movement, disavows the notion that the law should command that citizens be virtuous, explaining, "Law aims at human flourishing, but it does not command humans to flourish or prohibit the possession of a corrupt character."[69] Even Steven Wall, who defends "a presumption in favor of the legal enforcement of morals," makes clear:

> the criminal law is not in general a good means for helping people to live well. Noncoercive efforts to shape the ethical environment are preferable to those that rely on force and threats. And even when legal coercion is necessary, it is better if it does not punish, but instead makes it more difficult for people to engage in the disvaluable activity.[70]

As other scholars have pointed out, legislators keen on virtue promotion have many other tools at their disposal aside from criminal sanctions, including civil liability (to deter unjust behavior), mandatory disclosure laws (to enable us to make better, more just choices), tax policy and government subsidies (both of which can incentivize just action), qualifications for public benefits and public office, public education programs (to encourage virtue and justice), minimum-wage laws, social welfare programs, and income redistribution, among others.[71] As we move further away from conceptualizing virtue jurisprudence as merely punishing vice, the less controversial legislative virtue inculcation will be. A potentially more appealing way of conceptualizing virtue legislation is using the law to create an environment in which people can thrive, flourish, and, hopefully, treat each other justly.[72] Solum explains:

> for law to serve its end—human flourishing—it must accomplish two tasks. First, law must foster the conditions for "faring well"—that is, the law must create and maintain the material and social conditions for human flourishing. These include sufficient material abundance, security of persons and property, opportunities for meaningful work, a healthy environment, and so forth. Second, the law must foster the conditions for "doing well"—that is, the law must create and maintain the conditions for humans to develop their capacities—in Aristotelian terms, the human excellences or virtues.[73]

In line with Solum's point, Mark LeBar explains that Aristotelian virtue ethicists "can argue that despite the roots of a favored virtue ethical account in a specific account of human flourishing, a form of liberal neutrality can still be present in the political institutions endorsed by that account." He elaborates:

> Christine Swanton makes this case explicitly, arguing that while a strong form of liberal neutrality (understood as the nonpromotion of any specific conception of the good) is out

> of reach for an Aristotelian virtue ethicist, a weak form (understood as the nonprohibition of practices incompatible with that conception) is not only possible but very likely required by Aristotelian virtues properly understood. The Aristotelian virtue ethicist can argue for a weakly liberal state which engages in education and encourages a favored conception of human flourishing via e.g. tax and subsidy policies, so long as it does not engage in "legal moralism": barring practices just because they fail to satisfy or promote that conception.[74]

To sum up, the project of legislating virtue can be conceived in terms of fostering the peace and prosperity necessary, but not sufficient, to guarantee authentic human flourishing and a just society, rather than as merely a revitalization of long-discredited aspects of legal moralism involving the criminal punishment of vice. As a strategic matter, this is likely to make the project less objectionable to some (but not nearly all) antipaternalists.

CONCLUSION: COURAGE FOR VIRTUE LEGISLATORS?

Two major categories of challenges from distinct theoretical perspectives may be raised by what I have written here. The first group of challenges would come from those who have an utterly different conception of the relationship between normative legal theory and virtue jurisprudence from what is conceptualized in this chapter. Just as some philosophers do not see virtue ethics as a stand-alone rival to consequentialism and deontology in modern moral theory or ethics, it is conceivable that scholars endorsing virtue jurisprudence do not see it as a true normative alternative in legal theory. One might ask, then, if virtue jurisprudence does not entail the external aretaic evaluation of existing and proposed laws, then what does this scholarly movement entail? There are several possibilities. First, virtue-focused legal scholars might argue that they merely want legal consequentialists and deontologically oriented legal theorists to take account of character and virtue in their normative legal theories. For example, a legal consequentialist could factor the value or benefits of certain virtues into their moral calculations. This would be akin to a Kantian or a utilitarian writing about the importance of character or virtue within his or her respective deontological or consequentialist world views.

Second, one might view virtue jurisprudence as a largely explanatory tool. Those operating from this perspective might argue that they are merely observing that the content of existing laws or judicial decisions can be *explained* in some sense by the goal of virtue promotion or inculcation, whether or not that is a good thing. Thus, one might look at a federal antidiscrimination provision and opine that the requirements of the statutory text or judicial interpretations of the statute reflect, demonstrate, or illustrate legislative or judicial concern with certain justice-related virtues. One engaging in this type of analysis would be bracketing the question of whether such concern on behalf of lawmakers is normatively desirable.

Third, and finally, one might conceive of a form of virtue jurisprudence that does not entail virtue legislation. Thus, a theorist might focus on what it means for various key players in the legal system to be just or virtuous. Such a scholar might address ideal virtues or character of judges, jurors, police, prosecutors, and lawyers, among others. Such projects plausibly could be carried out without dedicating oneself to the legislative promotion of a particular version of justice or virtue.

The second theoretical challenge to this chapter is even more direct: one might claim that the core observation of what is presented here is essentially banal. A critic might argue that it is painfully obvious that a virtue legislation project that eschews the imposition by the state of one true vision of the good life and swears off the idea of using criminal sanctions to punish vice or compel just behavior will be less objectionable to antipaternalistic critics. Such a conception of virtue legislation is palatable, critics could claim, because it endorses a neutered version of virtue jurisprudence that is scarcely distinguishable from deontological and consequentialist legal theories.

What makes virtue jurisprudence appealing, it might be argued, is that it exuberantly rejects the laissez-faire, nonjudgmental view of both the means of regulation and the ultimate ends of the law that has prevailed for the past fifty years or so in US legal discourse. Those dissatisfied with the prevailing state of affairs in normative legal theory may thus opt for a more full-throated version of neo-Aristotelian virtue jurisprudence that entails a much more controversial but ultimately richer version of virtue legislation. Scholars and legislators ought to demonstrate the quintessential virtue of courage by employing audacious challenges to the existing regulatory order. Theoretical courage of this type would involve identifying cases where the commands of virtue ethics explicitly conflict with what consequentialist or deontological normative moral theories would prescribe.

To return to the soda portion size example discussed earlier, we saw that a consequentialist would consider the costs and benefits of the proposed regulation, whereas a deontologist would draw attention to whether limiting one's consumption of or purchasing options for soda violates consumer autonomy or freedom to choose. These are two competing moral perspectives employing an external normative theory to judge whether the proposed law is good. How should such an issue be analyzed under virtue jurisprudence? Irrespective of the ultimate outcome, tackling the question requires squarely addressing whether virtue jurisprudence entails (1) the legislative promotion of a particular conception of justice and human flourishing (which must be defined and defended) and (2) an evaluative methodology or standard for judging legal rules that is different not only in tone but in substance from consequentialist and deontological normative legal theories. Directly addressing these points (according to the hypothetical critic) would be what is potentially exciting about virtue legislation—legal scholars going out on a theoretical limb and arguing that regulators in a particular area should forbid or require some action in service of a particular, potentially narrow conception of eudaimonia or human flourishing.[75] Nevertheless, for reasons suggested by this chapter, virtue legislators have yet to proffer such a robust aretaic regulatory agenda.

NOTES

1. I recognize that "[t]he phrase 'normative legal theory' is ambiguous" (Solum 2006b, 1479) and that "[a]ttempting to categorize normative legal theories and then to generalize about them is fraught with peril" (Solum 2006b, 1464). West 2011 uses the term "normative jurisprudence," which I take to be the same as normative legal theory for my purposes.
2. See Burton 2013, 539; emphasis added. See also Wendel 2011, 1039: "A frankly normative argument is one that asserts that some desirable state of affairs will be brought about if the law is understood in a particular way, or possibly reformed along certain lines."
3. Burton 2013, 539: "Normative legal theories provide standards with which to evaluate the normativity of existing laws and proposals for law reform." This is quite different from exploring whether "moral considerations are relevant to figuring out what the law already is." Murphy 2014, 2.
4. Obviously, this is a rather controversial proposition. See Singer 2009, 934, disputing the view that "legal reasoning is . . . empty unless filled with some external theory."
5. See Baron, Pettit, and Slote 1997, 1.
6. Vermeule (2014, 390) uses the term "prescriptive theory" to cover claims about the best means to adopt, given stipulated ends.
7. Solum 2005, 495.
8. Solum 2006b, 1464.

9. See generally Kaplow and Shavell 2002. There is a large literature on Kaplow and Shavell's work that I will not cite here in the interests of space. Suffice it to say that there are many scholars in legal academia that dispute their core claims.
10. Oliver Wendell Holmes foresaw this more than a century ago, long before the rise of the law and economics movement. See Holmes 1897, 459: "For the rational study of the law . . . the man of the future is the man of statistics and the master of economics."
11. The leading judicial advocate of legal pragmatism is Judge Richard A. Posner. See, e.g., Posner 2008; 2003; 1999. Since the focus of this chapter is legislation, not judging, I will not address issues raised by forms of adjudicatory consequentialism or judicial pragmatism.
12. Edmonds 2014. Turiel, Dahl, and Besirevic discuss trolley-car situations in chapter 5 of this volume.
13. Solum 2006b, 1464.
14. See *N.Y. Statewide Coal. of Hispanic Chambers of Commerce v. N.Y.C. Dep't of Health & Mental Hygiene*, 23 N.Y.3d 681, 690 (2014) (describing the sixteen-ounce portion cap rule).
15. Ibid., 701.
16. See Wiley 2014, 52.
17. Conly 2013.
18. Tirosh 2012, 308.
19. Ibid., 270, 294.
20. Amaya and Lai 2013, 5.
21. Much of virtue jurisprudence is linked to neo-Aristotelian virtue ethics.
22. Solum 2013, 2. See also Farrelly and Solum 2008, 2–3, making a similar point.
23. See Solum 2006a, 91–92 (formulating a virtue-centered theory of judging); Solum 2003, 178.
24. Solum 2005, 478.
25. See George 2008, 24. See also Colombo 2012, 25–28. Yankah (2013, 79–81) questions the extent to which Aristotle meant for the law to be used as a tool to inculcate private virtue as opposed to civic virtue.
26. George 1993, 46. See also Yankah 2013, 62: "virtue jurists and non-liberal moralists of a certain kind believe that communities have an appropriate interest in the development of good personal character and a virtuous society and protecting both from decay through the normative guidance of the law."
27. For a critical survey of the state of virtue legislation as a form of virtue jurisprudence, see Kochan 2014, 315–322.
28. Not all scholars operating under the broad umbrella of virtue jurisprudence understand the field as necessarily entailing a legislative project of virtue inculcation. See generally Amaya and Lai 2013.

29. See Duff 2003, 215: "The antennae of traditional liberals will quiver at the suggestion that this is any part of the law's proper aim."
30. Dworkin 2016, defining paternalism as "the interference of a state or an individual with another person, against their will, and defended or motivated by a claim that the person interfered with will be better off or protected from harm."
31. Sandel 2009, 9.
32. See Huigens 2002, 445. Huigens has pressed this claim in many articles on the subject.
33. Yankah 2009, 1210.
34. Hill 2010, 1: "The term 'morals legislation' has been used to designate laws prohibiting activities such as consensual homosexual relations, abortion, adultery, fornication, prostitution, bestiality, bigamy, adult incest, sadomasochism, gambling, the use of illegal drugs, euthanasia, and assisted suicide, to name a few."
35. Ibid., 14: "The consensus today is that Hart demolished Devlin's argument." Scoccia 2013, 513: "Most commentators . . . agree that Hart was devastatingly effective in his critique of Devlin's defense of the legal enforcement of a society's positive morality."
36. Mill wrote: "the sole end for which mankind are warranted, individually or collectively, in interfering with the liberty of action of any of their number, is self-protection. That the only purpose for which power can be rightfully exercised over any member of a civilized community, against his will, is to prevent harm to others. His own good, either physical or moral, is not a sufficient warrant. He cannot rightfully be compelled to do or forbear because it will be better for him to do so, because it will make him happier, because, in the opinions of others, to do so would be wise, or even right." Mill 2003, 80.
37. But see Bernard E. Harcourt 1999, 109, arguing that "[t]he proliferation of conservative harm arguments has produced an ideological shift in the harm principle from its progressive origins," which has essentially caused the harm principle, as it was originally understood, to collapse.
38. *Obergefell v. Hodges*, 135 S. Ct. 2584 (2015), at 2607–2608.
39. Justice Kennedy's Millian move was hardly surprising. After all, Kennedy also wrote for the majority in *Lawrence v. Texas*, 539 U.S. 558 (2003), which declared Texas's antisodomy laws to be unconstitutional in an opinion that many observers believe was deeply indebted to Mill (though the extent of that debt is open to debate). See Lwin 2011, 409 and n. 75, noting that "many commentators have noted that *Lawrence* articulates many arguments found in *On Liberty*."
40. *Obergefell v. Hodges*, at 2622.
41. See Kochan 2014, 320: "Opponents of morals legislation lodge a variety of objections based on the indeterminacy and subjectivity of morals, the existence of moral relativism, the intrusion upon individual liberty and personal

autonomy associated with public dictating of morals, and the benefits of governmental neutrality."

42. See Wyman 2009, 1005.
43. See generally Yankah 2008, 1195: "Most would find the claim that the law is coercive uncontroversial."
44. Schauer 2015, 1.
45. Holmes 1897, 459.
46. See Stein 2004, 664–66; Wittlin 2011, 424, describing various mechanisms through which law shapes social norms and behavior.
47. Colombo 2012, 24.
48. Of course, I am not neglecting the possibility that law can also fail in its mission of changing behavior through various means. But at the very least, changing behavior is a possible outcome.
49. George 2008, 29 (footnote omitted); George 1993, 114: "Someone who refrains from vice merely to avoid being caught and punished under the law prohibiting the vice realizes no moral good (though he may avoid further moral harm)."
50. Brownlee 2015, 15.
51. Peñalver 2009, 864.
52. See Annas 2006, 516; Berges 2013, 67: "we should think not only that something is the right thing to do, but also that we have the desire to do it."
53. Julia Annas, *Applying Virtue to Ethics*, 32 J. OF APPLIED ETHICS 1, 2 (2015).
54. See Carson 2006, 10, stating that eudaimonia is not "coextensive with the classical utilitarian conception of happiness"; 11, explaining that Aristotle "argued for an objective standard of human happiness grounded in his metaphysical realism." I express no opinion about whether Carson's view of Aristotle is historically correct. For an argument against Aristotelian perfectionism, see Haybron 2006, 1.
55. The term *nudge* refers to Thaler and Sunstein 2008.
56. See generally Sunstein 2014.
57. Sunstein 2014, 63: "for the most part, behavioral economics have not sought to revisit people's ends, and their findings do not support ends paternalism." For more on the distinction between means and ends, see Sunstein 2014, 61–72. Sunstein is careful to note that the line between means paternalism and ends paternalism may be unclear at times (63).
58. Sunstein does endorse harder forms of paternalism in some cases. Sunstein 2014, 142, explains that "the master concept is social welfare, and that when the benefits justify the costs, harder forms of paternalism are not off-limits."
59. Exactly how "thick" is an open question. Clark 2005, 776–777: "virtues need not be defined with scientific or philosophical precision in order for them to be developed and articulated through public action."

60. I thank Mark LeBar for this insight. Moreover, depending on the form of virtue ethics we are endorsing, we may also want to know the relationship between the individual virtue of justice and eudaimonia. See Hursthouse and Pettigrove 2016: "although all standard versions of virtue ethics insist on that conceptual link between *virtue* and *eudaimonia*, further links are matters of dispute and generate different versions."
61. Kochan 2014, 321 (footnote omitted).
62. For works outside this volume, see, e.g., Bragues 2006, 349–353, discussing the virtue of justice, especially in reference to law and business; Cimino 2009, 717–718, asserting, "Justice encompasses two different ideals: lawfulness and fairness or equality, in the sense of reciprocity rather than dignity"; Solum 2006a, 172, stating that "humans that possess the virtue of justice are nominos—they have internalized the *nomoi* or deeply held and widely shared social norms of their communities."
63. Woodruff in chapter 1 of this volume.
64. Sim in chapter 9 of this volume. For more on Confucian thought and virtue ethics, see Wang and Solum 2013.
65. Hanley in chapter 2 of this volume.
66. Alexander and Peñalver 2009, 135, citing Nussbaum 2000 and Sen 1985. Martha Nussbaum more recently explicated her capabilities approach in Nussbaum 2011.
67. George and Peñalver 2009, 137–138 (footnotes omitted).
68. For an in-depth, thoughtful philosophical examination of eudaimonia and "living well," see LeBar 2013a.
69. LeBar 2013a, 9. Solum does acknowledge that "[a]n aretaic theory of legislation *might* support the criminalization of gambling, recreational intoxicants, and prostitution on the ground that these activities interfere with the development and maintenance of the virtues;" Solum 2013, 11; emphasis in original. But he states that "this is only a possibility—not an inevitable consequence of a virtue-centered theory of the ends of law."
70. Wall 2013, 470.
71. Brownlee 2015, 10: "The law can model decency through policies that are supportive of the people who are most vulnerable, such as policies of unemployment insurance, basic income, universal preventive health care, education and reeducation opportunities, community housing, effective systems for redress and compensation, contract laws that favor vulnerable parties, unconscionability doctrines, and constitutional protections of human rights." Kochan 2014, 318–319, describing different forms of "virtue-enhancing, virtue-inducing, or virtue-regulating legislation."
72. See George 1993, 47, discussing a "moral ecology which will help to shape, for better or worse, the morally self-constituting choices by which people form

their character, and in turn affect the milieu in which they *and others* will in future have to make such choices"; emphasis in original.

73. Solum 2013, 10.
74. LeBar 2013b, 277–278 (footnotes and citations omitted).
75. See Berges 2013, 70: "in a sense it would be disappointing not to be able to put forward a virtue ethical view on the bigger question of what the ultimate ends of the law should be."

WORKS CITED

Alexander, Gregory S., and Eduardo M. Peñalver. 2009. "Properties of Community." *Theoretical Inquiries in Law* 10: 127–159.

Amaya, Amalia, and Ho Hock Lai. 2013. "Of Law, Virtue, and Justice." In *Law, Virtue, and Justice*, edited by Amalia Amaya and Ho Hock Lai, 1–25. Portland: Hart Publishing.

Annas, Julia. 2006. "Virtue Ethics." In *The Oxford Handbook of Ethical Theory*, edited by David Copp, 515–536. Oxford: Oxford University Press.

Annas, Julia. 2015. "Applying Virtue to Ethics." *Journal of Applied Ethics* 32: 1–14.

Baron, Marcia W., Philip Pettit, and Michael Slote. 1997. *Three Methods of Ethics: A Debate*. Malden: Blackwell Publishers.

Berges, Sandrine. 2013. "Education and Paternalism: Plato on Virtue and the Law." In *Law, Virtue, and Justice*, edited by Amalia Amaya and Ho Hock Lai, 67–77. Portland: Hart Publishing.

Bragues, George. 2006. "Seek the Good Life, Not Money: The Aristotelian Approach to Business Ethics." *Journal of Business Ethics* 67: 341–357.

Brownlee, Kimberley. 2015. "What's Virtuous about the Law?" *Legal Theory* 21: 1–17.

Burton, Steven J. 2013. "Normative Legal Theories: The Case for Pluralism and Balancing." *Iowa Law Review* 98: 535–575.

Carson, Scott. 2006. "Eudaimonia." In *Encyclopedia of Philosophy*, 2nd ed., edited by Donald Borchert, 10. Detroit: Macmillan Reference USA.

Cimino, Chapin F. 2009. "Virtue and Contract Law." *Oregon Law Review* 88: 70–743.

Clark, Sherman J. 2005. "Law as Communitarian Virtue Ethics." *Buffalo Law Review* 53: 757–788.

Colombo, Ronald J. 2012. "Toward a Nexus of Virtue." *Washington and Lee Law Review* 69: 3–84.

Conly, Sarah. 2013. "Three Cheers for the Nanny State." *New York Times*, March 25, A23.

Duff, R. A. 2003. "The Limits of Virtue Jurisprudence." *Metaphilosophy* 34: 214–224.

Dworkin, Gerald. 2016. "Paternalism." In *The Stanford Encyclopedia of Philosophy*, edited by Edward N. Zalta. http://plato.stanford.edu/archives/sum2016/entries/paternalism.

Edmonds, David. 2014. *Would You Kill the Fat Man?* Princeton: Princeton University Press.

Farrelly, Colin, and Lawrence B. Solum. 2008. "An Introduction to Aretaic Theories of Law." In *Virtue Jurisprudence*, edited by Colin Farrelly and Lawrence B. Solum, 1–2. New York: Palgrave-Macmillan.

George, Robert P. 1993. *Making Men Moral: Civil Liberties and Public Morality*. New York: Oxford University Press.

George, Robert P. 2008. "The Central Tradition—Its Value and Limits." In *Virtue Jurisprudence*, edited by Colin Farrelly and Lawrence B. Solum, 24–50. New York: Palgrave-Macmillan.

Harcourt, Bernard E. 1999. "The Collapse of the Harm Principle." *Journal of Criminal Law and Criminology* 90: 109–194.

Haybron, Daniel M. 2006. "Well-Being and Virtue." *Journal of Ethics and Social Philosophy* 2: 1–27.

Hill, John Lawrence. 2010. "The Constitutional Status of Morals Legislation." *Kentucky Law Journal* 98: 1–66.

Holmes, Oliver Wendell. 1897. "The Path of the Law." *Harvard Law Review* 10: 457–478.

Huigens, Kyron. 2002. "Solving the Apprendi Puzzle." *Georgetown Law Journal* 90: 387–459.

Hursthouse, Rosalind, and Glen Pettigrove. 2016. "Virtue Ethics." In *The Stanford Encyclopedia of Philosophy*, edited by Edward N. Zalta. https://plato.stanford.edu/archives/win2016/entries/ethics-virtue/.

Kaplow, Louis, and Steven Shavell. 2002. *Fairness versus Welfare*. Cambridge: Harvard University Press.

Kochan, Donald J. 2014. "The Mask of Virtue: Theories of Aretaic Legislation in a Public Choice Perspective." *St. Louis University Law Journal* 58: 295–354.

LeBar, Mark. 2013a. *The Value of Living Well*. New York: Oxford University Press.

LeBar, Mark. 2013b. "Virtue and Politics." In *The Cambridge Companion to Virtue Ethics*, edited by Daniel C. Russell, 265–289. Cambridge, UK: Cambridge University Press.

Lwin, Michael. 2011. "Big Love: Perry v. Schwarzenegger and Polygamous Marriage." *Georgetown Journal of Law and Public Policy* 9: 393–438.

Mill, John Stuart. 2003 [1859]. *On Liberty*, edited by David Bromwich and George Kateb. New Haven: Yale University Press.

Murphy, Liam. 2014. *What Makes Law*. New York: Cambridge University Press.

Nussbaum, Martha C. 2000. *Women and Human Development*. New York: Cambridge University Press.

Nussbaum, Martha C. 2011. *Creating Capabilities: The Human Development Approach*. Cambridge: Belknap Press of Harvard University Press.
Peñalver, Eduardo M. 2009. "Land Virtues." *Cornell Law Review* 94: 821–887.
Posner, Richard A. 1999. *The Problematics of Moral and Legal Theory*. Cambridge: Belknap Press of Harvard University Press.
Posner, Richard A. 2003. *Law, Pragmatism, and Democracy*. Cambridge: Harvard University Press.
Posner, Richard A. 2008. *How Judges Think*. Cambridge: Harvard University Press.
Sandel, Michael J. 2009. *Justice: What's the Right Thing to Do?* New York: Farrar, Straus and Giroux.
Schauer, Frederick. 2015. *The Force of Law*. Cambridge: Harvard University Press.
Scoccia, Danny. 2013. "In Defense of 'Pure' Legal Moralism." *Criminal Law and Philosophy* 7: 513–530.
Sen, Amartya. 1985. *Commodities and Capabilities*. New York: Oxford University Press.
Singer, Joseph William. 2009. "Normative Methods for Lawyers." *UCLA Law Review* 56: 899–982.
Solum, Lawrence B. 2003. "Virtue Jurisprudence: A Virtue-Centered Theory of Judging." *Metaphilosophy* 34: 178–213.
Solum, Lawrence B. 2005. "The Aretaic Turn in Constitutional Theory." *Brooklyn Law Review* 70: 475–532.
Solum, Lawrence B. 2006a. "Natural Justice." *American Journal of Jurisprudence* 51: 65–105.
Solum, Lawrence B. 2006b. "Public Legal Reason." *Virginia Law Review* 92: 1449–1501.
Solum, Lawrence B. 2013. "Virtue Jurisprudence: Towards an Aretaic Theory of Law." In *Aristotle and the Philosophy of Law: Theory, Practice and Justice*, edited by Liesbeth Huppes-Cluysenaer and Nuno M. M. S. Coelho, 1–31. Dordrecht: Springer.
Stein, Michael Ashley. 2004. "Same Struggle, Different Difference: ADA Accommodations as Antidiscrimination." *University of Pennsylvania Law Review* 151: 579–673.
Sunstein, Cass R. 2014. *Why Nudge? The Politics of Libertarian Paternalism*. New Haven: Yale University Press.
Thaler, Richard H., and Cass R. Sunstein. 2008. *Nudge: Improving Decisions about Health, Wealth and Happiness*. New York: Penguin Books.
Tirosh, Yofi. 2012. "The Right to Be Fat." *Yale Journal of Health Policy, Law, and Ethics* 12: 264–335.
Vermeule, Adrian. 2014. "Connecting Positive and Normative Legal Theory." *University of Pennsylvania Journal of Constitutional Law* 10: 387–398.
Wall, Steven. 2013. "Enforcing Morality." *Criminal Law and Philosophy* 7: 455–471.

Wang, Linghao, and Lawrence B. Solum. 2013. "Confucian Virtue Jurisprudence." In *Law, Virtue, and Justice*, edited by Amalia Amaya and Ho Hock Lai, 106–135. Portland: Hart Publishing.

Wendel, W. Bradley. 2011. "Explanation in Legal Scholarship: The Inferential Structure of Doctrinal Legal Analysis." *Cornell Law Review* 96: 1035–1074.

West, Robin. 2011. *Normative Jurisprudence: An Introduction*. New York: Cambridge University Press.

Wiley, Lindsay F. 2014. "Health Law As Social Justice." *Cornell Journal of Law and Public Policy* 24: 47–105.

Wittlin, Maggie. 2011. "Buckling under Pressure: An Empirical Test of the Expressive Effects of Law." *Yale Journal on Regulation* 28: 49–469.

Wyman, Katrina M. 2009. "Should Property Scholars Embrace Virtue Ethics? A Skeptical Comment." *Cornell Law Review* 94: 991–1007.

Yankah, Ekow N. 2008. "The Force of Law: The Role of Coercion in Legal Norms." *University of Richmond Law Review* 42: 1195–1255.

Yankah, Ekow N. 2009. "Virtue's Domain." *University of Illinois Law Review* 2009: 1167–1212.

Yankah, Ekow N. 2013. "Legal Vices and Civic Virtue: Vice Crimes, Republicanism and the Corruption of Lawfulness." *Criminal Law and Philosophy* 7: 61–82.

INDEX

www.ingramcontent.com/pod-product-compliance
Ingram Content Group UK Ltd.
Pitfield, Milton Keynes, MK11 3LW, UK
UKHW021133160926
475595UK00020B/27